EDGAR
An Autobiography

Edgar Martínez with Larry Stone

30 YEARS

TRIUMPH
BOOKS

Library of Congress Cataloging-in-Publication Data available upon request.

This book is available in quantity at special discounts for your group or organization. For further information, contact:

Triumph Books LLC
814 North Franklin Street
Chicago, Illinois 60610
(312) 337-0747
www.triumphbooks.com

Printed in U.S.A.
ISBN: 978-1-62937-729-2
Design by Patricia Frey

For Holli, Alex, Tessa, and Jacqueline
—E.M.

For Mom, whose memory shines on, and the family she loved:
Dad; Judy and Esther; Lisa, Jessica, Meredith, and Jordan
—L.S.

Contents

Foreword

WHEN I THINK OF MY FRIEND EDGAR MARTÍNEZ, I think first of his incredible work ethic.

Well, first I think of that amazing mustache he had when we were teammates on the Mariners in 1989. I was just a 19-year-old rookie and couldn't grow any facial hair at all, so I was jealous of all the guys who could sport a mustache or goatee. The only thing I had was a 'fro—and Edgar had a little bit of that going, too.

But it was evident to me from the start that Edgar put in an unbelievable amount of work. People see what he did on the field, which led to a brilliant career that rightfully put him in the Hall of Fame in 2019. What they didn't see was what he did off the field. The eye exercises Edgar did for 20 to 30 minutes every single day to correct his vision problem. The hours in the weight room and the batting cage. They see the two batting titles, but not the work it took to accomplish that feat.

I was lucky enough to see it close up for the 11 seasons we were together in Seattle. I saw the countless hours Edgar spent preparing before each game. And I understood that the job he had for most of his career, designated hitter, is the hardest position in baseball. Playing in the field, you can sweat a little, get some flow and rhythm going. But as the DH, all you're doing is hitting. You have to go up to the plate cold. It's just hard. It would be like a basketball player who doesn't run up and down the court. You just stand in the corner, and if we pass it to you, you shoot.

Edgar found a way to make it work, though. He took that position to new heights. He transformed the DH spot from what it used to be, which was an older guy trying to hold on for a couple more years. After Edgar, teams looked for guys who were in their prime to DH. When he wasn't playing in the field, Edgar studied the game. He was one of the most prepared guys in baseball. Because he had to be. Whenever there was a pitching change, we'd go to Edgar to get a scouting report. He would tell us what pitches the guy threw, what tendencies he had. When Edgar got done, I would look over at Lee Elia, our hitting coach, and he'd nod his head yes.

It took a while for Edgar to get a starting job on the Mariners—and early in his career, he was a good defensive third baseman, too. He didn't show any frustration. He just worked harder. We had a logjam at third, and Jim Presley was ahead of Edgar, even though he was tearing up Triple-A. But when you can hit, they'll find a spot for you. And Edgar could hit. Every year for a decade-plus, he put up a .300 average, 25 to 30 homers, 40 to 50 doubles, 100 RBIs, and he could even steal a base when he needed to.

Edgar's night was four at-bats—five if he was lucky. So his mindset had to be different than ours. We could go out and play defense. He just had those at-bats to make an impact. It was impressive to see him do it day in and day out, to be ready for an at-bat after sitting for 30 to 40 minutes. He made a living doing that.

One great thing about that group we had in Seattle—Edgar and Jay Buhner and Dan Wilson and all the rest—is that we took care of each other. We were all in the same age group, and we all got along. We pushed each other, too, in a positive way. The only way to get better is to compete, and we'd do that every day in batting practice. Whether it was getting the guy over, home run derby, getting the guy in—it was a competition. But we all rooted for each other. The jealousy wasn't there. Edgar winning a batting title was like Jay or I winning a batting title, even though we didn't hit for him. We were just as excited when he won it as if we had won it ourselves.

That's the way we took care of each other. No one cared whose name was in the paper or not in the paper. As long as we went out and played and did our jobs, we didn't worry about who had the headlines. It was like, "Okay, if you want a headline, go ahead and do something to earn it."

Edgar was a funny guy, too. He had a dry humor—and sometimes he'd crack us up without even trying. You'd just look at him, and it was almost like how people say things about Rickey Henderson. We'd say, "There goes Gar."

When we were in the hitters meeting, as soon as someone said the word "cutter," we'd all look at Edgar. He'd say, "Everyone has a cutter. No one throws the ball straight anymore." It was no longer the sinker everyone was upset about; it was the cutter. Well, Gar made his living off the cutter. He hit nearly .600 against the guy with the best one, Mariano Rivera. Now they're going in the Hall of Fame together.

Early in his career, Edgar hit second, right in front of me. But I think when a guy hits as many doubles as Edgar did, and the No. 3 hitter keeps getting walked, you're going to make a change. Lou Piniella put Edgar at cleanup behind me. He wasn't the traditional fourth hitter, but he could do a lot more damage than most No. 4

hitters. He had a deadly combination of not striking out, doubling you to death, working the count, and having the ability to hit the ball out of the ballpark. And, oh yeah, he'd hit it down the right-field line as if he was a left-handed pull hitter.

Of course, Edgar and I will always be linked by the double he hit in Game 5 of the 1995 playoffs against the Yankees. It scored me from first base with the winning run to clinch the Division Series. That was an incredible year for all of us. I broke my wrist in May, and we eventually fell 13 games behind the Angels before making a miracle comeback. You look at how many people can carry a team for one, two, three, or maybe four days in a month. Between five guys, they carried it for 73 games. Then more than that after I came back. That's how determined the guys were to just keep fighting. So many guys stepped up. You hear about "next man up." That year, we stepped up as a team and were able to do something that was fun and exciting—not only for the players, but for the city of Seattle, and for baseball.

When Edgar stepped up against Jack McDowell in the 11th inning at the Kingdome, we were trailing the Yankees by one. Joey Cora was on third and I was sitting on first base as the winning run. What I was thinking was, "Give yourself a chance to score." If Edgar hits a double and I don't score, then maybe they get out of the inning and who knows what happens? I wanted to score for Edgar. I wanted to make it hard for Sammy Perlozzo, our third-base coach, to stop me. Make *him* have to come in and explain why he sent me or stopped me. You didn't want Lou to ask you that question: Why weren't you running? That's the worst feeling in the world.

Of course, Edgar hit it into the left-field corner and I scored from first to win the game. The players came out and mobbed me, and there's a famous picture of me smiling at the bottom of the pile. I'm just trying to get people off me! Don't forget, I had surgery three months earlier. That's why I rolled over the way I did, to protect my wrist. But sliding into home and having people jump up and down, that's one of the greatest feelings you can have as a player.

Playing with Edgar, being his teammate and friend, was another one of the joys of my career. I think it took a little longer for people to realize how good he was. But when you put his numbers up against everyone else's, you see how consistent he was. When I was growing up, the definition of a Hall of Famer was someone who was one of the most feared guys for 10 years. That's the way it was when my dad played, and that's the criteria I grew up believing.

With Edgar, the answer to that question was yes. I'm thrilled we're going to be teammates again in the Hall of Fame in Cooperstown. It was lonely being the only Seattle guy.

—Ken Griffey Jr.

Introduction

I DIDN'T PLAY BASEBALL to make the Hall of Fame.

I played for the pure joy of the game, and for the constant challenge of making myself a better player. I played for the relentless pursuit of winning, and how good it felt when that goal was achieved. I played for the camaraderie of a clubhouse and the enduring friendships of teammates. I played for the great fans who supported me every step of the way. I played for my family and for the people who got me started in baseball as a kid in Puerto Rico. I played for all those who stuck with me when it didn't appear that I was going to fulfill my dream of a professional career.

I am completely sincere when I say that personal accolades were not what drove me during my 18-year major-league career with the Seattle Mariners. In fact, my personality has always been to shy away from the spotlight. I have been happy to let others take center stage. During my career, I played with Ken Griffey Jr., Randy Johnson, Alex Rodriguez, and Ichiro, all of whom were legitimate superstars. Some people say that I was overshadowed, but that's not how I look at it.

I always felt appreciated and valued, both within the team and from those on the outside. My career was a blessing, from start to finish.

All that being said, I can't put into words the thrill when my cell phone rang on January 22 at 5:18 PM in my hotel room in New York. I knew who it was—though a couple of minutes earlier I had gotten a false alarm when the manufacturer of my CPAP machine had returned a service call. Talk about bad timing. This time, however, the call was the one I had been waiting 10 years to receive. Jack O'Connell, secretary-treasurer of the Baseball Writers' Association of America, was on the line. The phone was on speaker so that everyone could hear.

"I'm calling to tell you that the writers have elected you to the National Baseball Hall of Fame. Congratulations."

My family, gathered in the room with me, cheered. We all hugged and then my wife, Holli, led us in a toast. I didn't show much outward emotion, because I'd used a mental trick I learned during my baseball career to keep my composure. I concentrate on the moment, and don't let the past or the future overwhelm me. It worked for me in pressure situations at the plate, and it worked for me that day. But trust me, on the inside I was overwhelmed with joy and pride.

As you read this book, you will learn how close I came to never having a baseball career. I was nearly 20 years old and enrolled in college, preparing for a business career, when I signed with the Mariners out of a tryout camp I didn't even know was going to take place. I hit .173 in my first professional season, and spent several years stuck at Triple-A, waiting for a major-league job I wasn't sure was ever going to come. And then I endured a series of injuries that threatened to end my career prematurely.

But I persevered, and lasted through 18 mostly wonderful seasons, all of them in Seattle. I won a couple of batting titles. I honed the mental skills that helped me endure the inevitable setbacks that test every major-league ballplayer. I adjusted to and eventually embraced the new position of designated hitter that became my full-time home starting in 1995, which was also the season that the Mariners saved baseball in Seattle. I got a double against the Yankees in the playoffs that year that you might remember, too.

When I finally hung up my cleats for good after the 2004 season, I thought I had a shot at the Hall of Fame, but I suspected it was going to be a long, difficult road. I wasn't sure how the writers who vote would look at the fact that 72 percent of my plate appearances were as a designated hitter. And though I was very proud of my numbers—a .312 career batting average, .418 on-base percentage, and .515 slugging percentage—I didn't hit the milestones that voters look for, like 3,000 hits or 500 home runs.

And a long and difficult road it was. I received 36.2 percent of the vote in 2010, my first year of eligibility. You need 75 percent to be elected. When my total fell to 25.2 percent in 2014, my fifth year on the ballot, I began to think it might not happen. That same year, the Hall of Fame changed the eligibility rules. Instead of staying on the ballot for 15 years, candidates would remain for only 10. So I had just five more years, not 10, to raise my vote total from 25 percent to 75 percent. It looked nearly hopeless, particularly when I was still stuck of 27 percent in 2015. But I wasn't bitter at all. I considered it a great honor to even be considered, and I understood why some voters had hesitance. It wasn't something I stressed over. My attitude was always that it would be a great bonus if I got voted into the Hall of Fame, but it was not something that consumed or haunted me.

That's when some remarkable things started to happen. The Mariners did an amazing job of reaching out to voters with a package of statistics and information on my career, as well as testimonials from many great players already in the Hall of Fame. Many voters who were well-versed in analytics and sabermetrics took a new look at my career and looked deeper than just the raw numbers. And some influential writers and analysts began to write articles about how I was deserving of a Hall of Fame vote. The bias against a DH, which I had felt from my first day of eligibility—and before—started to be chipped away.

The result is that my vote total began creeping upwards. I received 43.4 percent in 2016 and 58.6 percent in 2017. I began to regain hope that I could make it, but I was also prepared for disappointment. In 2018, my next-to-last year on the ballot, it actually looked like it could happen. My wife, Holli, would frequently check the twitter and website of Ryan Thibodaux, whose Hall of Fame tracker tallied each vote as it was revealed. I tried to ignore all that, but Holli would always tell me when I picked up a new vote, so it was hard not to get excited. However, when the results were announced, I fell just short with 70.4 percent.

It was disappointing, but also highly encouraging. No one who had received at least 70 percent of the vote had ever failed to make the Hall of Fame. For the first time, I started to really believe it was going to happen—especially when Ryan's tracker showed me well above 75 percent once the voting resumed in December 2018. It was my last time on the ballot. Every time I received a new vote from someone who had passed me over before, Holli would let me know. Yet still, in the back of my mind, I was prepared for bad news when the vote was announced. I knew from experience that whatever the tracker said—and it had me hovering around 90 percent—I was going to lose votes from those who didn't reveal their ballots publicly. About six weeks before the BBWAA vote, Harold Baines was named to the Hall of Fame (along with reliever Lee Smith) by the 16-person Today's Game Era committee. That gave me even more hope. Harold was primarily a DH, just like me. I figured if he got in, then I probably would have a real good chance via the same committee, if the writers didn't vote me in.

My daughter Tessa turned 17 the day before the 2019 announcement, and she wanted to spend her birthday in Manhattan. So our family headed to New York to watch a Broadway play (*Book of Mormon*), try to get out of an escape room, and take Tessa out for a nice dinner. The next day—announcement day—seemed to go on forever. As I said later, the final 10 hours seemed to last longer than the previous 10 years. For the first time in the entire process, I felt nervous. I tried to stick to my daily routines, including a workout in the morning. In the afternoon, Holli and I slipped away to have a glass of wine and a quiet talk about what lay ahead. That helped relax me, but there was still a lot of nervous energy as the family sat in the hotel suite, just waiting. Our close family friend, Christi Downs, loosened us all up with some jokes.

When the phone call finally came, and I found out I was joining Mariano Rivera, Mike Mussina, and the late Roy Halladay (along with Baines and Smith) in the Cooperstown Class of 2019, it was exhilarating, emotional, and deeply rewarding. And I realized that in many ways, the long wait to get into the Hall of Fame, which had been so frustrating at times, was actually a blessing. If I had made it my first year, my kids would have been too young to fully appreciate what it meant. But now they were able to celebrate right along with Holli and me, which just made the moment even richer.

Naturally, such an honor causes a person to reflect on the journey that got them there. For me, it all began in New York City, took flight in Puerto Rico, and soared in Seattle—with lots of detours and delights along the way. Here is that story.

Chapter 1

How It All Started

MY MAJOR-LEAGUE BASEBALL CAREER was fulfilling beyond my wildest dreams—18 seasons, all with the Seattle Mariners, two batting titles, seven All-Star appearances, and a berth in the Hall of Fame. The life I have forged in Seattle, my adopted hometown, with my wife and soulmate, Holli, and our three kids, Alex, Tessa, and Jacqueline, has been a constant source of happiness and inspiration. I had a rewarding second chapter in the game I love as the Mariners' batting coach and will continue to work with the organization on hitting.

But I'm certain that none of it—not the association with lifelong friends and former teammates like Ken Griffey Jr., Randy Johnson, and Jay Buhner, not the Martínez Foundation that Holli and I started in 2008 that has raised hundreds of thousands of dollars to promote teachers of color, not "The Double" in the 1995 Division Series against the New York Yankees that may have saved baseball in Seattle and gets brought up to me virtually every day of my life by Mariners fans—would have happened if I had left my grandparents' house on that fateful day in 1974.

I was 11 years old, living contentedly with my grandpa, Mario Salgado, and grandma, Manuela Rivera, in the town of Dorado, Puerto Rico. We weren't rich, by any means, but they made sure that food was always on the table for me; my younger brother, Elliot; and my older sister, Sonia. Born in New York, I had moved as an infant to Dorado—specifically, to the neighborhood called Maguayo—when my parents split up. Sonia and I, along with our mom, who was pregnant with Elliot, moved in with her parents, Mario and Manuela, and that was my home. It was the only home I'd ever known, and not only was I happy, but I felt my grandparents needed me. And to me, they were my parents.

My mom moved back to New York and eventually got back together with my dad. They decided they wanted to get the family together and give it a second chance. My sister and brother, they were kind of excited about that. I was excited my mom and dad were getting back together, but I wasn't excited about going to New York and leaving my grandparents.

I loved living in Dorado, with my friends, with my grandparents, with my cousin Carmelo, with whom I was inseparable. Surrounded by rolling bluish hills and dense green pastureland, Dorado is located 17 miles to the west of San Juan. It is composed of seven neighborhoods, including Maguayo, with a cumulative population of about 35,000. As my friend and winter-league teammate Carlos Baerga once said, "It is a calm town, like Edgar. It is a town for him."

It isn't too far from the Dorado Beach Resort and Club, which is a former plantation once owned by Laurance Rockefeller. The country club is the home of the famous Dorado Beach East Course, a golf course designed by Robert Trent Jones and featuring a hole that was rated by Jack Nicklaus as one of the 10 best in the world. Chi Chi Rodríguez owns a mansion overlooking the course and the Atlantic

Ocean coastline beyond. But that seems like another world compared to Maguayo, an inland barrio of modest means. Yet to this day, I feel completely at home whenever I return. I'll buy a pincho (something like a chicken or beef shish kebab) from the vendor at the barbecue pit across from Felipe's Place, an open-air bar that is always one of my first stops. It's where people from the town go to hang out and relax. Calle 13, the narrow street where my childhood home still sits, isn't far away. Calle 13 has now been renamed Edgar Martínez Street, something I could never have dreamed back in those days.

I had started playing baseball, a game I immediately fell in love with. I didn't have any reason to go to New York, even though everyone tried to tell me how much I would love it there. I never told my sister and brother I didn't want to leave Maguayo. But I struggled with that in my mind. I told myself, "I'm not going. I'm not going to New York." I was thinking about my grandparents, and how they would get by without us when they were older. My grandmother had diabetes and heart issues. My grandfather was already losing his vision from an eye condition that eventually would leave him nearly blind. My brother and I helped him work on the car and truck that he drove to make his living. We helped him with the yard, and any work he needed done around the house. I didn't think he could do it without me. So with all those things put together, I said, "I'm not going." And I meant it.

At the time when I was expecting my father to pick all of us up to fly to New York, I went to the back of our house. There was a ladder, and I climbed it. I went on the roof, and I lay flat so no one could see me there. When the time came that my father had to go to the airport to catch a flight with us, I never came down, and no one knew I was up there. I could hear neighbors and everybody looking for me, calling my name. I just stayed there, praying no one would find me. I must have been up there for an hour, maybe longer.

3

My grandfather basically said to my parents, you have to leave him here. You're going to have a problem with him there. He doesn't want to live in New York. So Sonia and Elliot left, but I ended up staying in Puerto Rico. As my uncle, José Juan Rivera, told the *Seattle Times* in 2001, "Edgar's luggage was already packed. The luggage left. He stayed."

I remember it was so difficult. My brother and sister were close with me. It was tough, being apart from them, but I went through with it. I didn't really know what I was doing, not at that age, but I went with my feelings. I just felt great staying with them. Looking back all these years later, I feel like I did the right thing. I never had doubts or remorse about staying. But it did affect me. For a while, I had this strange feeling inside. One part of me was sad. I think that sadness stayed with me for a long time. It helped that Elliot eventually moved back to Puerto Rico and moved in with us, and now I have a very good relationship with my mom, who lives in Puerto Rico. My father passed away a few years ago.

I'm certain if I had gone to New York, my baseball career would have never gotten off the ground. Elliot had played Little League in Puerto Rico one year, and he was a power hitter from the left side. He could hit the ball a long way. But when he moved to New York, he never had a chance to advance his career. Our father worked in New York as a doorman in a building, and he wasn't a baseball fan. He wanted Elliot to get a vocation. For some reason, he wanted my brother to be a pilot, go to aviation school. Elliot didn't play ball in New York; he just went to school and pursued other interests. I don't think my dad would have let me play, either. It was like fate, in a way. My decision to stay in Dorado happened in a matter of minutes. It was far from the last time that fate intervened to guide me toward the glorious life I would wind up having.

My grandparents instilled in me a work ethic that I carried all the way to the major leagues. My grandfather had a variety of jobs over the years, but he was always working. At one point, he had a few trucks to transport gravel around the island. Later, he drove public transportation in his car, similar to a taxi. He owned the vehicles, so in addition to working five days a week, he'd spend the weekend tinkering with the vehicles, which always had something wrong with them. Most people rested on the weekend, but I never saw that. He wouldn't even take a half-day off. That just wasn't him. I would help him on weekends with the cars, trucks, or whatever else he was working on.

My grandmother was similar in a way. She was a homemaker, but she rarely rested. They showed me two important qualities—hard work and respect. Some people called me a perfectionist when it came to honing my baseball skills, and there's no question where that came from. My grandfather was very good at details. You had to do it right. If it didn't work quite the way he wanted, he would spend hours to make sure it worked. I was the same with hitting—I'd work at it until I got it right, whether it was my stance, my swing, or my approach. I might have blisters on my fingers, but I wasn't leaving the batting cage until I figured out whatever felt out of synch. I needed that perseverance when I was languishing in the minor leagues, year after year, getting a taste of major-league playing time in the late 1980s but unable to stick for a full season. That was the most frustrating time in my career, and there were points when I thought I might be traded by the Mariners—and that it might be best—but when the breakthrough came in 1990, it was that much sweeter.

The first time I really became aware of baseball was in 1971, when Roberto Clemente, who had grown up in Carolina, Puerto Rico, about 35 miles from Dorado, played for the Pittsburgh Pirates in the

World Series against Baltimore. Everyone on the island was riveted to that Series because of Clemente, the best player ever to come out of Puerto Rico. I was eight years old, and I was mesmerized not just watching the World Series, but watching my family watch the World Series. They were living and dying with every pitch, especially my aunt Wilma, who was a huge baseball fan. I have a vivid memory of watching a highlight of Clemente hitting a double, and Aunt Wilma screaming in the living room.

He ended up as the MVP of the World Series, batting .414 with two home runs, so there was a lot more cheering. I have a picture in my mind of a television being set up in my classroom so we could watch the games at school. It might have just been highlights, but the mental image I have is of our teacher putting the games on live. It's funny—one thing I remember is seeing Baltimore first baseman Boog Powell, who was 6-foot-4, 230 pounds, and thinking, "Wow, he's huge."

After that, I paid more attention to baseball. There was a plot of land very close to our house where all of us would play. I started Little League at age 11, and from that point on, I played baseball for the next 30 years, until I retired in 2004. Sadly, Clemente died on New Year's Eve just a year later, when his plane crashed while he was on a relief mission to deliver supplies in Nicaragua after a major earthquake. Once again, I remember Aunt Wilma's reaction, though this time instead of celebration, it was tears and sobbing when the news came over the television. I cried, too. Every young Puerto Rican boy wanted to be the next Clemente, including me. That's why one of the greatest honors of my entire career was winning the Roberto Clemente Award in 2004, which reflects not just baseball but sportsmanship and community service.

Just three weeks after I played my final game, I received it at the World Series that year in St. Louis from Roberto's widow, Vera, and his children. I was the first Puerto Rican ever to win the award, which has a treasured place in my home. Clemente is in the Hall of Fame, and joining him there will be the ultimate thrill. Orlando Cepeda, Roberto Alomar, and Iván Rodríguez are the only other Puerto Ricans in the Hall.

I was hooked on baseball almost instantly. I loved the game so much. In Puerto Rico back then, we didn't have what the kids have today, so many choices, like video games and computers. In Maguayo, playing baseball was a way for me to entertain myself. I would go out and hit rocks with a broomstick. My grandfather had a pile of pebbles and rocks in the backyard from various construction projects, and in my mind, I would picture myself being like Roberto Clemente. I would pretend it was different situations in a game, and hit the rocks, imagining I was in a major-league stadium. I would do that for an hour, maybe longer, day after day, for years. I did it so much that I cleared out all the rocks from the backyard, which wasn't necessarily appreciated by our neighbors. I remember that my grandfather bought me my first uniform around that time—striped, with my name sewn on the back. I couldn't have been prouder.

Sometimes it would be raining and I would try to hit the drops as they fell from the gutter of the house. I had a small baseball glove, and I would get a golf ball and throw it against the driveway wall. That was how I practiced defense, catching ground balls off the wall, or pretending I was a first baseman receiving a throw from an infielder. I would put baby powder in the area of the driveway where my grandfather would park the car on slick tiles. Then I would run and slide. The powder made the slide smoother. Some days, Carmelo and I would pitch bottle caps to each other. Carmelo started early teaching me to hit the ball to right field, which was a big advantage in my career. We didn't have the best equipment, but we were creative in finding ways to play or practice every day. And we loved every minute of it. We lived for baseball.

My grandpa was a big baseball fan, too. When the Puerto Rican winter league—which is now named after my childhood hero, Roberto Clemente—started in November, his team was Santurce, a town nearby. Every night, he would grab the radio and turn on the game. Listening to the Santurce games was his favorite thing to do, and I would listen with him, entranced. My grandfather was a big part of introducing the game to me, all the nuances and intricacies. He would always criticize the manager, second-guessing his decisions. That was a great memory, listening to my grandfather's passion over Santurce. We would talk about baseball for a couple of hours, dissecting it as we listened together on the radio, and it just added to my love of the game, my knowledge of it, and my desire to be great at it.

His favorite player was Tony Pérez, the Hall of Famer from Cincinnati's "Big Red Machine." Though he was born in Cuba, Pérez became an adopted Puerto Rican from playing so many years in our winter league. We both loved Tony Pérez. He was such a clutch hitter, and had such a flair. Years later, when I played in the big leagues, I got to meet Tony several times, and tell him what he meant to me as a child.

Another favorite growing up was José Cruz Sr., who was a great player with the Houston Astros. When I was with the Mariners, one of my teammates was José Cruz Jr., his son. I got to play against his dad in the winter league when I was just starting and José Sr. was an older player. That was a huge thrill. One time, when I was about 11, Orlando Cepeda and a couple of other players came to Maguayo to put on a baseball clinic. I have a strong memory of Cepeda taking batting practice and hitting a towering fly ball. I couldn't believe how high that thing was. I don't remember much else about that clinic other than that fly ball into the stratosphere. That's when I started to realize that major leaguers were a different breed, and it provided more motivation for me to get there. I played with and against some of the greatest players in history—including Griffey, who was the best I ever saw, and guys like Tony Gwynn, Wade Boggs, and Frank Thomas— but those heroes of my youth still have a special place in my heart.

I played in Little League, and also a league called the Tomás Palmares League when I was about 13 or 14. That was a tough league. I remember thinking, these kids are much bigger than me, but that just pushed me harder. In Little League, I was always the best hitter. I was the No. 1 player on the team, and then I moved to this league, and man, these kids were bigger than me, and stronger. That league, I didn't play much. After that, pretty much all the teams I played on—Mickey Mantle League, Sandy Koufax League—I was the best hitter on the team.

Then I played semipro at age 18—Double-A we called it—and I was still the best hitter. I set the doubles record and hit well over .400. We got $50 to $100 a game, which was a way for us to have some cash. Since Dorado didn't have a team, I was recruited by the nearby town of Vega Alta, which was the home of the Molina brothers, Bengie, Yadier, and José, all catchers who would play in the major leagues. Bengie and José won a World Series ring with the Angels, and Yadier has won two with the Cardinals. He'll be in the Hall of Fame one day. I played with their father, Benjamin, who surprisingly was an infielder, not a catcher—a switch-hitter. Benjamin had a big, fun personality, but sadly he died a few years ago of a heart attack—on a baseball field in Puerto Rico, coaching a youth team. Playing on that team was a great experience.

When I started playing in more advanced leagues, my grandfather would use his transportation van to drive me and several teammates to all our road games. He would drive us all over the island, sometimes on long trips that would last several hours. He loved to do that, and he loved to watch me play. He would often sit in the dugout during the game, taking it all in. He didn't second-guess the manager, though, like he did with Santurce—at least not out loud. Though my father wasn't around, my grandfather was a big part of my baseball life growing up.

Looking back, I think my success as a hitter in my youth—and into professional ball—could be traced to the drills I did in my backyard, hitting those rocks and throwing the ball against the wall. I did it so often I developed the motor skills and hand-eye coordination that served me well in baseball. I remember as soon as I started playing catch, I didn't have any problem catching the ball like a lot of the other kids. And as soon as I faced pitching, I could hit it. Hitting little pebbles and bottle caps, throwing a golf ball against a wall, day after day, I think I developed all those skills faster than the other kids. The bottle caps would never go straight, so it was great training for hitting breaking pitches.

At holiday time, we'd take round ornaments off the Christmas tree, remove the foam from inside, smash it into a smaller, harder ball that was more compact, and then put tape around it. That's all we needed to play a game of baseball—that and a plastic toy bat, again taped up to make it heavier. We'd throw pitches to each other—fastballs, changeups, breaking balls. We were very resourceful in finding ways to play baseball, because we loved it so much. And all that repetition honed our skills.

My cousin Carmelo was such a huge influence in my baseball career, a huge part of my following through with the game. He's two years older, and I watched his successes and used them to motivate me. One thing about Carmelo, no one outworked him, and he taught me how to train and prepare. He organized training sessions for all of us who had higher baseball aspirations. I'd go to his house, which was right down the street, three houses away, and we'd do aerobics and running and then go to the stadium for hitting and fielding practice. There was not much weight training yet, but that would come later and be influential in advancing my career when I was stalled in the minor leagues. Once Carmelo signed professionally, he would come home each winter with a new set of drills for me to work on, and new thoughts on my batting stance and swing that were incredibly helpful.

CARMELO MARTÍNEZ

Everything was baseball for us, even though at a young age we didn't play on the same teams, because we were one year apart. But we practiced together and played a lot of Wiffle ball games, when we weren't hitting bottle caps or rocks with a broomstick. We were always at a ballpark.

Not only that, Edgar was a hard worker. I think he outworked everyone. That's one big reason he had the success he did. Even when we'd stay out late and come back late, Edgar would get up early in the morning and go out and do his baseball work. He was committed. The ballpark was right down the street, and we'd go early in the morning until my mom would come and tell us to get home, it was getting late, or Edgar's grandpa would come and get us to wash the van.

I used to go over to his house almost every day. Edgar's grandpa was a little more strict with him, and I think that helped him, too. You can see what type of person Edgar is—a very straight, honest person. His grandpa drove a transport—like a taxi—and we'd wash it every day. I'd help him and Elliot, his brother, and then Edgar would take us for a short ride, afterward.

For him at that time, his grandparents were his mom and dad. He was used to his grandparents. That's why he chose to stay. The love and care they gave him made him do something like that. He didn't want to go back with his parents, even though right now he has a good relationship with his mom.

Maguayo is the type of town where everyone helps each other. Because it's so small, everyone is close. Baseball is the No. 1 thing there. I was the first one to come out into the major leagues, and then a lot of guys followed—José Lind, Onix Concepción, and others. We all grew up together, and we all practiced together. When I made it to the big leagues (in 1983), I set up the first hitting machine. Me and Edgar would take 400 to 500 swings a day. Then Carlos Baerga, Luis Aguayo, and others who would go on to the major leagues, a group of them, would all come in and hit off the machine. Then we'd all go to the park and take ground balls.

The Rural League, that's where we all learned how to play hard, and play with high intensity. It was town against town, and there are a lot of rival teams. Even though Edgar faced guys who were more experienced, he held his own, even though he doesn't think so, because he has such high standards. He was a good hitter in that league.

One time, and I always remind him of this, we were supposed to go out together to the Carnival in Dorado. We were set to meet by the ballpark. He didn't show up, but his car was there, so I knew he went with somebody else. I knew how to open his car with a screwdriver, so I opened it. They had cut the grass at the park that day, so I put all the grass inside the car. He didn't get mad—he just cracked up. That's Edgar. I was the troublemaker. He was the quiet guy. He hasn't changed. Same guy.

Because he was older, Carmelo was always in higher leagues than me. But one year, he joined us on a neighborhood team in what was called the Rural League, after his other season finished. He was developing a great reputation as a power hitter, the Bambino of the area. Everyone knew Carmelo, and the scouts were starting to notice, too. Everyone was super excited to have Carmelo join our team in the Rural League. That was the only time we played together until we became professionals and were teammates each winter on the San Juan Senadores of the top pro league in Puerto Rico.

Carmelo was becoming a big deal on the island, much more so than me as we came up. Everyone would talk about how far he could hit the ball, and that's what the scouts were looking for. He was burly and strong. I was skinny back then. I could hit the ball and was a good fielder, mostly at second base and third base—I even pitched sometimes and had success—but I wasn't much of a home run hitter. The professional scouts overlooked me, but Carmelo had a few tryouts.

Nowadays, players from Puerto Rico are subject to the MLB draft, but back then it was open season. Players were essentially free agents and could sign with whichever team they wanted once they turned 16. So when there was a top prospect like Carmelo, the competition among the scouts was intense. They all fell in love with his power. In 1978, when I was 15 and he had just graduated high school, Carmelo signed with the Chicago Cubs and went to Florida to start his professional career. Carmelo ended up playing nine years in the major leagues and he still works for the Cubs as a minor-league field coordinator. The youth center in the middle of Maguayo where we learned the game has been renamed Centro Comunal Carmelo Martínez.

The Cubs gave me a tryout—Carmelo had a lot to do with that, I found out later—but they didn't make me an offer to sign. They didn't think I was fast enough, nor did I have enough power. My swing back then is what is called "inside out"—I hit line drives, mostly to the opposite field, though I could pull the ball as well at times; just not often enough, or far enough, to suit them. Ironically, that approach would lead me to great success in the major leagues, but the scouts were looking for someone who could crush the ball a long way, and that wasn't me. I had a tryout with the Montreal Expos, as well, but they thought I was too skinny. That wasn't too far off—I weighed 165 pounds soaking wet in those days.

I had a yearning to play professional baseball, one I possessed from the time I first picked up a broomstick in the backyard. But I was beginning to believe that it wasn't going to happen, so I developed a fallback plan: I would go to school to study business. I still loved playing baseball, but I wanted to make sure I could set myself up for a good job if baseball didn't work out—and my hopes were dwindling. Most prospects in Puerto Rico had already signed by the time they got out of high school. If they hadn't signed by then, it was rare to get another look, because the scouts had already moved on to younger players. So after I graduated high school, I enrolled at American University, which had a campus in Dorado.

I felt good about it—I enjoyed studying, and I enjoyed working. And so I started doing both. I could see myself managing a store one day—that was a goal. I was going to school from 6:00 PM to 10:00 PM, Monday through Friday, taking business administration courses. Then I worked the night shift from 11:00 PM to 7:00 AM. When I got home, I'd sleep until about 1:00 PM, and then I would go practice baseball from 3:00 until about 4:30 in the afternoon with Carmelo, when he was home for the winter, and another friend of ours in pro ball, Juan López. I'd race home, take a shower, grab a bite to eat, and head off to classes, and then do it all over again. It was hectic, it was crazy, but I loved it.

I had two different jobs at that time. One was at the Westinghouse plant, where my job was to calibrate an electrical breaker box for commercial applications, such as yachts and commercial boats. I also did some welding. The other place I worked was a pharmaceutical company that made kits for the heart, and I worked on packaging these kits. About 12 of us would run the machine, and eventually I became the supervisor of the shift.

I was only making about $4 an hour, but I thought I had it pretty good, and I was quite content. I had a girlfriend, I had saved enough to buy a nice car, and I was preparing myself for my future by getting an education. I was making even more money playing baseball on the weekends. I was 19 years old and going places, I thought. But that place wasn't professional baseball.

That all changed one day, completely out the blue, in 1982. I had absolutely no idea that day, but my life was about to take another one of those dramatic turns that would shape my future. It was two weeks before my 20th birthday. The owner of the semipro team I played for owed me some money, because he hadn't paid me for several games. I think he felt bad about it, and to make up for it, he decided to get me to a tryout that the Mariners were having in Bayamón, which is about 10 miles from Dorado. I had just finished my night shift at Westinghouse and headed home for my nap. The owner was waiting in front of my house.

"Get dressed and grab your glove, we're heading to Bayamón for a tryout," he told me.

I hadn't heard a word about the tryout. If he hadn't stopped by, I never would have known about it. I'd probably still be in Puerto Rico, working behind a desk, running a company, or managing a store. But he drove me to the field, Estadio Juan Ramón Loubriel, where there were about 30 other hopeful kids. I had been through this drill before, and I wasn't particularly hopeful. I remember being so tired—I hadn't slept in more than 24 hours—that I could barely swing a bat.

There were two Mariners scouts running the camp—Coco Laboy and Marty Martínez, who wasn't any relation to me. Marty had grown up in Cuba and played seven years in the majors as an infielder. Judging infielders was his specialty, and the Mariners trusted him, as I would find out, to my everlasting gratitude. It was like most of the

15

other tryouts I had gone to. I took some ground balls at shortstop, making throws to first base. I took some swings against a pitcher, and I'm pretty sure I ran the 60-yard dash so they could see how fast I was. I thought I had done well, but I wasn't expecting much, because I'd been disappointed before. My power was still lacking, and I figured that would be a deal-breaker again.

But Martínez—whom I had no idea at the time would become a major influence in my career, a sort of father figure when I struggled in the minor leagues—took a liking to me. He told Bob Finnigan of the *Seattle Times* years later that he had heard from the other scouts not to waste his time on me, that I didn't have enough speed or power to make it worth his while. "I never did listen much to other scouts," Marty told Finnigan. "I had my own idea on things. I liked his bat, of course. I liked his hands. And he threw the ball so accurately. A little, funny motion but perfect to first base all the time. I thought he'd make a good middle infielder."

JEFF SCOTT
Bellingham Manager, 1979–1983; Mariners Player Development, 1983–85

I got a phone call form Marty. He said, "I want to sign this kid." Marty was Cuban, and he spoke definite Spanglish. "Scotty, I like this kid. But he's a little old." And theoretically, he was. Marty told me what he thought Edgar could do.

Back then, you don't anticipate him being the type of hitter he ended up being. People don't remember, but until he hurt his hamstring in Vancouver, Edgar was the best defensive third baseman in the organization. Marty said, "I want to sign this kid. He wants $5,000, but I can sign him for four." Back then, $5,000 in Seattle was a big deal. As we all know, George

Argyros, the owner, was not a spendthrift. Five grand was meaningful. We weren't all that involved in the Latin market, even Puerto Rico. We didn't have the resources to do all that.

But I told Marty, "If you like that kid so much"—and he said he liked his makeup, his tools—"give him $5,000."

Marty said, "He'll take four."

I said, "If he doesn't sign because you wouldn't give him $5,000, I'm going to fire you."

If I recall, he left the tryout without signing him. Marty was heading to the Dominican Republic to look at more kids. He had a three- or four-hour wait at the airport in San Juan. Edgar and his grandfather came to the airport and signed for $4,000.

The offer from the Mariners was $4,000. As excited as I was to finally be wanted by a major-league team, I thought that was too low, and I didn't want to sign. I was going to give up my job, my education, my car, my girlfriend—my future—for just $4,000? What happened if I didn't succeed in pro ball? I would have to start all over again, and I would have lost valuable years. It just didn't add up to me. I'm a very practical person, and I knew the odds of me making it to the major leagues were not good. It's not that I didn't have confidence in my ability, but I was also realistic. I knew how many kids, particularly Latin kids, signed contracts and flooded the minor leagues. Most ended up coming home. When I calculated the odds, I felt the better route for me was to stay home and keep working. I thought I would spend my bonus money, get cut, and then be without a job. I wanted at least $5,000, but Marty wouldn't budge.

That's when Carmelo went to work on me. Of course, I consulted with him, because he was already in pro ball and knew what it took to make it and what kind of lifestyle I would face. Plus, I just trusted him and his opinion. I knew he had my best interests at heart. We were as close as brothers. I vividly remember a fierce game of ping pong, where we batted the ball back and forth and also batted back and forth the question of whether or not I should take Marty's offer. I told him why I was leaning against it. He told me why I was crazy. Carmelo told me that I needed to take a chance. But most importantly, he insisted that I could make it. He had seen the other pro players, and he told me that I could not only compete, but I could surpass them. It was his belief in my ability that swayed me. I decided to take the Mariners' offer.

But I still had to convince my grandfather. Initially, he was thinking like me. He didn't like the risk of giving up my job and leaving college. He was against me signing, and I would not have done it without his blessing. But my godfather, Juan Rivera, stepped in and talked to my grandfather, who didn't think that $4,000 was enough. Neither did I, for that matter. Juan pleaded with him to just give me a chance. Rivera's clinching argument was that the great Roberto Clemente had signed for $400. He told my grandfather, "Look where he went in baseball. If Clemente could sign for $400, Edgar can sign for $4,000." How could he argue with that? My grandfather eventually gave his blessing.

Carmelo and my godfather, Juan Rivera, made it happen. I told Marty I would accept the Mariners' offer. It wasn't until years later that I read this quote from Marty in the *Seattle Times*: "You know, the Mariners were trying to save a buck back then. But if Edgar had pushed me, I'd have given him the other $1,000." I wish I had known that then! But I just didn't know how to negotiate, and I didn't feel like I was in a position of strength. As it was, the Mariners signed one other player from that camp, a catcher named Luis Vega, and they gave him $5,000!

Laboy, the other scout, liked him a lot, apparently. Laboy had played five years in the majors with the Montreal Expos. I remember wondering, why is Vega getting more? We were teammates on the semipro team, and I was the best hitter, not him. But I didn't say anything. Luis wound up playing just two seasons in the lower minors and batted a mere .221. I was right. But I have no complaints—I ended up making a lot of money in major-league baseball, far more than I could have ever dreamed. Carmelo's instincts were right, and I am forever grateful that he pushed me.

I think Marty recognized right away my ability to catch the ball and make accurate throws. As a hitter, he liked that I was able to cover both sides of the plate and make contact. I wasn't just a big pull hitter. I used the whole field—just like Carmelo taught me. What had caused other teams to pass me by was what attracted Marty to me. Marty said later that the Montreal scout, the one who had rejected me, laughed when he found out the Mariners had signed me. He thought that at age 20, I was too old to start a career in the low minors, and that I wouldn't make it anyway. But I was ready to find out.

CARMELO MARTÍNEZ

I signed in 1978, right after I graduated high school. I was 18. The scout who signed me was Pedrín Zorrilla, the same scout that found Roberto Clemente. At my tryout, I went to the ballpark and hit two home runs—inside-the-park home runs. The fence was 600 feet away, and I hit a couple of one-hoppers off the wall. They gave me $6,000 to sign, and I thought that was a fortune. I talked to that same scout about Edgar, and he told me that Edgar was too slow to play second base, and didn't have enough power to play third base. I told him the power would come, but he wasn't interested. A couple of other teams looked at him, but Edgar didn't want to sign. He was going to school and working.

I kept pushing him—take a chance, take a chance. He finally did, and the rest is history. When the Mariners made their offer—$4,000—I told him, the money is in the big leagues, not the signing bonus. And I told him he could get to the big leagues. I finally convinced him, after a lot of arguing. It was hard for him to make that decision, very hard.

The second part was convincing his grandfather, who was getting old. Edgar was doing most of the stuff around the house. It would have been hard to survive without Edgar, and that was playing on Edgar's mind. But he did survive. Elliot, his brother, ended up helping the grandparents. It was José Juan Rivera who helped convince Edgar's grandfather. José was one of our mentors—whenever we had an activity at the ballpark, he would cook for us. He was influential to all of us ballplayers.

Another very influential person was Mako Oliveras, our first manager when we played in the Puerto Rican winter league. He is a legend in Puerto Rico, the winningest manager in professional baseball, and he gave great advice to Edgar and me. He gave us both our first chance. His first year in winter ball, Edgar went 0-for-50-something. He wanted to quit. Then he came back the next year and hit over .400.

I knew from the start that Edgar was a better hitter than me. I just took more chances. I was a power hitter, an aggressive hitter. He was a thinking hitter, always trying to find a way to get better on his approach and mental game. Then when he got stronger, it all came together. He was a workaholic, man. He hit the weights. He still does, even in his fifties. I didn't do that. I thought I had enough power. Maybe I should have. Edgar's work ethic is incredible—not just a physical work ethic, but mental. He started reading a lot of books on how to use his mind. I tell people, "I taught him well." I stayed behind, but I taught him well.

What a crazy turn my life had taken. All of a sudden, I was a professional baseball player—the dream I had always had, but had almost given up on. Once again, fate had intervened. If I had gone with my parents to New York, none of this would have happened. If I had missed that tryout in Bayamón, none of this would have happened. And if I had turned down the Mariners' offer, none of this would have happened.

But all of it happened. Back then, barely 20 years old and wondering if I had made the right choice, I had no idea where it was all going to lead. There was a good chance it was going to lead me right back to Dorado, but I was going to give it everything I had. Carmelo's words had given me confidence. I said goodbye to my grandfather and grandmother, packed up a suitcase, and headed off to the Mariners' rookie league team to start my baseball career.

Chapter 2

Breaking In

I SIGNED WITH THE MARINERS in December 1982, and the following June I got in an airplane and headed to Bellingham, Washington, a place I knew almost nothing about, where they spoke a language of which I had scant understanding. I had only been to the United States a couple of times since I left New York to move to Puerto Rico as an infant. There were some short trips to see my parents in New York, and a tournament in New Mexico when I was a teenager and our team qualified for the Mickey Mantle League World Series. But those were just a couple of weeks, tops. This time, I was going to be gone for the entire summer, playing for the Bellingham Mariners.

In other words, it was a new adventure in a new world. I was scared, nervous, and excited all at the same time. There were so many unknowns. I would be by myself, trying to meet new people, adjusting to an unfamiliar environment, not knowing the language—and oh yeah, trying to prove that I belonged in professional baseball. It was daunting, but I looked forward to the challenge.

A bunch of Latin players from the Dominican Republic, Venezuela, and Puerto Rico were on the flight with me. And when we got there,

Jeff Scott, who was to be our manager in Bellingham, as well as being the Mariners' assistant farm director, was there to pick us up. He loaded all his players in a van and drove us about 100 miles north to Bellingham, Washington, which is about 20 miles shy of the Canadian border. I remember that we drove right by the Kingdome, where the Mariners played at the time, and Jeff pointed it out to us. Of course, all of us were thinking, "It would be cool to play there one day."

But that day seemed far, far away. I had just turned 20, which made me kind of old for short-season rookie league. But I was just like everyone else on the "Baby Mariners," as they called us. We were all trying to make ourselves stand out so that we could keep advancing up the ladder. It was tough at the beginning. The biggest thing that struck me right away was the weather. It was a jolt. I was used to Puerto Rico, of course, where it was warm all year round. In Bellingham, it was cold, even in the summertime. At least it felt that way to me. And I was lonely. It was the first time I had ever been away from my grandparents for an extended time, and I missed them and worried about them. There were no cell phones in those days, but I found a way to call them pretty much every day, even if it meant walking to a store or a gas station to find a pay phone.

I rented a house in Bellingham with three other Latin players, including Luis Vega—the catcher that signed out of the same tryout camp as me—and a Venezuelan first baseman named Pablo Moncerratt. It was an adventure, all of us trying to make our way in a new country and succeed in baseball. We bonded around that and got to be good friends.

The Latin players tended to hang out together, mostly because of the language barrier, but I became friends with some of the other guys on the team, too, like Dave Hengel, an outfielder from California that I played with at every level of pro ball, including for a time with the

Mariners. One vivid memory I have is when me and my roommates crashed a party that some other players were having. It was a toga party—this was 1983, just a few years after *Animal House* came out—and so we all got blankets to use as togas and walked into the party.

Living without my family was the biggest adjustment, along with learning the basics, like cooking, doing my own wash, ironing my clothes. All those things had been done for me at home. It was a big adjustment for my grandparents as well when I left home. My cousin would bring them the newspaper every day during my career. Because my grandfather's eyesight was failing, my cousin would read to him what I was doing on the field. He was able to appreciate my accomplishments in that way.

I only knew a few basic words of English at that time. I couldn't even put them together into a sentence, and I struggled to understand other people when they were talking. Today, teams have language instruction for their foreign players, but they didn't have that back then. We were pretty much on our own. So what I did was make sure I watched American television shows, and listen closely to try to pick up words and figure out the meaning. I remember I'd watch *The Jeffersons, The Bob Newhart Show*, and later *Married with Children*—a lot of sitcoms. There were no tutors. I learned by watching television, listening to the radio, and just being around the other players. It was hard at first, I'm not going to lie, because we all need communication as humans. But as I slowly began to pick up the language, it got easier.

What wasn't so easy for me that year, it turned out, was playing professional baseball. We were in the Northwest League, riding buses to places in Washington and Oregon like Walla Walla, Spokane, Eugene, Salem, and Bend. I just couldn't ever get going offensively. At the end of the season, my average was .173. It's still hard for me to fathom that number, nearly 40 years later. I had just 18 hits in 104 at-bats. I didn't hit any homers, and had just two extra-base hits—one double and one triple. I couldn't believe it. I was used to being the best hitter on every team I was on, and I couldn't even get my average up to .200.

The funny thing is, every time I came to the plate I felt like I was going to get a hit. My confidence was so strong—which made it even more frustrating. I was like, "What's going on? I'm not getting hits." That had never happened to me before. I remember one game getting to first base and telling the coach, "I'm seeing the ball so good, and my swing feels so good, and I'm still not hitting anything." What I remember is that I was swinging through fastballs. I was always a contact hitter and had been able to barrel balls my whole life. I was asking myself, "I feel so good; why am I missing it?"

My mind stayed positive the whole time, though. I didn't feel any pressure, for some reason. Of course, that was my first year using wood bats, except for one league in Puerto Rico. That took a little getting used to, and so did hitting in the cold weather. But that's not an excuse. My recollection of that season is just that I was shocked I wasn't hitting, but I felt great. Still, .173 is .173. I was afraid that my pro career was over already, and that I'd made a horrible mistake leaving my old life behind.

TODO FRANCIS
Teammate, Bellingham Mariners, 1983

What most impressed me about Edgar was his defense. His hands were awesome. Edgar's nickname was "Pops," because when you played catch with him, the ball never stayed in his glove. He popped it out so fricking quick. And even though he hit a buck-seventy, when you looked at him in batting practice, you knew. If you knew baseball players, you knew this guy could play. We all would go, "This dude is unbelievably good."

The other thing was his character. Edgar was the greatest dude ever. Unflappable. All the Latin guys on the Bellingham team looked up to him like he was king. Even though he had just come over from Puerto Rico and didn't know anyone, they all looked up to him. Basically, it was how he carried himself. His cousin, Carmelo Martínez, had just broken into the big leagues that year with the Cubs, so that gave him some extra credibility, too.

Jeff Scott, our manager, called me into his office at the end of the season and I was sure I was being released. I really liked Jeff. He was a guy that all the players looked up to and respected, almost like a father figure. I remember being very, very attentive to everything he said. We were all very young, and he looked out for us, tried to help make us more comfortable. But I thought he was going to tell me to pack my bags and go home. Instead, he said, "How would you like to go to the instructional league?"

Wow, what a relief! Thinking back now, I'm wondering if there was a clause in my contract where they couldn't release me after the first season. Marty Martínez, the scout that signed me, would have been the one to answer this. At any rate, I immediately said, "I'd love to go." I went from thinking I was being fired to getting chosen for the instructional league, where teams sent the prospects they thought had the most potential. I heard later that Marty and Jeff had to talk Hal Keller, the Mariners' general manager, into sending me to instructional league. Instructional league took place in Tempe, Arizona, where the Mariners held spring training in those days. Bellingham had won our division of the Northwest League, and Jeff had another message for me when he called me in his office: he said I was going to play every day in the playoffs. Up until that time, I had been splitting time at third with other players, not getting regular playing time.

In a 1992 article in the *Seattle Times*, Marty Martínez said of my .173 season, "If he was with any other team they would have cut him, but we were patient. Being Latin had a lot of do with it. I don't know why, but you need more patience with Latin players. I think it helped him, too, that we didn't have a third baseman in winter ball."

TODD FRANCIS
Teammate, Bellingham Mariners, 1983

He was never going to be released. He might have thought that, but you saw how he carried himself. You watched batting practice, and he put on a clinic. We had guys like Darrel Akerfelds, Bill Wilkinson, guys who would play in the big leagues, and we all knew. We'd say, "This guy is fricking great." You can't really tell about a guy until you get 200 at-bats. Edgar had never been in the United States, couldn't order from McDonald's, couldn't go to Wendy's. That's life-changing. But at 4:30 in batting practice, he was hitting rockets. If you saw him take BP, he was the best player on the field. If you saw him take infield, he was the best player on the field. He would have been a defensive wizard at third base if his hamstrings had held up. His hand-eye coordination was off the charts.

You know what else about Bellingham? Worst hitting background I've ever seen in my life. The fence was low, with a neighborhood behind the fence. You'd get a hanging curveball in Bellingham and it would hit three streetlights. You'd say, "Where did the ball go?" Then Edgar went to Wausau, with a great hitting background, and he hit .300.

We ended up losing the title to Medford, but that was a real turning point in my career—yet another juncture when it could have taken a completely different route. It could have ended right there. But when we had that meeting, it eased my mind. I thought, "Well, if I'm going to instructional league, I guess I'm going to get another shot." That helped a lot. In Tempe, we'd practice in the morning and play games against other teams in Arizona, every day for about a month. I played really well in instructional league, both offensively and defensively. I hit .340 in fact. That was confirmation in my own mind that I could play at this level—especially that I could hit up here. And that gave the organization confidence to send me to full-season Single-A the following year.

JEFF SCOTT
Bellingham Manager, 1979–1983; Mariners Player Development, 1983–85

I threw batting practice in those days, and Edgar never hit a ball out of the ballpark in BP. Nowhere, home or road. He only had four or five RBIs, and no homers. But I remembered I had managed Jim Presley, who was a 17-year-old high school kid when we drafted him. He played the whole summer for me, and played a lot more than Edgar, and he never hit a home run, either, and never hit a ball out of the park in batting practice. He became a pretty good major-league hitter. I had experienced enough situations of young kids in the Northwest League, which is a college league, and they just needed time to catch up. Darnell Coles hit .200. It's not an uncommon thing. Edgar went up to the Midwest League the next year and took off.

Once he got to Instructional League, in fact, the other coaches and managers realized he had a chance to be a really good player. Even the two or three scouts from our organization that had come to see him during the season, they were impressed. Edgar told me a few years later in winter ball, "Scotty, I thought I'd be released after that first year."

I said, "Why did you think that? You played half the time, and we took you to instructional league." Marty and I talked Hal Keller into sending him to instructional league.

Hal didn't want to send him, but Edgar did well, and Hal said, "I'm pleasantly surprised." Hal Keller was a genius. When we signed Edgar and he came up to Bellingham, Hal didn't even know we had signed him. He was director of scouting and player development, and I was his assistant. He said, "You handle all that other crap." He saw Edgar in Bellingham for the first time during the year and said, "I like this kid." I said later, "Then why was it so hard to talk you into letting him play in instructional league?" He said, "I thought he'd be overmatched. You proved me wrong."

I said, "No, Edgar proved you wrong."

We took care of them when they got to Bellingham, but they do a better job in today's world. More people are involved. We had eating arrangements for them, made sure we got them housed. There wasn't host families like now. We had to get them apartments. Edgar had never been out West, and of course there was the language barrier. His English back then was not like today. I'm sure some of that stuff played a role in how they play.

Most all the players lived in the same apartment complex—they were good working with us—and it was close enough they'd walk to the park. Not many guys in a rookie summer league are driving. The game would be over, and half an hour later you'd see 20 of them walking up the highway. Travel days were fun. They'd be pulling their suitcases right down the street. One distinctive thing about Bellingham, the clubhouse was huge. It was a football locker room for Western Washington University. You had to walk across the parking lot to get to the baseball field. I had no office. The trainer and I shared a big old table. It was all open season. There were no secrets. Everyone could see and hear everything.

The first year I managed in Bellingham, 1979, I had no coaches and 40 players. I actually had quite a few Puerto Rican kids, seven or eight. Only one spoke decent English, and he was my translator. My Spanish was *un poquito*. I could understand more than I could speak, except for the dirty words. But I learned early, the language of baseball is universal. So when it comes to doing things on the field, doing drills, fundamentals, cutoffs, relays, I never had any trouble communicating in that regard. I'm sure if we were sitting down and I was trying to talk to them and get in their head if they needed help with something above and beyond, that was tougher for them. In all honesty, that was Marty's role. He was a roving instructor, and jack-of-all-trades. He spent a lot of time with those kids. He was their daddy, including Edgar, and later Omar Vizquel. When Marty would get to town, I'd say, "Find out if there's any problems, Marty. Let me know so we could solve them."

Edgar didn't talk much. He got along fine with everybody, but I'm sure it was harder for him than I realized. I wasn't exactly a grizzled veteran. I was 24 the first year I managed in Bellingham. Edgar was pretty skinny back then. When he signed, he could run—he was a tick above an average runner—he could throw, he had good hands, good range. If he hadn't become a DH, he could have played first base his whole career. But when he got hurt, Alvin [Davis] was there, and he wasn't going to supplant him. In my opinion, he would have been an above-average third baseman. I've heard people say he was a defensive liability. He wasn't a defensive liability.

He had a good swing and made solid contact. He just didn't drive the ball as much as he needed at the time. In my mind, he was doing fine. He just happened to be hitting .170. I'm sure I told him that others before you went through the same thing, so don't get discouraged. I don't remember any real heart-to-heart talks. We were not in the business of signing kids and releasing them because they didn't do what we wanted the first couple of months. But Latin players heard a lot of stories about that. I'm sure those thoughts go through their head.

In 1984, I was assigned to the Wausau Timbers of the Midwest League. Before the season, I went back to Tempe for my first spring training as a pro. That's kind of a blur now, but the one thing I remember happened on the last day, when they held a race from the left-field line to the fence and then back. I was never known for my speed, even back then, although I was much thinner than I would become, and my legs were still in good shape, which wouldn't be the case later in my career. I was determined to win. And, somehow, I did win. That's a good example of how competitive I was throughout my career (I'm a little better now that I'm retired). People might not realize that, because I'm quiet and low-key. But I wanted to be first, or I wanted to win, or I wanted to be the best. That was something burning within me. Other players would say, "Oh, man, why do we have to run?" I'd say, "I'm going to win this."

I had this attitude with pretty much anything. I remember when I got to the majors, my teammate Mickey Brantley (whose son, Michael, has been a great player) had the same kind of personality. We were always talking about racing, and we each boasted that we could beat the other guy. Finally, we set up a race. I beat him—and he was much faster than me. But I had that strong desire to win and be the best. Early in my career, it was more of a personal thing. In the minor leagues, especially the low minors, it's mainly about surviving, and you have to be a little selfish. I was motivated to prove to other people I was very good. And I was probably trying to prove it to myself as well. Later, I learned that winning is a lot of fun, and it's not so much fun when you lose. I transferred that passion and drive to the team, and channeled my competitiveness into trying to lift us to success.

I had a temper, too—another thing that might surprise people. I think it had to do with that desire and competitiveness. I remember punching the bat rack one time in Single-A. I had my moments where it comes out. Maybe it's because things are building for a while and I tend to hold it tight. All of a sudden, it just explodes. That was the case the one and only time in my career I charged the mound.

It was 2001 and we were playing the Angels in Anaheim during the last week of the season in October. I was holding it in, holding it in, holding it in. I had been hit like eight times that year. It seemed like every time I played in Anaheim, I would get hit. Eventually, I'd had enough. When Lou Pote, the Angels pitcher, hit me that game on my right hand (and the ball then ricocheted off my cheek), I remember the thought just came into my head: start running to the mound.

It was like my emotions took over. My teammate Mike Cameron told the writers afterward, "They flicked a switch in Edgar I've never seen before." And John McLaren, our bench coach, said later, "He was the raging bull of all time. I've never seen a man's eyes get like that… I would never mess with Edgar. He was one of those quiet guys that would clean your clock. It took six of us to pull him off."

I charged the mound and was just about to swing but the Angels catcher, my old friend from Puerto Rico, Bengie Molina, grabbed my arm. And that's when Boonie—Bret Boone—saved me. My hand was basically tied by Molina, and so the pitcher had a clear shot at me. But Boonie was the baserunner at first base, and he charged over, grabbed the pitcher, and held him back. If it wasn't for Boonie, I'd probably have had a broken nose, which wouldn't have been good, because that was the year we won 116 games and we were about to start the playoffs. Luckily, I didn't get hurt—and I got all that frustration off my chest. I did get a fine from Major League Baseball—$1,000, if I recall. All the other fights we had during my career, including a couple of big brawls with Milwaukee and Baltimore, I played the peacemaker.

I didn't get ejected from a game until August 23, 1996—seven years into my career as an everyday player. In an important game at Fenway

Park—we were fighting to stay alive in the playoff race—our entire team was frustrated with the ball-strike calls of home-plate umpire Ted Barrett. Ted would have a long career, and was a good ump, but at that time he was a substitute umpire just breaking in.

Anyway, there was a pitch to me that he called a strike "that appeared well inside," according to the *Seattle Times.* Two pitches later, he called strike three on "on a pitch that appeared four to six inches outside," said the *Times,* which continued: "Martínez wheeled and let loose." I told the reporters after the game, "I honestly can't remember what I said to him to get tossed. Before that, I told him to call pitches the same for both teams. He had been squeezing [our starter, Terry] Mulholland and giving [Boston pitcher Tom] Gordon a lot." I soon had company in the clubhouse—our manager, Lou Piniella, was thrown out later that inning and Joey Cora was tossed an inning later. Sometimes, you just can't control yourself. But other than that fight, I had just one other ejection in my career, also for arguing balls-and-strikes.

The other incident that people like to talk about occurred in spring training shortly after we moved into the new facility in Peoria, Arizona. The sound system was near my locker, and it was always playing really loud. One day, when everyone was sitting around the clubhouse, I stood up, got my bat, and smashed the stereo. I acted like I was really mad and serious, but I wasn't. It was just kind of a joke. I was doing it for fun for the guys. There were pieces of the radio scattered all over the place, and people were stunned, like, "What the heck just happened here?" I went back to weighing my bats without saying a word. A lot of people thought I was mad, and some probably still do, but honestly, I wasn't. The next day, I came in with a new sound system for the clubhouse.

RICK GRIFFIN
Mariners Athletic Trainer, 1983–2017

No, he was not joking. It was in spring training, and they put in a new system. We were over in Peoria now and everyone was all excited. Edgar was in this one corner, and Jay was across from him, and a couple of the other big-name guys were there. They put the speaker right above Edgar. And after the workouts, they'd turn it up super loud. Edgar would go over and turn it down because it was too loud and he didn't like it. He said they needed to move the speaker somewhere if they were going to turn it up so loud.

It was after a game one day, I heard all this screaming and yelling. I ran out of the training room, and Edgar had a bat and he was smashing the speaker. He destroyed it. Then he kicked it and pushed it out of the way. Then he said something like, "No more loud music." Everyone was like, "Oh, my God, Edgar snapped, did you see that?" They couldn't believe that he snapped. The next day he went and bought a brand-new stereo system that was better. But he made them put the speaker way on the other side.

He could snap. He never snapped on the field, except that time in Anaheim, but he would have these little mini-snaps in the clubhouse. He would get really, really upset.

MIKE BLOWERS
Former Mariners Third Baseman

I like how quiet Edgar was all the time. Understated all the time, for somebody who was so great at what he was doing. I thought that was one of the coolest things. Junior was the biggest star in the game. We would travel, and he was *the* thing everyone wanted to see. And then there was just the steady Edgar right behind him all the time, doing his thing. Which between the two of them was a pretty cool dynamic.

I didn't see the stereo incident, but I heard about it shortly after. I wasn't in the room when it happened. From the way it was explained to me, he had had enough. He had asked to turn it down a number of different occasions. We're talking days, right. He finally had had enough. From what I understand, he calmly walked across, beat this thing to smithereens with his bat, and then calmly walked back and sat at his locker. When people were telling me, I was actually cracking up laughing. I thought it was awesome, just because it was so out of character for Gar. But the man had had enough, and that was it. That ended that whole situation. To hear the way he went about it was just perfect Edgar. You could visualize the whole thing. Aside from probably the aggression of it, it was just perfect.

One of the things I do remember, which was awesome, involved Armando Benítez, the closer for Baltimore. He threw at that time as hard as anyone in the game. I'll never forget one night he drills Edgar. Edgar obviously was not happy about it. It was the very next day, he's facing Benítez again in the ninth, and Edgar took him deep in Camden. It was one of the few times he hit a home run, and he watched it. Which was pretty awesome—one, that he was able to do that, and two, just for him to let Benítez know: I recognize what you did, and here you go, which is pretty cool. Everyone would love to do that, but it's a hard thing to do. Edgar was good enough to pull it off.

I remember another time at Safeco when a young pitcher—whose name escapes me—threw one at my head. I stood up and stared at him, and the next pitch I hit a home run. It looked to me like he was trying to intimidate me, so that was satisfying.

But that was still light years away.

Back then in 1984, I still wasn't sure I would ever get to the major leagues when I reported to the Midwest League for my second pro season. Wausau was a small town in Wisconsin—and it was even colder than Bellingham. For one thing, we started the season in April, instead of June like we did in Bellingham, and there was even some snow at times, I remember. Once again, I lived in a house, this time with a couple of teammates from Venezuela, one of whom was married, so his wife lived with us, too. I have good memories of living in that house. It was very homey. I even remember how the house smelled, because it was older. For the most part, we got along well.

There was a bar with music where a lot of the single guys used to hang out. This was another bus league, traveling to small towns in Wisconsin, Iowa, and Illinois. Some of the trips were 10, 12 hours. I liked to read on the bus but sometimes I would pop in a cassette tape (remember, this was the 1980s) to pass the time. I liked reggae, plus Michael Jackson was getting big, and so was Prince. I'd listen to their music a lot. We'd stop at places like Dunkin' Donuts and Waffle House to eat. It wasn't glamorous, let me tell you.

Oh, and the car we drove was a story in itself. Ernesto Gomez and I chipped in and bought an old Volkswagen for about $300. The windows hardly worked, the tailpipe was falling on the ground, and it was really loud. Every time we saw a police car, one of us would say, "A cop!" and we'd put it in neutral and let it idle on the side of the road. We made sure we didn't press on the gas pedal. We were always thinking, "This thing is going to leave us in the street one day." But it got us through. We had a to tie a couple of shoelaces together to try to secure the tailpipe to the bumper, so it wouldn't drag on the ground.

MIKE WISHNEVSKI

Teammate, Wausau, 1984; Chattanooga, 1986; Calgary, 1987–88

Edgar and Ernie Gomez had a blue VW Beetle, and at the end of the season, they didn't know what to do with it. So my brother Bob, who went on to play in the minor leagues himself, bought it.

On the field, I picked up where I had left off in instructional ball. I continued to make adjustments. I started out right away hitting well, which helped my confidence, and wound up with a .303 average. I had 32 doubles, 15 homers, and even stole 11 bases.

Looking back now and asking the question of why I didn't hit in Bellingham, one big thing was that we had five third basemen, and Jeff Scott wanted to play everybody. That meant I didn't play every day. Whether it was because he wanted to play the other guys or because I wasn't hitting, I don't know. But it was hard to get in a rhythm. Throughout my career, even in the majors, when I would sit a few days or be sidelined with an injury, it always took me a while to get in a groove. Even in my best years, once interleague play started and I'd sit for a few days in National League parks because they didn't have a DH, it would take me a while to get my swing back. In Wausau, though, I was an everyday player. I remember getting into a rhythm, and after that I felt normal at the plate. That was a big factor in my success.

The manager, Greg Mahlberg, was good for me. I remember him getting all of us together to talk baseball, go over the game, discuss ways to improve. But in those days, I was a very private person. I still didn't feel comfortable communicating. I was very into myself, my own space, not interacting with a lot of people. I was here to do my job, do it well, and then go home when I was done. It's funny—now I almost feel like English is my first language. Living in Seattle, I speak it more than I do Spanish, and it comes very naturally. But it took a long time to feel comfortable. Even after I had been in the minor leagues for a few years, I still felt a little uneasy conversing.

One person who really helped in those days was Marty Martínez. He was a roving instructor, and also later a coach, and when he'd come to town, he'd talk to us, especially the Latin players, and make sure we were okay. He'd give advice on how to do things in the minor leagues that was very helpful. I didn't have much communication at all with anyone else in the Mariner organization, so his feedback was very important. Marty was a father figure for all of us—not just me, but Omar Vizquel, Mario Díaz, and the other Latin players in the organization at the time. We were all like his sons. Marty was always protecting us, but he'd do it in a funny way. He had a great sense of humor.

Marty Martínez was a very important person in my life, and I was very sad when he passed away in 2007. I was glad he got to manage the Mariners for one day in 1986, a year before I got to the major leagues. The Mariners fired Chuck Cottier in midseason and hired Dick Williams, but Marty was the interim manager on May 9 while Dick was on his way. He lost to the Boston Red Sox, but for one day, Marty Martínez was a major-league manager. It's in the record books.

GREG MAHLBERG
Wausau Manager, 1984
Edgar was a real pleasure to have. He was one of the few guys, I never had to worry about him doing something. He always did his job, always worked hard. In time you could tell he was going to get better and better and better.

He was so young and just starting out when I had him. He had it in him to get really good, but I'll be honest, I never imagined Hall of Fame. I think his confidence was down a little after the season he had in Bellingham, but he was so young. It was his first time out of his own country, out of his own culture. Other Latinos were there, but I think he felt a little uncomfortable. I don't blame him.

We worked a lot. We did a lot with his hitting, and his fielding. He came right along. I kept telling him, just keep working hard, you're doing fine. Especially in his situation, I wanted to make him feel part of what was going on. I could understand how he felt being away from home, basically on his own. His English wasn't perfect, but it was pretty good. I used to get Marty Martínez, our infield coach, to help me out quite a bit if I needed to explain something in more detail.

Edgar was a real good fielder, and he worked hard at it. He was a pretty big kid, and they were thinking he was going to get much bigger and might have to move to first base. He worked hard on coming in on balls, going to his left and right, to get better. He always had a very accurate, strong arm. It was just a matter of doing repetition. And he'd do it. That was the neat thing about Edgar.

I remember a story. He couldn't get the signs. I made special signs just for him. I even told Marty, we'll make special signs, anything he wants. But he couldn't get the signs. It would frustrate me and the team. We'd have the hit-and-run on and he wouldn't pick it up. But he figured it out.

I always thought he had a really good swing, and he worked hard to develop it. Edgar had great hand-eye coordination. The organization had kind of lost a little bit of hope for him [coming off Bellingham] but they still thought of him as a prospect. I always thought he had it in him because of his work ethic. From really when he was a kid, he always wanted to do whatever he could. Not only with the swing and working on that, but he'd do all kinds of cage work, soft toss. For fielding, he'd come out and I'd roll him balls. He just did it forever.

Wausau wasn't a bad place to live. We had a lot of families where kids could stay. There was a pretty good booster club. It was a small community, a rural community, a different type of culture. Some of the people there back then, especially with a Latino, they kind of shied away a little sometimes. It could be lonely, especially if you didn't have other teammates. Just their food, for one thing. You have to think about that. They're used to beans and rice, and here we are eating hot dogs and hamburgers. It was different.

Edgar was the standout. He was in the voting of the league for MVP. I think he came damn close. He was just a pleasure to have. If you had a son, that's who you'd want him to be like.

MIKE WISHNEVSKI
Teammate, Wausau, 1984; Chattanooga, 1986; Calgary, 1987–88

When we first met, we used to go to Denny's because there were pictures on the menu. Edgar and I were in Wausau, Chattanooga, and Calgary together. And we were in big-league camp together. We just traveled along. Edgar was as good a friend as you could ask for in a game where sometimes you're hoping the guy at the plate in your position doesn't get a hit; you're looking for opportunity. Edgar was quiet around most people, but he could be hilarious.

I think Edgar lost three years of big-league time being stuck in the minors. But he never complained. His perseverance was amazing. His attitude was, I know I'm better than what's there, and eventually they will figure it out. Hopefully sooner than later.

Edgar was very accurate throwing the ball. One time, he short-hopped Brick Smith, our first baseman. We got the guy out anyway, and afterward,

Brick stuck his chest out and said, "Hey, what was that?" Because Edgar never skipped one to Brick. It was always chest high.

He had great range, and you didn't see a lot of balls tipping off his glove. Him and Mario Díaz would play catch, but it was a game they played where they never caught the ball. It would ricochet out of the pocket of the glove and land in their hand, and they'd see how fast they could go back and forth. He said they did that as kids. If you didn't know they were doing it and a double-play was happening, you'd think they must have caught it, but it was popping out of the heel of their glove.

I could see that Edgar was going to get to the big leagues. I knew he'd be an excellent hitter in the bigs. I think he honed his skills once he got to the big leagues. In Chattanooga, it was 471 feet to center with a 30-foot wall. I can't tell you how many drives Edgar hit that the center fielder ran down. He was robbed of a lot of homers. Once he got to Triple-A, you could see Edgar needed to be up top. He had the skill and talent to play third base up top. He finally got his chance and never looked back.

After the season in Wausau, I felt much better about my career. I had hit .300 in a professional league, and the unease that crept in after I hit .173 in 1983 was fading. I was 21 years old and at least I knew that I would have another season in pro ball. I went back home to Dorado to take a break, but it wasn't really a break. I'd still go to the stadium every day and practice. And when November came, I was back at it with the San Juan Senadores of Liga de Béisbol Profesional de Puerto Rico (now named Liga de Béisbol Profesional Roberto Clemente, which is fitting). Playing winter ball in Puerto Rico, which I did for the next decade-plus, was a huge part of my development. It was also a thrill to play in the same league that I had watched with my grandpa growing up, the same league that so many great players had played in, from Puerto Rican idols like Clemente and Orlando Cepeda to American superstars like Hank Aaron and Willie Mays. My grandpa used to tell me about Hank Aaron playing second base for the Caguas Criollos, and about Orlando Cepeda's father, who was an amazing hitter just like his son.

The league had hit some hard times in the late 1970s and early 1980s. But that changed with the next generation, which was one of the best in the history of the island. We had so many great players in their prime—Roberto Alomar, Sandy Alomar, Rubén Sierra, Juan González, Carlos Delgado, Carlos Baerga, Bernie Williams, and many, many more—including Carmelo, who was named the league's MVP playing for Bayamón in 1982–83 (and again as my teammate on San Juan in 1993–94). Almost all of them understand how important it was to remember their roots, and to give back. It was humbling to go back to the same fields and old clubhouses you played in when you were struggling to make it. It also reminded you why you played baseball in the first place—because you loved it.

Not only did I feel an obligation to play in Puerto Rico each winter, but I thoroughly enjoyed it. I loved the atmosphere, the color, the excitement of the fans, and the fun of the game. It was just different. Everyone wanted to win, of course, but it was a more relaxed atmosphere. And for a young guy like me to play for the Senadores, one of the most famous teams in Puerto Rico, was special.

Dickie Thon, who was a major-league star with the Houston Astros before his career was marred by a beaning, was on that team. So was Baerga, who was becoming a star with the Indians. I was just trying to make my name in those days. The quality of play was very high, which I firmly believe helped me get a head-start when I went back to spring training. Even after I became an established major-leaguer, I kept playing. I had the mentality that this was my job, and I needed to work at it all year. I also had the belief that playing every day made me better. When I got to Arizona, I didn't have to get in shape. I didn't have to work on my mechanics. I was already sharp. I feel winter ball was extremely beneficial to my career. My skills kept getting better the more I played.

My breakout year in the winter league came in 1989–90, when I hit .424 for San Juan to become the first player in Puerto Rico to hit .400 since Luke Easter hit .402 for a famous Mayagüez team in 1948–49. I had 56 hits in 132 at-bats, with 37 walks to bring me over the 150 plate appearances necessary to qualify for the batting title. I was named co-MVP of the league that year, along with Baerga, who hit .341 with four homers and 35 runs batted in. It was unreal. When you have so few at-bats, your average can fluctuate. You can be .400 today, and then drop to .220 by the end of the week. But from Day One, I was very consistent and kept my average high. The down days were very few. I was hitting from line to line, covering the whole field.

Mako Oliveras, my manager in San Juan, was another very important person in my career. We all grew up with him on the Senadores (which later changed its name to the Metros for a few years)—Carmelo, Carlos Baerga, and a lot of others. We were his guys. He called us his "Pillos," which translates literally to "teeth," but it's a fun word that means "young rascals." We were all young compared to the rest of the league, but he helped us be contenders, and we were going to the playoffs.

Mako put a lot of trust in me as a young player, and that gave me a lot of confidence. He was always high on my talent, when maybe others weren't. Even as a young player, he kept giving me opportunities. Even though the league in Puerto Rico is about winning, he had a good eye for promising young players, and he'd stand by you even if you were struggling. And my first year in the league, I really struggled, with a long hitless streak. That was very hard, but Mako stuck with me. Every day, I was in the lineup. He'd say, "Just go and play. You're going to come out of it." I would hit the ball good, and right at somebody. I would hit the ball soft, and right at somebody. It was one of those tough stretches. But he was right. I came out of it, and eventually hit .400.

When that winter-league season in which I hit .400 ended, I reported to camp with the Mariners for the 1990 season, which turned out to be the first year I stayed in the major leagues all season, hitting .302. I don't think that's a coincidence. My strong showing in Puerto Rico set me up to succeed in the majors that year. My favorite year in the winter league, though, was 1994–95, when all the top players in Puerto Rico were together on what came to be known as "The Dream Team" that won the Caribbean World Series. I'll talk more about that later, but playing at such a high level of competition all winter set me up for the greatest year of my career with the Mariners in 1995— another topic I'll get back to, in depth, I promise.

In those early days, I was making more money playing in Puerto Rico than I was in the minors. I made about $5,000 a month playing for San Juan when I first started, then it got bumped up to between $8,000 and $10,000 a month when I became more established. In Bellingham, I made about $800 a month, so I needed that winter-league money. Heck, I made more on the night shift at Westinghouse before I signed than I did at Bellingham—which was one of the reasons it had been such an agonizing decision to turn pro. I was living a pretty comfortable life back then, and all of a sudden I was barely getting by in Bellingham and Wausau. In the minors, you had to pay clubhouse dues to cover your food and such. You had to make sure you didn't waste a penny, which meant no frivolous expenses. I remember some of the guys buying stuff they didn't need, and they didn't have the money to pay their dues, and they got in trouble. That was a no-no. I was pretty good at managing what little money I had.

MAKO OLIVERAS
Former Manager, San Juan Senadores/Metros

I'm 72 and still coaching. I refuse to give it up. I learned a long time ago, I can rest when I die.

I think it was 1988 when I was manager for the Metros of San Juan, we signed Edgar. Edgar always was a real quiet type of guy, low-key, didn't talk much. He talked with his bat. And I remember that for some reason, I liked his bat. His cousin Carmelo was on the team, too. I decided to play Edgar at third base, and at the beginning, he had a little trouble hitting. He was hitting a buck-eighty, maybe lower, but I stuck with him. I kept putting him out there. My owner and general manager wanted me to play someone else. I went against their orders. I said, "He's my third baseman, and he's going to play." I was cocky back then. Edgar hit .400 the next year. Line drives everywhere. I tell you, he was a very smart hitter. He was the type of player that used to sit in the dugout, not say anything. I saw him staring at the pitcher. He was looking for an advantage, like, sometimes he puts his glove this way, and it's a curve. When he puts it the other way, it's a fastball. He was a master of that.

What really stands out, he had great glove. I never saw Edgar make an errant throw. Every time he threw the ball to first base, it was right on the money. Edgar was a manager's dream as a player. He never complained; whatever you asked him to do, he'd do it quietly. He still is like that.

Edgar spent a lot of years in Triple-A for the Mariners. For some reason, Seattle never brought him up. I used to manage Edmonton, the Triple-A team for the Angels, when he was at Calgary, and he wore me out. Omar Vizquel was on that team, too. I remember Tom Romanesco, a former umpire, became director of player development for the Padres. He came around, and I told him, "There's a third baseman that for some reason they don't bring up to the big leagues, and he's going to be a great player." That year, the Padres tried to get him in the Rule 5 draft or something, but that was the year he came to the big leagues with Seattle and never went down. Edgar was so quiet, he wouldn't talk about how he felt being stuck in the minors. I never heard him complain.

Edgar was raised by his grandparents. He was living with them when I met him. He treated them with so much love—very respectful. Edgar's the type of guy, you wish your daughter would find someone like him. He built a batting cage at the house, and we all used to go there. Especially on days off, the whole team would go there. He was a great friend to everyone. I'm getting goosebumps talking about it. He was special for me. I love the kid. The way he treated his grandparents, the way he acted, he was an outstanding human being. His town, Maguayo, everyone there is like a family. You say something wrong about Edgar Martínez in Maguayo, you'll have to be fighting all day long.

Here in Puerto Rico, Edgar Martínez is the silent hero. He was never a guy that liked to be interviewed. They don't talk about him the way they used to talk about Clemente and Cepeda. He's the other way around. He was low-key, and still is. Everyone is waiting for that moment they put Edgar in the Hall of Fame. If there's somebody that deserved to be in a long time ago, his name is Edgar Martínez. I'm going to take out my savings because I want to be there in Cooperstown.

Edgar could be so naïve back then. I remember one time, he had a sports car, and he stopped to make a phone call. In those days, there were pay phones on the corner. He stopped, and they robbed him. But even then, he never complained.

Okay, about that robbery Mako mentioned. I had a Mazda RX-7, and after a winter-league game, I was on my way to a carnival and I wanted to say hi to my girlfriend. There were no cell phones in those days, so I stopped at a pay phone. Bad idea. I parked, and as soon as I grabbed the phone and started talking, this other car parked next to me, with four guys in it. The driver got out, pulled out a gun, and put it to my head. I was just stunned. I said to myself, "If this guy doesn't kill me, those other guys are going to." I don't know if they had guns, but they probably did. So I just said, "Don't shoot." The guy kind of calmed down, and they left—with my car.

A guy had been driving by and saw what happened. He turned around and when they left, he said, "Get in the car, get in the car, I saw what happened." We kind of chased them a little bit—not the greatest idea. Eventually, I ended up at a friend's house, and he said, "Okay, let's go. I might know where this car is." He grabbed his dad's gun. Another bad idea. We went to this narrow road in the middle of nowhere. I said, "I don't know what we're doing here. What are we going to do?" We didn't see anything and ended up leaving. I reported the incident to the police, and the next day I got a call that the car was found. But when I picked it up, there were no tires, or seats, or radio. They had dismantled the car. I fixed it up with new tires, new seats. But it never worked quite the same, because it looked like they abused it.

If it sounds scary, believe me, it was. I was kind of traumatized for a little bit, in fact. I remember I looked over my shoulder all the time. What it did was make me aware that there are some places you have to be careful. It was a lesson I learned again a few years later when I was playing in Chattanooga in Double-A. I was living in an apartment with catcher Dan Firova and his wife and kids. One day, I was walking their nanny back to her apartment, which was in the same complex.

We passed one door, two doors, three doors, and suddenly someone opened the door to an apartment and pointed a gun—basically straight at me. He stared, and then went back inside and closed the door. It looked to me like he was waiting for someone, and thought we were them. We got out of their quickly. I got the nanny home and hustled back to our apartment. That was pretty scary, too.

Believe it or not, I got mixed up in one other incident, back when I was much younger. I wasn't even in pro ball yet. This one I'm not proud of, even though I didn't do anything. I was at a bar with some buddies, and one of my friends got in a fight and punched a guy. That guy got really mad and apparently went to his car to get a gun! We thought he was leaving, so we went to our car to leave, too. But he started walking toward us with the gun, and he was pointing it at us and talking. Luckily, one of his friends calmed him down. He got in his car, we got in ours, and we figured the whole thing was over. We drove off.

But within a minute or two, he was right behind us—and I was driving! I tried to speed off and get away from him. I had my brother with me and I didn't want him involved in something like this. All the rest of the guys were older—I grew up with older friends. One of them was a police officer, and he told me, "Don't run away." I wanted to say, "But there's a guy with a gun right behind us!" We ended up on the highway, stopped on opposite sides of the road. And this guy starts shooting our way. We got down on the ground, and we could hear these shots going in the bushes. We could see it. I don't think he tried to hit us, but he tried to give us a good scare.

Eventually, the cop said, "He shot all his shots. I know that gun, he only has five bullets." And when the guy got in his car and tried to get away, my cop friend said, "Now we're going to chase him."

I said, "Then you drive." At that point, though, I calmed him down. Like I said, I was with my brother, and I told my friends, "My grandfather is going to kill me." The cop backed off, and the other guy was gone anyway. That was the end of it. My grandfather never found out. He would have been so mad. I was shaken up, as you'd expect—I had never experienced anything like that. I'm thankful that all those incidents ended without any harm—just lessons learned.

Okay, back to baseball. In 1985, I moved one notch up the ladder again and started the year at Double-A with the Chattanooga Lookouts. That was definitely the toughest league I played in—and frustratingly, I would play there for the next two seasons. The ballpark was the biggest in the minor leagues, and the pitching was a lot better than I had been facing. All the teams sent their best prospects to Double-A. I faced pitchers like Tom Glavine, David Wells, Todd Stottlemyre, José Mesa, Bobby Thigpen, Jim Clancy, Floyd Youmans, Mark Leiter, Tim Belcher, Eric Plunk, and many others who threw hard and would go on to have big-league success. The upshot was there was a lot of learning that went on for me at Chattanooga. I was up and down a lot. The first year, I hit .258, and the second year, I hit .264. But the good thing was that I walked a lot—71 times the first year and 89 the second, bringing my on-base percentage up to .378 and .383, respectively. My home runs were down—three one year, six the next—but I attribute some of that to the cavernous ballpark. Whenever I hit the ball good, it seemed like it went nowhere.

There were times of frustration, but truthfully, I wasn't frustrated. Not yet, anyway. I was just trying to get better, trying to be as productive as I could. I wasn't really worried about my career. I think going up through the minor leagues, other than at the end of my season in Bellingham, I wasn't worried about my career. I was trying to do the best I could each day. I didn't think, "My career is going nowhere." I was enjoying the process, enjoying my time in the minor leagues. I didn't stress too much about the future at that point.

My manager in 1985 was Bill Plummer, who became an important figure in my career. He was also my manager for three seasons at Triple-A Calgary, when I was shuttling back and forth between the majors and minors while Jim Presley and Darnell Coles held down third base in Seattle. And when I won my first batting title in 1992, he was my manager with the Mariners—his only year in that job. Bill was very good for me. He played a big role in showing me how to play the game, including what to do in situations that come up for every ballplayer, which is more important than most people realize.

I remember one time, in Triple-A, I made the last out, hitting a fly ball to right field on a 3-1 count. He called me into his office after the game and said, "If you're going to swing 3-0, 3-1, you've got to make sure it's a pitch you can pull and drive it out of the park." He taught me how to think more about game situations—when to move runners over, that kind of thing. I learned how to play the game the right way under Plummer in Double-A and Triple-A.

Those were learning years. Plummer was big on playing the game the right way. I think that carried over to the rest of my career, even later when I was playing with Lou with those great Mariners lineups. I was always very aware of when I needed to move the runner over. It didn't matter if we were up by four runs, five runs, I would try to move him, even if it meant giving myself up. If we were down, I would take a pitch, try to find a way to get on base. I was aware of the pitcher; if he didn't have good command, I would be more patient. Those kinds of things. My approach to hitting was always middle of the field, because by percentage, pitchers throw more middle away. Those are the kinds of things I learned from Bill.

BILL PLUMMER
Chattanooga Manager, 1985; Calgary Manager, 1987–89;
Mariners Manager, 1992

I first saw Edgar at spring training and he ended up with me at Double-A in '85. Really, one of the biggest things I remember in Chattanooga is he was one of our hardest workers. We all stayed in the same apartment complex, players and the manager and coaches. I remember guys would be swimming in the pool and he was in the weight room at the complex—and it was hot in Chattanooga in the summer. He was always working hard, always ready to play. He didn't have a great year—he hit about .250 in the Southern League—but he played well at third base. He was a pretty good third baseman, an accurate thrower. The next year, I moved up to Calgary—Triple-A—and he went back to Double-A. I don't think he spoke to me for about a year because I didn't take him with me. When he did come up, he hit about .380 in Calgary.

Edgar was a great kid, always fun to manage. I remember a day game we had in Calgary, early in the spring, about 30 degrees. He said it was the coldest game he ever played in, being from Puerto Rico. One of the greatest things I remember about him, Jim Lefebvre had taken over as manager of the Mariners [in 1989], and Edgar had a chance to make the club. We kept telling Jim to let him play third. I remember Lefebvre sent him up as a pinch-hitter against all the good closers. Edgar would hit a double down the left-field line, a double down the right-field line, like he always does. Pretty soon, he was starting.

He was one of the best right-handed hitters I've ever seen. He was really special. You didn't see many right-handed hitters that could handle everything, and hit the ball hard from line to line. The more he played, the better his power got. He always had a great glove, and one of the most accurate arms I ever saw, but then he got hurt in the majors. The biggest problem was that his knee got worse and his range got worse because of it. What a hitter, though. I don't care if he was a DH or not, he was a great hitter.

R.J. HARRISON
Chattanooga Manager, 1986

After the year he played in Wausau, we brought him to the Instructional League and started playing him all around the infield. As an organization, we thought his glove was greater than his bat. Edgar was really a gifted defensive player at the time. We brought him in thinking his route to the big leagues was as a utility player.

When you look retrospectively, Edgar was kind of ahead of his time as far as the hitter he was. He had the ability to use the whole field, and really drove a lot of balls to the opposite field, but he didn't have home run power. Back then, the profile of corner infielders was power—home run power. In that same league, Mark McGwire was playing third base in Huntsville, Ken Caminiti was playing third base in Columbus. They were the prototypical profile of a third baseman. I think we took for granted how advanced Edgar was as a hitter, and spent too much time dwelling on his lack of home run power.

Edgar was quiet, obviously a good teammate. In those days, we only had a couple of Latin players on the ballclub. Culturally, he was one of those guys that did his talking with his bat and glove. He always did the right things. I never had to worry about Edgar—just put him in the lineup and let him play.

The story I tell people most is about how we misunderstood him, mis-evaluated him just because of the stereotypical profile we had in those days. Now, we would understand the way he swung the bat and the way he used the field, and especially the ability, for lack of a better term, to stay inside the ball and drive it to the opposite field. The terminology was an inside-out hitter. No, he wasn't. He was just a really good hitter. One that saw the ball, wasn't afraid to hit deep in the count, a lot of things that really were before their time. It would be fun to see a hitter like him in today's game. His major-league career literally had just about the same amount of strikeouts [1,202] as base on balls [1,283]. That doesn't happen in the world of baseball we live in.

As I said earlier, off the field I was living with Dan Firova (a veteran catcher who'd already had a cup of coffee in the big leagues with the Mariners), his wife, and their two kids. Dan was a fun-loving guy with a great sense of humor. They helped keep it light for me in Chattanooga. We weren't very good in 1985, finishing 66–77, but the Triple-A Calgary Cannons had a good squad that year and they called me up to the Cannons near the end of the year for the Pacific Coast League playoffs. In 20 games, I hit .353 with 14 RBIs, so I was able to end the season on a good note with a lot of confidence. One thing that struck me right away was that the stadium in Calgary was a lot better place for hitting. And believe me, I would get to know it well, playing for Calgary in large parts of 1987, '88, and '89. I was so close to sticking in the major leagues that I could taste it—but taking that final step turned out to be an excruciating process that would test the limits of my patience.

DAN FIROVA
Chattanooga Roommate, 1984
I was looking for a roommate because we weren't making that much money. I had my wife with me, and also my daughter and son, D.J. and Chanel. Also, my wife was expecting one on the way. Edgar volunteered to move

in with us and help us out, finance-wise, by splitting the rent. He had his own room. He helped us out a lot. You couldn't ask for a better roommate. Edgar was a quiet guy, and his English was broken, of course. I tried to communicate with him in English so he could learn more. One time, my son was in a walker, and Edgar was taking a bath. The walker hit the door and opened it up, and all we heard was, "D.J., close the door, close the door. The door." D.J. couldn't even walk. We still laugh about that.

It might have been too early in his career to see what kind of hitter he was going to become, because what really looked good for Edgar was as a defensive player. He could really pick it at third base. His bat wasn't that great at that time in Double-A. He did well, but it wasn't something where you said, "This guy can really tear the cover off the ball." He eventually got better and better and got to where he's at.

We drifted apart after that. I went to Triple-A the next year and then became a free agent and moved on to the Cubs, then the Indians. He went his way and blossomed. I was with the Nationals in 2016 and '17 as the bullpen coach, and we played the Mariners at home in D.C. I didn't know until the last day that Edgar was the hitting coach, so I didn't get to talk to him. He was over on that side and I didn't even know. That's too bad. But I can tell people I roomed with that guy, and he's a Hall of Famer. I have bragging rights.

Chapter 3

Up and Down

I STARTED THE 1987 SEASON in Triple-A with the Calgary Cannons, which meant that I was one step away from the major leagues. Little did I know how difficult it would be to take that final step—at least without stepping right back to the minors.

Once again, Bill Plummer was my manager, which led to a sense of comfort. So did the fact I had done well with Calgary in the playoffs in 1985. The first thing I noticed when I got to Calgary was that the stadium was so much better for hitting than Chattanooga. And all the ballparks around the Pacific Coast League were good hitters' parks, except Vancouver. The ball would go nowhere in Vancouver. A few years later, when I was with the Mariners, a major development in my career (not positive) would occur in Vancouver, but that's a story for later. There's a reason the PCL is known as a hitters' league. You'd be in places like Colorado Springs and Albuquerque, with the high elevation and light air, and the ball would fly. I remember a doubleheader in Colorado Springs where I had seven or eight hits in the two games. It was good hitting pretty much all around that league.

The other thing I noticed was that in Triple-A, the pitchers didn't throw as hard as they did in Double-A. I know that sounds weird, but most teams put their top prospects, the young flamethrowers, in Double-A. Everyone threw hard, it seemed. But Triple-A staffs were filled with veteran pitchers, guys who had been around but never quite established themselves in the major leagues. These guys were a little older and really knew how to pitch, so it was a different kind of a challenge.

I liked Calgary a lot. It was completely the opposite of Chattanooga. Not just the weather—the atmosphere was different, too. I made friends pretty much right away and had a great experience in Canada. My roommate that year was Mario Díaz, whom I had met in Double-A. Mario was an infielder from Puerto Rico, and we became roomies and friends. When Mario made it up to the Mariners, I roomed with Julio Solano, a pitcher from the Dominican Republic.

RUSS PARKER
Former Calgary Owner

When Edgar came to Calgary, it was because our third baseman came down with an injury and we were in need of a third baseman. Bill Haywood, the Mariners farm director at the time, came up to me with a long face. I remember it so well. He said, "Oh, Russ, we were able to find you a third baseman, but he's not going to hit much for you. He's got a good glove, though." I remember it like it was yesterday. It was Edgar, and he wasn't too far wrong at first. When he first came up, he hit little flares to the opposite field, and I wondered if he was going to hit. But no one I witnessed ever worked harder at becoming a hitter. He was there early, he listened, stayed for extra work. The next time he came back to Calgary, those flairs turned into line drives in the gap and home runs, and he became the MVP of the Coast League.

The other thing about Edgar—he came to us three or four times when he was sent down from Seattle. Players were allowed 72 hours to report, and some took 71 hours. I remember some guys who came back and had their chins down and bemoaned this or that—I shouldn't be here. That was quite normal for a lot of Triple-A players when they were sent back. But Edgar would be here the next morning, or early afternoon, I swear. That was him. He didn't need 72 hours. He had the right attitude. It was sort of like, "Okay, where's the batting cage?"

I hit well in 1987, right from the beginning. In 129 games, I batted .329, which was fifth-best in the PCL. I had 31 doubles, which was third in the league. I hit 10 homers and drove in 66 runs. I made the PCL All-Star team and was also named the top defensive third baseman in the league by *Baseball America* magazine, keeping with my reputation back then as a good defensive player who needed to develop offensively. The power was slowly starting to come, but I knew I had to get stronger. I think most importantly, I walked 82 times and put up a .434 on-base percentage, fourth-best in the PCL.

Getting on base via walks became a big part of my game. In my career, I put up an on-base percentage of .418 over 18 seasons. That's one point higher than Stan Musial, and 21st highest in the history of baseball. Of the people ahead of me, 14 are in the Hall of Fame. I walked more than 100 times in four different seasons (consecutively from 1995 to '98, one of just 29 players in history with at least 100 walks in four straight seasons). In four other seasons, I walked more than 90 times.

I was very proud of my batting eye. I felt I was a better hitter the more pitches I saw. I wasn't a good first-pitch hitter (or so I thought; I checked the statistics, and in 557 at-bats over the course of my career—roughly the equivalent of a full season—I hit .384 on first pitches, with 36 homers and 156 RBIs). But I think that was because I learned when was the right time to swing at the first pitch. If I swung, it was because I was absolutely sure what was coming. I preferred to go deep into the count, so you could see all his pitches. The more pitches I saw, the more efficient I was, and the better I felt I was. Batting with two strikes never worried me, until I got late in my career and I couldn't see well.

But in these years, I didn't mind two strikes at all. Actually, I felt my best swings were with two strikes, because I wasn't trying too hard. It was just, wait and see the ball. Instead of "swing hard," my mindset was "swing quick." In addition, I'm helping the team because that guy is working more. In my ideal lineup, every batter from one to nine would see five pitches or more. That way, the pitcher is out of the game in the fifth inning. And if you're going that deep into the count, you're going to draw a lot of walks, which also helps the team. It's not like I was thinking much about putting up a .400 on-base percentage. No one focused on that in those days. I just had pride in drawing walks, swinging at good pitches, and not getting out of my strike zone. That way, I would make the pitcher work, and I'd get good pitches to hit. If not, I was satisfied to take a walk.

Really, it's amazing I was known for my batting eye considering how hard I had to work on my eyes. I have a condition called strabismus, which means that I was unable to align my eyes when looking at an object—not a good thing when the object is a baseball coming at 95 mph. In layman's terms, I'm cross-eyed, and my eyes don't work in tandem. One of them—my right eye—wandered. The Mariners' optometrist, Dr. Douglas Nikaitani, said he's never run across another position player in the major leagues with strabismus, nor have any of his colleagues. In fact, one major-league eye doctor with over 40 years of experience in the game told Dr. Nikaitani he's never heard of anyone doing what I did.

I had known I had some kind of issue with my eyes since way back in grade school. My grandparents took me to the eye doctor, and they prescribed these special glasses. I never used them. I couldn't get used to them, and I felt like, I can see fine, so why do I need them? My vision was actually strong—20/20. I didn't have any problems functioning, but because I was cross-eyed, kids at school would tease me. There was a popular cartoon character called Clarence, the Cross-Eyed Lion, and kids would call me Clarence. I can laugh about it now, but at the time, it bothered me. Not enough to push back, though. I was never the kind of guy that would get into altercations over things like that.

It wasn't until I reached my first major-league camp in 1987 that I was examined by Dr. Nikaitani and diagnosed with strabismus. Now I had a name and explanation for my problem, and Dr. Nikaitani took it upon himself to come up with a plan to help me deal with it. I was still in the minor leagues at the time, going up to Seattle and back down, but he worked up a program of eye exercises that helped me focus my eyes. I did these exercises every day for the rest of my career. I could not have had the success I did without them. Every day, after lunch, I'd spend half an hour to 45 minutes on my eye exercises. And then right before the game, about 6:00 PM for a night game, I would do them for another 15 to 20 minutes just to make sure everything was working right.

One exercise involved a card that had two circles of different colors with letters inside. I had to work to bring the two circles together so they appeared to me as one circle, and the letters spelled out a sentence. Once I did that, and it was all fully centered, it meant my eyes were working together. At the beginning, it was really hard to accomplish, but once I got good at it, I started moving my head at the angle I used when I looked at the pitcher. Eventually, it got to the point I'd lock in quick. The more accomplished I got at it, the better I felt, and I would see the ball better at the plate.

Another exercise involved tying a cord with three beads—they were colored red, yellow, and green—to the doorknob, and then bringing it close to my nose. I would change my eyesight as I looked from bead to bead to bead. I would also do depth perception drills in which Dr. Nikaitani gave me what appeared to be pieces of glass, but they were actually lenses of different prescription and I'd have to change from one to another. There were cards I looked at, almost like holograms, and behind it would be an object like, say, a flower, and behind that something else, and I'd have to bring them together. He had all different kinds of unique exercises for me, but the idea was get my eyes to work fast, and to work together. And the only way to succeed was to do these drills every day. It became a part of my routine, an hour that I built into every single day, basically for 18-plus years.

DR. DOUGLAS NIKAITANI
Former Mariners Optometrist

I first saw Edgar during the minor-league physicals in the mid-80s. I would always screen the muscles. I wasn't expecting to see anything like this, but when I saw it, it was surprising. I mentioned maybe we could work on it at some point. I just thought it would be an opportunity to work with someone who had a significant problem, and I wanted to find out if I could do more than just be a regular eye doctor and actually help someone to enhance their vision.

I went about looking through a medical library. I worked at a hospital and I got all the articles I could on his type of problem. A lot of the articles had to do with kids that had the problem. I looked for training and anything I could find. There wasn't a lot. I joined the International Academy of Sports Vision to talk to other professional sports physicians if anyone in baseball had any experience with anyone with strabismus, and they didn't.

Strabismus is when the eyes don't align correctly. A lot of time the players would ask me, "What's wrong with Edgar's eye?" because he was dominant in his left eye—as a right-handed hitter, that's a good thing as far as I could assess from my studies of dominancy. But whenever he was fatigued or not focusing or not concentrating fully, his eye would naturally go out. And it would go out significantly. That was his natural state. That's why when he was in the clubhouse or walking around, guys knew there was something wrong. Most of the time, he was relaxing, not concentrating, and his eye was going out. Even when he was talking to you, his right eye was turned out.

Essentially, he had to really concentrate a lot to pull his eye in. When he was tracking the ball he had to pull it in even more. It was very difficult to do. That's why he did the exercises diligently, because he knew he had to protect himself. The motivation was good, in a sense, as a doctor, because this guy *had* to do it. His livelihood was at stake. It didn't take much from me. I wasn't the kind of guy who ever pushed anything on anybody.

So I just started doing some basic things with him, and then I realized I had to come up with some unique things for him to do. He would challenge me, because if something wasn't quite enough, I had to come up with something else. We had that type of relationship where I could run things by him and he would give me an honest assessment of what I was coming up with and whether it was helpful.

63

He had a lot of passion. He bought in fully to what we were doing. He got the best out of me in that I really wanted to help him, and I really enjoyed working with him. It was just a real good arrangement for us together. In the beginning, I was pretty new at all this. I didn't know how rare it really was. I saw a lot of strabismus in my practice because I was in a medical practice. So I wasn't surprised by it, per se, but I was a little surprised he had it. It wasn't until I went through 30 years I realized nobody else had it. I talked to another guy who worked 40 years in baseball and he didn't have any position players with strabismus. It's really amazing.

I think about someone like Shaquem Griffin of the Seahawks, he's got part of one arm missing, and how the public and social media responds to this in such an amazing way. If he became All-Pro, it would be one of the most amazing stories in sports. There's so much adulation now for a guy with a handicap, Shaquem Griffin, but people didn't realize Edgar had an even greater problem, in a sense, because the problem for him was that he could get killed. Because when he lost the pitch, it was super-dangerous for him.

He broke his hand that one time when Dennis Martínez hit him. He lost the pitch. I remember telling him, if he loses it, he'll never find it again, so just get your head out of the way, and your hands out of the way, and duck. That's why he did that later in his career, even when they threw the ball right down the middle at times, because he lost it. Just to protect himself.

I feel he overcame such a great barrier that if people knew that, they would rally around him in the same way. But people don't really realize what he overcame. I lived it with him, so I know how difficult it was. How dangerous it was, on top of that. He was risking his life when he went up to bat. He overcame a lot, and he deserves a lot more credit than he's ever gotten. I never have expressed it that way.

What are my true thoughts? That's really my thinking, that it's a pretty miraculous thing. If people really understood it, they'd put him in the Hall of Fame right now. There wouldn't be any question about it.

What he did, that you might not know, is he suppressed his eye. When you get an eye deviation at an early age, the brain decides that, hey, double vision is dangerous, let's shut down the center of vision in that eye. So when his eye went outward, he didn't see double because his central vision shut down. As a hitter, that's even more dangerous, because you lose depth perception, you lose the ability to judge velocity when you're using one eye. So suddenly you're looking at the pitch, you see the release point, and then you go to one eye. You can't even tell how fast it's coming, and then momentarily there's a loss of where the ball is. Just think how dangerous that is when the ball is coming toward your face.

That's why I told him after he broke his hand, "Just duck. I don't care. As soon as you lose it you'll never get it back. You have 0.4 seconds—a 90 mph fastball, 0.4 seconds; high 90s, even less time. Just protect your hands and your head. Just don't worry about anything else. If it looks crazy, it looks crazy." He did that from then on. He even had a home run a few times after ducking. Because the pitcher got freaked. If you're throwing a pitch and you throw it right down the middle, and the guy jumps out of the way like it's coming at his head, what are you going to think? I remember seeing that once. One of the next pitches, he hit for a home run. The pitcher came back with something similar and he hit it out of the park. He's thinking, I've got this guy, he's freaking out. Maybe there's some crazy movement on this pitch I didn't realize, I'll throw the same pitch.

Basically, over time sometimes it deviates a little more. It just happens. We get old, lose a little bit of elasticity or whatever in our body, and that's what happened. That's why he kept telling me—and I don't know if he really meant it, but he kept saying, "I'm going to retire, I'm going to retire."

65

He kept saying that probably five years before he retired. Maybe it was to challenge me. Maybe he really believed it, that, "Hey, I can't do it."

When he didn't do his exercises during the off-season and he came in for spring, his eyes were way worse than anybody you take off the street. It was way worse. I'd run some of my tests on him to see where he was at, and I'd go, "Edgar, you didn't do your exercises, did you?"

He'd go, "No, I didn't do them during the off-season. I needed to relax."

I said, "Wow, you better start doing them then." If he wasn't picking up early in the season, and he was hitting maybe .270, if it dropped to .250, he would really freak out and he would call me. I knew we would have to ratchet it up.

He would usually say, "You've got to give me something new. I got to try something else. You've got to come up with something else." And he would challenge me.

His eye exercises were basically to enhance his depth perception, get his eyes to work together, and make sure they were locked in. Because if he did them enough, he could feel when he looked at things that his depth perception was on, his eyes were lining up, and he was tracking the ball well. But as soon as that eye started shifting, it was dangerous.

There were various exercises, but most of them had to do with tests that would allow you to see 3D, and the 3D would ensure that both eyes were on equally, focusing equally, everything was working evenly, and that's what I wanted. Everything he did, I would really stress that all the tests were making sure that both eyes were on equally, and the dominant eye wasn't overpowered. Because as soon as the dominant eye was overpowered, the other eye would drift out. So I had to get the other eye to be stronger so it would line up and stay there and track the ball. All the tests had checks where he could tell. I had tests where he could literally tell he was using both eyes by getting the right response.

There was one time in May 1999 when I really had trouble picking up the ball out of the pitcher's hand. I would see it from the release point but then lose it, or it wouldn't be where I thought it was—just a little off. You can figure out for yourself how dangerous that can be. Throughout the course of my career, this would happen from time to time, where I'd lose track of the ball. I learned to tuck my head out of the way and pull my hands out of danger. I would try to just think fastball, fastball, fastball, because then I see it better. But the times I start looking for a breaking ball, and it's a fastball, I would lose it. So I have to think fastball. When I got hit by Dennis Martínez on Opening Day in 1994, that's what happened—I was looking breaking ball, and I couldn't get out of the way.

Usually, it would be fine on the next pitch. But this time, back in 1999, it wasn't getting better. I even flew to Chicago to consult with a specialist, but it still didn't get better. As I told Ken Rosenthal (then of *Sporting News*) when he wrote about the incident in 2001, "I tried everything. I was doing everything I always did to prepare myself. But still, it wasn't enough." There was fear among the Mariners' medical and baseball staff that I would have to go on the disabled list, or even, in the worst-case scenario, retire at age 36. But I was bound and determined not to let that happen.

So on an off day for the Mariners, May 16, Dr. Nikaitani came to my home for an emergency session. What resulted was the most intense session we ever had. He put my charts on the wall and had me work on fusing them, as usual, but while I was doing that, he confronted me with a barrage of sensory challenges—math problems that he shouted out and I had to solve, and martial arts kicks that I had to block. He even began firing tennis balls at me that I had to bat away. Dr. Nikaitani said he was trying to bring in all my senses to challenge my visual system. I'll let him tell the story from an expert's point of view.

DR. DOUGLAS NIKAITANI
Former Mariners Optometrist

Any time his average would drop, I would tell my wife, "He's going to call me soon. I've got to think of something new, because he's going to say, 'What I've been doing isn't working anymore. You've got to come up with something else.'" I'd always be tinkering—What can I make, what can I do, to help him? That's what happened that time in '99, when they were going to put him on the DL because Lou Piniella was afraid he would get killed. Because he was literally having such bad at-bats at that point they could tell he was not seeing the ball. He was totally losing it. And yet even that time he was able to overcome it.

I was driving to his place, and I was playing some tennis so I had some balls in the car. I was thinking, "Hey, if I need this, I'm going to try some unique things on him." Really, I had him do his regular tests where he fused targets, but I said I've got to do more because it's not enough. That's when I took out the balls. It was in his house. I remember his son, Alex, was really small then and his wife thought I was crazy. I was throwing balls at him and having him block the balls. I introduced math questions while I was doing it, and then I did the martial arts stuff, throwing punches at him and basically he had to block them. I was throwing stuff at vital parts of his body, finger jabs and kicks to the groins, stuff like that. I was even bumping him at times, to really get his system… I overloaded him. I overloaded his stimulus regarding his vision so that anything in baseball would be easy. Everything I tried to do for him was to try to make seeing the ball easy compared to the drills he had to do, where everything was harder. That was the idea.

He's a great guy and everything, but I saw him at times when he was struggling. He's just like anybody else, he's a human. He's got doubts. Like when he said he was going to retire. I dealt with all that. I just really tried to be there for him and always give him encouragement and say, "We're going to get through this." Try to be a rock for him. I wanted him to have the best career he could and last as long as he could. He surprised me, really, that he kept playing those last few years. And he had some really good years. That was amazing to me, actually, deep down.

Did that session in 1999 work? Did it ever! I was in the lineup the next day at the Kingdome against the Minnesota Twins. I went 3-for-3 with two walks and two home runs—my first home runs in 29 games. The following day, we faced the Twins again—and believe it or not, I hit three more home runs. That was five homers in two games, the best stretch of my career. I was just the 23rd player in history to hit five homers in back-to-back games—a feat first accomplished by Hall of Famer Cap Anson in 1897.

Even though I told the media that the power surge was because I had altered my hitting mechanics, the truth is that Dr. Nikaitani's creative regimen had fixed my eye problem. I told Rosenthal, "I felt different. I could see the ball more. I was able to pick up the rotation." From that off day when we worked together until the end of the 1999 season, I hit .355/.456/.601 in 108 games, and then I had many more good years to follow. Dr. Nikaitani deserves a lot of credit for the success I had in my career. He was more than an eye doctor. He also knew that the mind is connected to the vision. I became more aware of how to connect the mind to help me see better. He made a big difference for me to stay in the game a long time.

I think it helped that, as I said, I had really good vision; it's just that my muscles didn't work correctly. I also believe that all those drills I used to do when I was a kid in Puerto Rico—the pebbles I would hit that were very tiny, hitting rain drops, those type of things I would do on a daily basis like throwing the ball against a wall, hitting bottle caps with a broomstick—all of it developed a lot of my hand-eye coordination. And also developed my belief and confidence that I was really good at this. That combination actually is part of being able to succeed with the eye condition I have. It's not only the skill. I think it's more the belief and confidence that I'm really good at this. So I didn't focus on my eyes as an ailment. I always believed I was normal, until someone found out about it. They would say, "Do you have this condition?"

I'd say, "No, I'm normal."

DR. DOUGLAS NIKAITANI
Former Mariners Optometrist

I watched the games [against the Twins after the session] and I was scared. I was scared for him. Because Rick [Griffin, the Mariners' athletic trainer] told me how afraid Lou was, and Rick was worried, too. They really wanted to put him on the DL. Edgar was begging them, I guess—please, one more chance, one more, one more. They said, one more only this time. So when I'm watching, I'm thinking, what happens if he gets hit? What happens if something happens? It's my fault; I'm endorsing this when maybe I should have said he should go on the DL and we could just work on some exercises. So of course I was apprehensive. But when he hit those home runs I was really happy for him. I was elated for him.

RICK GRIFFIN
Mariners Athletic Trainer, 1983–2017

There's a lot of amazing things about Edgar, about his personality and his character, his morals, his work ethic. One of the key ones was his eye condition. Probably anybody else that had it, they would not be able to play. He refused to let that get to him. Dr. Nikaitani and Edgar worked very closely together. Back when personal computers were first coming out, he would make Edgar these eye-exercise discs, and when all the other guys on the plane were playing cards or screwing around, or whatever, Edgar's back on his computer, and he's watching these discs. He's doing these eye exercises, visualization training, and different types of things to strengthen the muscles in his eyes. In between at-bats, he'd go up to the clubhouse and he would do that. He had all these little tricks. He had this box of all these things. He had little beads and little balls and things he would use to get his eyes stronger. That was Dr. Nikaitani that made him do all those things.

Sometimes his eyes would get really bad and he'd go through a two- or three-day stretch where he'd just really struggle. If you think back, you'd see Edgar a lot of times, he would take a pitch, and he would lean back. The reason he would do that is because his eye would go off and he wouldn't be able to track the ball and so he didn't know where the ball was. He would just move because he didn't know where it was going. The pitcher in that situation thought, well, he didn't see that pitch or he didn't pick up that pitch very well. Edgar used that to his advantage: "Well, that guy thinks I didn't see that." Then he would wait for it, and he would hit it.

Jay used to make fun of it. He called him "Mr. Magoo." That was his nickname. Jay called him Mr. Magoo because of his eyes. You'd be talking to Edgar and his eye would go off to the side. He'd pop it back in place. Like, boink.

Edgar's probably got a lot of guys that are super important to him, but Nikaitani's got to be way at the top. Because he really helped him. He instilled in Edgar the belief that even though you have this, you can still play, you can still do well, but it takes a lot of work. What he did every day to do those exercises is amazing. We can't get guys to do shoulder exercises, but he'd do those things every single day. I'll have young players ask me, "What do you need to be successful in the big leagues?" I say, "You've got to have the three Ds. If you don't have the three Ds you'll never make it. You've got to have drive, determination, and desire." Edgar had all of them. He had more Ds than that. Discipline, for sure.

WILLIE SANCHEZ
Agent

I'll never forget, he was at a batting cage, and there were 100 tennis balls and they all had a number on them. At a certain speed, he could tell you the number on the tennis ball. This was one of the drills he did for his eyes. I said, "Are you kidding me?"

Edgar said, "Get in there, Willie." They had the machine at 20 mph, and I still couldn't see the numbers. He got in, and they had it at 70, 80 mph, and he was reading every number. I was just amazed. He did his exercises every day.

I'd say, "Let's go out, let's have lunch."

"No," he'd say, "I have to do my eye exercises." It was quite the dedication.

I think what happened was, to compensate for my eye condition, I had to study the pitcher and his tendencies. I would also learn how each catcher called a game, and I would use those tendencies to my advantage. From talking to people and reading about it, I learned that because of my condition, my mind actually helped me see better, as counter-intuitive as that might sound. I needed to visualize the fastball in order to prepare for the velocity and movement. The same with a breaking ball. I had to understand the shape, the velocity.

If I saw it in my head first, I had a better chance to connect. Sometimes, when I didn't know what was coming, and it was a breaking ball, I would lose the ball. I knew, "Okay, that's my condition." Because my mind wasn't connected, it wasn't helping me see it. I was a guess hitter. I would guess what the pitcher was going to throw, although I don't think "guess" is the right word. I got good at anticipating what he was going to throw. So good that if he threw me another pitch, I would take it. I was so 100 percent sure what he was going to throw that anything else caught me by surprise.

One postscript: I had surgery on my eyes about three years ago to try and correct the condition. I held off on having it done during my career because Dr. Nikaitani told me there was some risk involved, including the possibility of double vision if it didn't go well. I wasn't willing to take that chance. When I had the surgery, I went back to the doctor to see how much I improved, and it was only about 15 to 20 percent. I thought it was going to be much greater. The doctor said he could do additional surgery, but I decided against it.

DR. DOUGLAS NIKAITANI
Former Mariners Optometrist

We used to talk about visualization and all those things. I remember reading about Hank Aaron and how he would lay down before the game. He would visualize a pitcher. He said, all the fastballs are a little bit different. A fastball is not a fastball. Every one has a little cut on it, or a little movement on it. Some stay level, some sink it, they throw a two-seamer vs. a four-seamer, all these different things. Hank Aaron would just visualize that.

I remember talking to Edgar about that, and visualizing things, what pitchers would do. One time, he had visualized a pitch coming before the pitcher threw it, so when he hit it—I think it was off-speed—he hit it without delay. A lot of times you see on high-motion film how guys have a little delay on off-speed. They'll stride and hold back slightly. But he hit it like it was a fastball, because his mind had already cued into that. His timing and subconscious had already clicked in so that he saw it. I said, "Man, that's amazing, he hit it like a fastball." Griffey used to do that too, same thing. I saw very few players do that, but there was something they saw out of the hand or something they visualized before, and they were so relaxed that their internal mechanism in their brain took over their body, and they had the right timing, even though the pitch was totally different than a fastball. Hey, that's really something.

Edgar studied, but I think there was something even more than that. Because he was intent about that, and maybe his visualization, he could anticipate things to such a high level that his body would respond. Versus "see the ball, hit the ball." He would see it, but his body would do the right thing, timing wise. That was because of his hard work.

R.J. Harrison, my manager at Chattanooga in 1986, harped on me to be more aggressive early in the count. I would take a lot of pitches, and I almost always took the first pitch. That might have been one of the reasons my numbers weren't so good at that stage of my career, because I was always behind in the count. R.J. worked with me on being more aggressive, but throughout my career, I just felt better going deep in the count. I told R.J. I wanted to get familiar with the pitcher, but I wonder, without being aware, if it might have been because I couldn't pick up the ball. At that point, I wasn't doing any eye exercises. I felt better getting familiar with the pitcher and hitting deep in the counts so I could anticipate what was coming. Even in the big leagues at the beginning, I was like that.

R.J. HARRISON
Chattanooga Manager, 1986

Even more so than getting him to be aggressive early in the count, we were just trying to get him to that point of, just go ahead and let it out. Go ahead and hit the ball in the gap or hit the ball out of the ballpark. Ultimately, as he grew and got stronger and got even more confidence, Edgar grew into that guy, really without sacrificing his patience and selectivity. Edgar never struck out 100 times in a year until his last season in the big leagues.

Edgar was very patient as a young player. He didn't strike out, walked a lot. As an organization, we wanted him to grow into that third-base profile, be a guy who was a run producer. At that time, we almost felt he was more of an old-school No. 2 hitter because of his ability to handle the bat and shoot the ball to right field. Those were the discussions we had as an organization, hoping for him to grow into what he eventually grew into. Injuries precluded him from staying on the field defensively. People who never saw Edgar defensively, and only know him as a DH, missed a lot. He was a wonderful third baseman.

We had a great team in Calgary in 1987, finishing with the best record in the Pacific Coast League at 84–57. But we wound up losing to Albuquerque, three games to one, in the best-of-five league championship. As soon as the series ended, on September 11, Bill Plummer called me into his office in Albuquerque and gave me the news I had been waiting for my whole life: I was going to the big leagues! I had been called up to the major leagues. Eight of us from the Calgary team were called up together: pitcher Clay Parker, catcher Jerry Narron, first baseman Brick Smith, infielder Mario Díaz, and outfielders Dave Hengel, Donell Nixon, and Jim Weaver. In an article in the *Seattle Times*, the Mariners' director of player development, Bill Haywood, gave summaries of all the new players. Here's what he said about me:

"His glove is his strength. Hitting over .300 is a pleasant surprise. If he could hit for more power, he has a chance to make it next year. I see a utility role for him, third base, second base. I'm not sure if he can play short."

I guess I still had some convincing to do.

I was excited, of course, and called my grandparents and Carmelo to tell them the news, but mostly I was numb. It wasn't until we flew to Seattle and walked into the clubhouse at the Kingdome that I really got excited. The Mariners were on the way to a losing season, but I didn't care. I was 24 years old, and in awe of the big-league atmosphere. I knew most of the players from spring training, and a few had played with me in the minors, but I still felt like an outsider. Three guys in particular played a huge role in welcoming me to the team and teaching me how to handle myself in the big leagues—Alvin Davis, Harold Reynolds, and Dave Valle.

They were always encouraging, always helping me out, always talking to me. They wanted to make sure I was comfortable, and they really meant it. They wanted me to succeed. Ken Phelps was another one who was always there for me. The way they welcomed me is how I tried to treat young players once I became a veteran. I never forgot what it felt like to be the wide-eyed newcomer.

ALVIN DAVIS
Former Mariners First Baseman
Most veterans are very willing to take young players under their wing, but on the other side, guys have to have the wisdom and humility to listen. It's a two-way street, and that's not automatic. One thing I appreciated about

Edgar—and many others—was his willingness to learn. He didn't step into the clubhouse and say, "I'm taking over."

I feel the pride of an older brother with Edgar. I had the same feeling when Junior [Ken Griffey Jr.] was inducted in the Hall of Fame. Edgar deserves all the credit in the world for being a learner, a student of the game, of the craft, a guy who really wanted to be a good major-league player, if not a great one. He was willing to do the things and have the conversations necessary to get there. Junior was different. Junior was the first "can't-miss" guy that literally didn't miss. He grew up in a clubhouse with his dad. When he got to the big leagues, he was young, and he didn't have a lot of questions. He probably had more answers than questions.

Edgar was a little different. He had to grind and he knew that. It's not that Junior didn't grind, but he didn't have any detractors. He was the first overall pick in the draft, so the industry told Junior how good he was and could be. Back during this era in the '80s and '90s, players' labels were based on what you couldn't do. That's a different way of referencing the labels Edgar had—can't hit for enough power, not a prototypical third baseman, doesn't run well enough to profile as a corner outfielder, where his bat could have fit. That was a constant narrative during that time. And Edgar fought through it, overcame it, and became what he was—a superstar. He was the epitome of that old movie in the '70s—speak softly and carry a big stick. That's Edgar from Day One. He let his game do the talking. He was always a great teammate, always ready to have a conversation about the game, a winner through and through. Edgar Martínez was the guy you wanted at the dish with the game on the line or when you needed to score a big run. He was a tremendously tough out his entire career."

Dick Williams was the Mariners' manager. He was 58 years old and already a legend, having won two World Series titles with the Oakland

A's and pennants with the Red Sox and Padres, as well as having stints with the Expos and Angels. He made the Hall of Fame in 2008. Seattle was Dick's final stop. At the time, only 11 managers in history had won more games than him. The Mariners had never had a winning season in the franchise's history, and Williams was trying hard to bring them above .500. He wouldn't quite make it, although we finally got there three years after he got fired in 1988.

Dick was a little bit irascible, and could be intimidating, but what struck me was how quiet he was during the game—a far cry from Lou Piniella, who would be my manager for the bulk of my career. Lou was always engaging with the players, while Dick basically stood there with his arms folded. Ozzie Virgil was Williams' guy—he was Dick's bench coach wherever he managed, and Ozzie was the one Dick would use to talk to the players. Ozzie would tell you to get ready when Dick was going to put you in the game. On very rare occasions, Dick would praise you when you did something he liked. Once in spring training, we were facing the Padres and my cousin Carmelo was hitting. He faked a bunt, so I moved up a little bit. Carmelo hit a ground ball to me, and I made a good play to my left and threw him out. Dick told me, "Great play." That was about as much as I heard from Dick Williams.

He was very firm and demanding. One time, I was on second base with no outs. Glenn Wilson, one of our outfielders, hit a ground ball to shortstop, right at me, and I didn't go to third base. The inning ended with me stranded on base. When I came into the dugout, Dick barked, "You've got to take chances!" He didn't say it to me, he just said it to everybody, which makes you feel even worse. You know who he's talking to. That was his style. I understood that he wanted to deliver a message, so no one else makes the same mistakes. He wanted to stress that you should be aggressive. That was his thing.

When I was called up, Dick Williams had never seen me play. He told the writers, "I wouldn't know Edgar Martínez if he walked across the infield and waved hello to me. The only thing I know about him is he's Latin, so he doesn't have blond hair."

As excited as I was about being in the majors, I was also very nervous, wondering when I was going to get in a game. Fortunately, Dick put me in right away. On September 12, we were playing the White Sox at the Kingdome. In the bottom of the sixth inning, Jim Presley drew a walk, and I made my major-league debut as, of all things, a pinch-runner. Considering my speed, or lack of it, that makes people laugh. Dave Valle promptly grounded into a double-play, which means I wasn't out there on the base paths very long. We had an 11–1 lead at the time, so it was a good way to break in without the pressure of a close game.

I took over at third base in the top of the seventh, and in the bottom of the eighth I stepped to the plate for the first time. There were two outs, no one on base, and Ray Searage, a veteran left-hander, was on the mound. I wish I could say I hit a home run, but it wasn't quite that heroic. I fouled out to the first baseman. I was so nervous and excited that I sprinted full speed all the way to first base, even though the ball was clearly way foul. I remember Frank Howard, our first base coach, calling out for me to stop. It was pretty funny.

I started at third base two days later against the Indians and batted seventh in the order. There were 7,839 fans in the stands, but it felt like 50,000. In the top of the second, I made two consecutive diving plays to rob hits from Jay Bell and Andy Allanson. That helped calm my nerves, which was a good thing. Leading off the bottom of the second, I stepped into the batter's box for my second major-league at-bat. On the mound for Cleveland was Reggie Ritter, a right-hander. I ripped a ball off the right-field wall, and when it bounced around a little bit, I made it to third base—one of just 15 triples I would hit in my entire career in 8,674 plate appearances! It was an indescribable feeling. You've been playing baseball since you were nine or 10 years old. You started playing because you idolize baseball players. The journey is like a dream, and finally you're on that stage and you get your first hit—the first of 2,247, it turned out. It's an amazing feeling, one I'll never forget. My teammates gave me the ball, but I don't know where it is now. Somewhere along the line, I lost it. But I'll never lose the memory.

Mario Díaz—my old roommate—followed with a ground out to second, and I scored my first major-league run. I wound up going 1-for-4 in the game with a hit by pitch and a strikeout.

I started a total of 10 games at third base in the final month and hit .372 overall (16-for-43) with five doubles and two triples. I didn't make any errors, either. Jim Presley, the Mariners' regular third baseman, came down with the flu, so I got several starts in a row and went 7-for-15 (.467) to start my career. In one game against the Rangers, I had a single, double, and triple. I came up in the eighth with a chance for a cycle if I homered, but I grounded out.

I never did get a cycle in the major leagues—although I came close a few other times. On May 20, 1990, in Cleveland, I had a single, home run, and triple in my first three at-bats. The hard ones were out of the way, and I always considered myself a doubles hitter. My next time up, with a chance for the first cycle in Mariners history, I hit one to the gap in right-center, but Cory Snyder ran it down. The game went into extra innings, and I had one more at-bat in the 10th inning, with two outs and one on. I hit the ball hard to left—so hard that it went over the fence. No cycle, but it was the first two-homer game of my career and the margin of an 8–7 victory. I'll take it.

Then, in back-to-back games in July 1991, I fell one hit shy of the cycle each time. In a 14–3 win over the Indians on July 14 at the Kingdome, I already had a single, triple, and home run when I came up in the eighth. I hit one into the right-field corner, which would have been a sure double, but it was barely foul. I ended up walking, and didn't get up again. The very next night, playing the Yankees, I needed a home run in my last at-bat for a cycle. Facing left-hander Steve Howe, I swung hard and hit a fly to center field that Bernie Williams caught. I didn't swing for the fences very often, but that was one of those times. "I was trying to hit one out for sure," I told the reporters after the game. What's amazing is that in each of those cases, I already had the triple, which is by far the hardest part of the cycle, especially for me. I couldn't quite finish it out, though. Jay Buhner wound up getting the first cycle in Mariners' history against the A's in 1993.

I got a hit in each of my first seven starts after my call-up, and Dick Williams told the writers, "He looks good out there. He doesn't get rattled. He's been real steady."

I was thrilled with my first stint in the major leagues. As I told Bob Finnigan of the *Seattle Times*, the meal money we were making— $47.50 a day, which was $332 on a seven-day road trip—was just a little less than I was making at Calgary, "but the year before, in Double-A, that was my paycheck."

I felt like I made an impression on the Mariners and showed that I was ready to play in the major leagues, even if it was as a utility player to start out. I couldn't wait until spring training in 1988, when I thought I would get a chance to make the team and maybe be the regular third baseman.

It didn't work out quite that way. Late in spring training, I was sent back down to Calgary. Also shipped out to Calgary in the same cutdown was a young shortstop from Venezuela named Omar Vizquel. Marty Martínez, the same Mariners' scout who signed me in 1982, had signed Omar for the Mariners in April of 1984. His bonus was $2,500—even less than mine. It was a pretty good bargain. Omar went on to have a fantastic 24-year career, one that should put him in the Hall of Fame eventually.

When you hit it to Omar, you knew it was a sure out. No question, he was the best fielding shortstop I played with or saw (although I never got to watch Ozzie Smith). No one knew at that time if he was going to hit enough to be an everyday player, but you could tell he knew the strike zone. And he developed into a very solid major-league hitter, with 2,877 hits. Omar and I were teammates for five years with the Mariners, and even roommates for one season. One thing about Omar—nothing bothered him. He was just a relaxed guy.

The Mariners decided to stick with Jim Presley as their everyday third baseman in 1988. It was understandable—he had made the All-Star team in 1986, and hit 24 homers with 88 RBIs in 1987. The problem for me was that Jim was just 26 years old—only one year older than me. And then, in July 1988, the Mariners made a trade to get back another third baseman, Darnell Coles, who had been Seattle's first-round draft pick in 1980 but was traded in 1985 to Detroit. Darnell was 26, too.

There seemed to be a logjam at third base in the Mariners' system, and I couldn't help but wonder what it meant for me. There had been talk in the off-season that the Mariners would move first baseman Alvin Davis to DH, and put Jim Presley at first so I could get a shot at third base. There were also a lot of trade rumors all winter involving Presley: Presley to the Blue Jays for Jesse Barfield. Presley to the White Sox for Harold Baines. But when the season started, Alvin was at first and Presley was back at third.

So I was headed back for my third stint in Calgary in 1988—and to make things worse, on the very last day of spring training in Tempe, playing in a Triple-A game, a bad-hop grounder came up and hit me in the face, breaking my nose. That required surgery that put me out of action for a couple of weeks.

But I didn't have to wait long to get back to Seattle. When Presley got off to a rough start, both at the plate and in the field, I was called up on May 10, just as the Mariners were about to start a four-city, 12-game road trip. I joined the team in Toronto and was thrown right in the starting lineup at third base. The Mariners had gotten off to a 14–18 start, and Presley was the third regular to get benched as Williams tried to spark the team. Jim was hitting just .217 with four homers and 14 RBI, and the trade rumors about Presley-for-Barfield were heating up again. Williams told the media, "We need better offense and defense at third. Presley has been having a rough time and maybe a few days off will help him. But if Martínez catches fire, you never know. We're not bringing Martínez up to sit."

I started three games in a row, but then I sat for 10 days, and finally on May 31, I was sent back down to Calgary. In 14 at-bats, I had just two hits, a .143 average, and they told me I needed to play every day. That was disappointing, but I kept raking in Calgary, despite missing some games here and there with tendinitis in my knee. I caught fire in August, going 16-for-26 in one stretch to raise my average to .365, just two points behind Phoenix's Francisco Meléndez. I wound up hitting .363 and won the PCL batting title by two points over Meléndez. I also led the league in on-base percentage at .467, slugged .517, and finished third in OPS at .983. For the second year in a row, I was named the Cannons' MVP and made the PCL All-Star team. That earned me another call-up to the major leagues when the rosters expanded on September 1.

When I rejoined the Mariners, quite a lot had changed on the ballclub since I was sent down in late May. With the team struggling at 23–33, Dick Williams had been fired as manager on June 6 and replaced on an interim basis by his first-base coach, Jim Snyder. Dick Balderson, the general manager, was fired on July 27 and replaced by Woody Woodward, who had worked in the front office of the Phillies and Yankees. As I mentioned, the Mariners had also traded to bring back Darnell Coles—who became another competitor for the third-base job. And less than a week before he was dismissed, Balderson made his best trade—over the objections of our owner, George Argyros—when he sent our slugging first baseman, Ken Phelps, to the Yankees, for a 23-year-old outfielder named Jay Buhner, a top prospect in the Yankees' farm system.

You've probably seen the scene on *Seinfeld* where George Costanza's father says to George Steinbrenner: "What the hell did you trade Jay Buhner for?!? He had 30 home runs, and over 100 RBIs last year. He's got a rocket for an arm. You don't know what the hell you're doin'!" And Steinbrenner replies: "Well, Buhner was a good prospect, no question about it. But my baseball people loved Ken Phelps' bat. They kept saying 'Ken Phelps, Ken Phelps.'"

I loved Ken Phelps, too. He had been very nice to me when I was a young player coming up. Toward the end of my first year in the major leagues, he pulled me aside and told me I needed to get stronger. He urged me to really hit the weights, and said that lifting would benefit my career. That's one of the first times I really gave serious consideration to weight training—and he was right. I gradually changed myself into a guy who could hit the ball out of the ballpark and became the Mariners' cleanup hitter for the bulk of my career.

As sorry as I was to see Ken go, getting Buhner on the Mariners turned out to be a great thing for me—Jay and I became very good friends—and fantastic for the Mariners. The organization, which began as an expansion team in 1977, was only 12 years old, and we were struggling to break through and become relevant. The Mariners would go on to lose 93 games in 1988—the 12th straight year with a losing record. It would be a couple more seasons before we finally finished above .500. But we were slowly amassing talent.

Ken Griffey Jr. was our first-round pick—No. 1 overall—in 1987 and broke into the majors in 1989 at the age of 19. In May of that same year we traded for Randy Johnson—two first-ballot Hall of Famers. Omar Vizquel was a rookie shortstop for us in 1989. Tino Martínez was on his way up the minor-league system. But Buhner (who still had hair back in those days) became one of the real catalysts to help get us to the next level, along with Lou Piniella (who ironically was the Yankees manager when the Buhner-Phelps trade was made). Like Lou, Jay had a burning desire to win, and his intensity rubbed off on everybody else. Plus, he was just a great player. He really did have a rocket for an arm, and he could hit!

Like me, it took a while for Jay to get his chance—much longer than he wanted—but when he did, he became a fixture in right field. From 1991 to '97, Jay averaged 32 home runs a year, hitting 40 homers or more three years in a row, 1995–97. And his attitude rubbed off on me. As I told a reporter in 1999, "Jay helps me all the time. When you start doubting yourself, you need positive things, and that's Jay."

I didn't play much in September after my call-up this time—just three starts and 18 at-bats—but I had seven hits, including three doubles, to raise my average from .143 to .281, which looks a lot better on the baseball card. Now I waited to see who the Mariners would hire as manager, and if I would finally get my chance next spring, in 1989.

Once again, there were trade rumors all winter involving Presley—who had actually asked the organization to trade him—but when spring training rolled around in 1989, Jim was still on the team. So was Darnell Coles, whom the Mariners had sent to the Arizona instructional league to reacquaint himself with third base after a few years in the outfield. Woodward said Coles was the fallback option in case they traded Presley, whose average had dropped to .230 in 1988. It looked like I was realistically fighting for a utility job, or I might be crowded out altogether.

But remember, I was coming off a batting title in the PCL. At age 25, I felt I was ready for my shot. I had surgery on my left knee on October 4, but it was relatively minor, and I was ready to go when spring training rolled around.

Our new manager was Jim Lefebvre, who had been a coach with the Oakland A's. The A's had won the American League pennant the year before, though they lost the World Series to the Dodgers (thanks to Kirk Gibson's home run and Orel Hershiser's pitching). Jim had a real upbeat attitude—a little different than Dick Williams. He loved to talk hitting. One thing I credit to Jim was my approach with men on base. One day, I was struggling, and he came to me and said, "You know, just focus on the middle of the field. Hit it to the middle of the field when you have men on base." The day he told me that, we were in New York, and I hit a home run to center field, just with that in mind. The next at-bat, I also got a hit. After that, I started approaching middle of the field with men on base and I became more productive that way. That hadn't been my mindset before.

No one was paying much attention to me—or anyone else—in the spring of '89, because all the focus was on Ken Griffey Jr., who was in his first major-league camp with a chance to make the team. Even though Junior was just 19, you could already tell he was going to be a superstar. And he played so well that spring, hitting close to .400 most of camp, that the Mariners had no choice but to put him on their roster, and stick him in center field every day. Griffey wasn't just the best player in our camp. He was the best player in the Cactus League.

That wasn't our only drama. Mark Langston, our ace, was entering his final year before free agency, and if he didn't get a multiyear deal, it appeared likely that he would be traded. Buhner, Omar, and myself were all fighting to make the Opening Day roster for the first time. There was more talk of moving Presley to first base to push Alvin Davis to DH and open a spot for me—but Darnell was also lurking. Rumors of a trade for third baseman Howard Johnson of the Mets were also floating around.

I ended up having an okay spring, hitting .254 with a couple of homers, and made the team as a backup infielder, one of five rookies on the Opening Day roster. Jim Presley was still the third baseman at the end of camp, and Coles was in the outfield, for now. Omar made the roster, too, when the regular shortstop, Rey Quinones, began the season on the disabled list. Jay was sent to Calgary, despite a team-leading four homers in the spring. He was upset, but that's Jay.

As mentioned, Junior made it impossible to send him down, finishing the spring with a .359 average and a team-record 21 RBIs. But on the final day of camp, Lefebvre called Ken into his office and told him the Mariners had traded for Atlanta's Dale Murphy, who would be the Mariners' center fielder. That meant Griffey was going down to the minors. With Junior in near tears, Lefebvre asked him if he knew what day it was. At that point, Lefebvre opened a door to the outside corridor, where the entire team was gathered. We all yelled, "April Fools!" Mark Langston, who had the same thing done to him in 1984, was the ringleader of that prank.

It was exciting to break camp with the big-league team for the first time—and even more exciting to start on Opening Day when Presley couldn't play because of a sore right hand. It helped relax me slightly that there were four of us rookies in the lineup in Oakland to face A's ace Dave Stewart in the opener: me at third base and batting eighth, Vizquel at short, Greg Briley in right, and Griffey in center— the latter drawing by far the most attention. In typical Junior fashion, he hit a double to the center-field wall off Stewart in his first major-league at-bat, but we lost 3–2. I had a decent game, fielding all my chances cleanly and driving in our first run with a fifth-inning single. Afterwards, I told reporters, "I feel half and half. Good about my play, bad about the game. But I feel we can play with anyone, and this game showed it."

Later in April, the Mariners traded Quinones to Pittsburgh, which made Omar, at age 22, our regular shortstop. But when Presley healed, I played only sporadically at third base and I struggled both offensively and defensively. One of the few bright spots came on May 6, when I finally hit my first major-league home run in the 143rd plate appearance of my career. It was a two-run shot to left field at Baltimore's Memorial Stadium off Orioles' lefty Jeff Ballard in the second game of a doubleheader sweep. It came on a 1-2 pitch, and according to the *Seattle Times*, "Ballard was shocked." He might not have been the only one.

You want to know something funny? I don't remember anything about that home run. That was typical. Not only don't I remember my first homer, I don't remember my last one (which Baseball Reference tells me occurred on September 25, 2004, off Texas's Chris Young— No. 309 of my career). To me, home runs were not these things you had to make a big deal of. What I will still remember, instead, are some swings that always stay in my mind, because it was the way I wanted to swing. All the practice, visualization, and mechanics meshed perfectly.

There was one double in the Kingdome against Mark Langston over the shortstop's head. It's a feel to it, just the timing and the swing path. It was so smooth. To me, that can be sweeter and more satisfying than a home run. It doesn't feel like you're trying. It's like in golf, when your best shots are the ones you're not trying to hit hard. Something like that. I will still remember some of those swings where the ball just jumped off my bat, and it's the smoothest swing. The ones where I tried really hard, the ball really didn't jump. It doesn't go anywhere. I hit a home run in Oakland that barely went out, but I felt it was so smooth, so effortless. I hit one early in my career in Cleveland against Greg Swindell, and same thing. There was a double in Kansas City. I have a handful of swings I remember.

But that first home run off Jeff Ballard? Sorry, I've got nothing. The thing was, I was so introverted, I wouldn't know who anybody was. I was just playing baseball. Who's that on the mound? I don't know, not unless it was someone famous that everyone was talking about. What I would do is keep watching and watching—"Well, he throws a fastball, it's straight, and a breaking ball, a changeup. Okay, that's it." That's where everything ended. As I matured more and more and was in the league longer, I started getting familiar with more of the pitchers. But in those early days, 1987 to '89, I was oblivious to most of them. Like I said, I was just playing baseball.

The team was hanging around the .500 mark, and on May 25 we made a blockbuster trade. Langston, our best pitcher, went to the Montreal Expos along with pitcher Mike Campbell, a minor-league teammate of mine, for pitchers Gene Harris, Brian Holman, and a tall, long-haired lefty named Randy Johnson. The deal would change the course of Mariners' history—but the immediate effect for me was not good. To make room on the roster for Johnson and Holman, I was optioned back to Calgary.

This was getting familiar. It was the fifth (but not the last) time I was sent back to Calgary. With a .344 average in Triple-A, I didn't feel like I had much to prove. But my numbers with Seattle didn't make a very strong case for me. I was hitting .229 with just a .590 OPS (.304 on-base percentage, .286 slugging percentage). I had two extra-base hits in 79 plate appearances.

It was the beginning of a yo-yo season. Two weeks later, Presley was suffering back spasms, so I got called back up to the Mariners. As always, I had little trouble hitting PCL pitching and sported a .333 average with two homers and nine RBIs in 12 games since being sent down. With Presley hurting, I started four games in a row for the Mariners and had eight hits in 14 at-bats, including another home run, this one off Frank Wills at the Skydome in Toronto. To me, it wasn't any secret—I played better when I played regularly. My defense improved as well.

"I didn't play that much before [being sent down] and I was not as loose or comfortable," I told reporters. "But when I was sent down I played every day and I found my rhythm and was more comfortable and secure with myself."

But I still didn't get regular playing time, and my bat cooled off again. When Presley's back healed up, he started getting the bulk of the time. I was sent back down to Calgary on August 8. I had a .235 average with two homers and 18 RBIs in 54 games. I still had just six extra-base hits.

I'll admit, I was down. I was wondering where my career was going, and whether I was going to be just a Triple-A player. I was struggling with that, and I think it was affecting my performance. I was too much in my own mind. I needed to be 100 percent focused on the game, but the future of my career was preoccupying me.

I came back up to the Mariners one more time when the rosters expanded in September. Once again, my numbers in Calgary looked great. I hit .345 for the season, on top of the .363 I hit in 1988, and .329 in 1987, and .353 in 1985. But when the year ended, I had a .240 average in 65 games to show for my time in Seattle in 1989. In 196 plate appearances, I had just seven extra-base hits. I knew some things had to change for me, mentally and physically. For the first time, I began to wonder if my future might be somewhere other than the Mariners.

Chapter 4

Making It

A COUPLE OF IMPORTANT THINGS happened before the 1990 season, and both figured to be good for my career. At least on paper. First of all, I hit .424 in the winter league, so I was full of confidence about my hitting. Even though the season was delayed by a 32-day lockout that wiped out most of spring training and pushed back the start of the season, I felt I was in top form. And then in January, the Mariners traded Jim Presley, their starting third baseman since 1985, to the Atlanta Braves.

I was optimistic that I'd finally get a legitimate shot, but only cautiously so, because Darnell Coles was still there, and he had played a lot of third base in 1989. There was even talk of moving Greg Briley or—believe it or not—Tino Martínez to third base. It was pretty clear that I still wasn't foremost in their plans, despite tearing up Triple-A for the past three seasons.

I wasn't too happy to read this quote from Jim Lefebvre at the outset of spring training: "Darnell goes into camp as our third baseman." And here's another quote from Lefebvre in February: "I think Darnell Coles is going to surprise a lot of people. He knows there is no one in the wings, just Edgar Martínez to back him up. I think it is time for him to realize that he belongs at third, because to play that position you have to be an athlete. And Darnell Coles is an athlete."

With spring training cut to three weeks, I didn't have much time to make my case. The good news was that rosters were expanded to 27 for the first few weeks of the season because of the lockout, which increased my chances of making the team. I made it—I don't think I could have handled another trip to Calgary—but Darnell Coles was handed the third-base job. I was a utility infielder, with the thought that I could play second base if need be. In fact, the Mariners had experimented with me at second base in instructional league, and it later came out that they were exploring trade options involving our second baseman, Harold Reynolds, with the thought of possibly moving me there.

As it turned out, I actually started at third base on Opening Day in Anaheim when Darnell had back spasms—just like last year when Jim Presley was hurt and I started on Opening Day. I had two hits against the Angels, including a single to drive in our first run in a 7–4 win. Ken Griffey Jr., beginning his second season and rapidly becoming a national star, had four hits, including a three-run home run. After the game, we presented the game ball in the clubhouse to our new owner, Jeff Smulyan, who had purchased the team from George Argyros.

I started the next night (and got a double), and the night after that. But when Darnell's back healed, he moved into the third-base job, and I moved to the bench. My frustration with my situation had been growing, even though I was careful to never let that show. Whenever I was sent down, I would report immediately, even though you're given 72 hours. Some guys are so upset they take a couple of days to show up to the minors, but I always had the sense that this is what you do, this is your job, so go do it. I think that goes back to observing my grandfather, and his work ethic. What are you going to do for two days? Nothing. So just go and do your job. That was the attitude I took. There was also a realization that I couldn't control anything else. The best strategy was to go and perform well. Don't complain.

In all my quotes to the media, I said I was fine with my progress in the organization and not growing impatient. I felt that was the smart thing to say. I wasn't a guy who was going to start a conflict. I was aware that if I said something that was perceived to be the wrong thing, it probably would work against me. So I said what I thought was the right thing. But inside, it was bothering me. I never went to management. Instead, my conversations would be with my agent, Willie Sanchez. At one point, I remember Willie said maybe there would be a trade to the Dodgers. I guess he'd heard some whispers. At that point, my career was at a crossroads. I could make it with the Mariners, I could go back to Triple-A, or I could be traded. I wasn't sure what was going to happen.

Well, I never went back to the minors, except for four games at Jacksonville in 1993 on a rehabilitation assignment after I injured my hamstring. And I didn't get traded, though I would be involved in various rumors over the years. I never left as a free agent, either, although there was one time much later in my career when I briefly considered it, which I'll discuss later. I didn't know any of this in 1990, however, as I sat on the bench in April and wondered when my break would come. It was a very uneasy time. Up until this point, I had been given brief stints at third base, but it was always as a backup plan. The Mariners had never fully committed to me. In 246 at-bats strung out over three seasons, I hit just .268 with two homers.

That was all about to change—out of necessity, or even desperation, more than anything else.

Darnell Coles went through an early stretch where he really struggled. In his first six games of the season, he made five errors and was hitting just .182. Our record was 2–7—and this was a team everyone thought had a chance to finally contend. As a ballclub, we were on a pace for 210 errors. Lefebvre told the media, "We've got to make some adjustments. These are big leaguers. You've got to be able to catch and throw."

After a loss to the Twins on April 18 in which Darnell made two errors, I started at third base in Oakland the next night. They basically didn't have anyone else, but I didn't look at it that way. It was another chance—and maybe my best one. In that game, I had three hits, including two doubles. Two of the hits were off Dave Stewart, who would win 22 games that year and finish third in the Cy Young voting. It earned me another start the next night—one of the most famous games in Mariners' history. Our pitcher, Brian Holman, had a perfect game for 26 batters. But with two outs in the ninth inning, pinch-hitter Ken Phelps—the former Mariner—hit a home run off Holman. Brian was so close to putting his name in the record books—man, that hurt. He got the next batter out to complete the 6–1 victory, but what an agonizing finish to come one out from a perfecto. I had a hit and scored a run in that game, but Brian was the story of the night.

After that, Lefebvre just kept writing my name in the lineup, putting me in the seven hole between Pete O'Brien and Dave Valle. And I was hitting. I had a four-hit game against the Yankees at Yankee Stadium on April 25—including my first homer of the year off Eric Plunk that was estimated at more than 410 feet to left-center—to raise my average to .343. Lefebvre told the reporters he was going to keep me at third base. "Edgar got hot, and when you're hot you keep playing," he said.

Well, Darnell Coles never played third base for the Mariners again. He got a little bit of time in right field and at first base, but on June 18, hitting just .215, Coles was traded to the Detroit Tigers for outfielder Tracy Jones. By that time, I was settled in as the everyday third baseman and had my average at .310. After all those years of sitting behind Jim Presley and Darnell Coles, after all the frustration of being shuttled back and forth to Calgary, it appeared that I had finally won the job, at age 27.

JIM PRESLEY
Former Mariners Third Baseman

The first time I saw Edgar was when we played Calgary in an exhibition game. I said, "This guy is legit. He can flat-out hit, no doubt about it." And Marty Martínez, who signed him, said the same thing. I knew about him coming up. I had been there six years, and it was time for me to move on. I even told Woody [Woodward, the general manager], "Hey, this kid is ready. If you want to trade me, I understand." Then he got a bad knee and they said they weren't sure he could play on turf every day. It's hard enough when you're healthy. But it was time for me to move on, and they needed to make room for Edgar. I told Woody there were two teams I wanted to go to, the Cubs and Atlanta. He said, "I've got good news for you. You're going to Atlanta."

It was the right move, and I was happy for Edgar. Like I said, he was ready. He could swing. He could have been in the big leagues earlier. I was supposed to be traded to the Baltimore Orioles the year before that, but something nixed the trade. I would have loved to play with Ripken and those guys. There was no doubt Edgar was going to be a great hitter in the bigs, and if his leg had stayed healthy, he would have been a really, really good defensive third baseman. Edgar handled the situation well, though, when he was stuck behind us. Darnell was probably one of the best athletes I've ever seen. They drafted him as a shortstop the year after me. I told Hal [former GM Hal Keller], "This kid can play shortstop." It would have been good to have him and me playing that side of the infield. They should have shifted him. But instead they drafted Spike Owen.

I had no animosity toward Edgar. I really liked him. We didn't have much interaction, but he was a good guy, and I loved him as a player. The Mariners needed him in the lineup just for his bat alone. Even in Triple-A, you could just tell he was the best hitter on the field. Great eye at the plate, great discipline, and he stayed inside the ball. All the things you try to teach, he just did it naturally. All Edgar needed was a chance.

That's not to say that everything went smoothly. Far from it. On May 6, for instance, I had maybe the worst game of my career. In a win over the Orioles, I committed four errors to tie a major-league record. It turns out that one of the people who set that record while playing for the Dodgers was Jim Lefebvre—my manager. He used that fact to try to console me. But I still felt really bad. Here I had been given the third-base job partly because Coles was struggling with his fielding, and I have a four-error game. I do remember that I thought two of those errors shouldn't have been called by the official scorer, including one on a ball that Craig Worthington just smoked. It didn't even touch my glove and should have been ruled a hit. There were also two grounders I booted, and one throwing error. I guess I looked so bad that the official scorer must have thought, "This guy is terrible," and didn't give me the benefit of the doubt.

That game actually had a huge effect on my career—a positive one, ultimately. I let it play with my mind so much that I was losing my confidence in the field. That compelled me to do research on the mental side of baseball, and how I could turn that negativity into positivity. I'll get into far more detail on that in the next chapter, because I firmly believe that the mind plays a huge, underrated role in baseball performance. It certainly did in my career, and I worked on that aspect of the game just as hard as I worked on hitting and fielding mechanics.

On that night at the Kingdome, though, I was just embarrassed. I felt bad for Randy Johnson, our pitcher, who gave up four unearned runs because of me. But I was very relieved we came back to win the game 5–4. It's a lot harder to deal with four errors when you lose the game, and you feel responsible. Lefebvre called me into his office after the game to tell me about his own four-error game, and to relax. He assured me he would keep sending me out to third base. It probably helped that I was hitting .320. I was the 22nd third baseman in history to have four errors in a game, so at least I knew I wasn't alone. In fact, Mike Blowers—who would replace me as the Mariners' third baseman in 1995 and became a good friend—had done it just a week earlier with the Yankees. Steve Kelley, columnist for the *Seattle Times*, was impressed that I talked to reporters after the game. He wrote:

"You learn a lot about a player by the way he handles a doomed day. Martínez could have hidden from reporters after the game. He could have refused to talk. He could have sneaked out a side door, or mumbled a few one-word answers. But Martínez, 27, sat by his locker and answered all questions, offering no excuses for his dog-day afternoon."

What I told Kelley was, "All that was in my mind was that, whatever happens, we've got to win. I didn't want to go home today knowing that we lost because I made errors. I made four errors. It happens. Sometimes you try too hard, but I don't think that contributed to me making errors."

I also made a little bit of a joke: "Randy shouldn't have let them hit the ball to me," and then I added, "I was terrible. No excuses. I was just terrible." It made me feel a little better when Randy stopped by my locker and said, "Forget it, Edgar. We won the game and that's the main thing."

At least I was able to help Randy out later in the season. On June 2 at the Kingdome, he threw the first no-hitter in Mariners' history against the Tigers, and I made a pretty good play in the fourth inning to cut off a ball in the hole by Chet Lemon.

On the night after the four-error game, I cleanly fielded the first ball hit to me and threw the runner out. The crowd at the Kingdome let out a big, sarcastic roar. Unfortunately, that wasn't the end of my defensive struggles in 1990. I wound up committing 27 errors, which was the most in the American League at any position (and just one short of the major-league lead of 28 by Howard Johnson of the Mets). What's more, I played in just 144 games because of a variety of injuries—strained hamstring (both left and right), sprained finger, and, most seriously, a sore knee that bothered me off and on all year.

All those errors were extremely frustrating, because throughout my career I had been known as a strong defensive player, and I took a lot of pride in my fielding. In fact, it was my glove more than my bat that drew attention in the minor leagues. But in addition to the loss of confidence that I talked about after the four-error game, I felt I was getting in bad habits as my knee got worse and worse, until finally I needed surgery after the season.

I felt I became kind of sloppy moving around. I found that I was "in between" a lot. In other words, I wasn't moving quickly enough to get a good hop, and that makes it much tougher on you to make the play. I would miss a lot of balls by being in-between. What I remember most, though, is that instead of keeping my hands in front of me, I would keep them at my side. The result was that anything sharp that was hit at me, I would react late. Those were the struggles I had when my knee was bugging me. The next spring, we had a new infield coach named Ron Clark, and he really helped me. He would harp on me to keep my hands in front of me. I'm not sure where that bad habit came from, but I think when you're in pain, the mind goes too. Ron also worked with me on first-step quickness, which in turn helped me get better hops to field. I improved quite a bit in 1991, with my error total cut nearly in half to 15. It's amazing what relatively good health, a clear mind, and good habits can do.

One thing I did consistently all season was hit. I kept my average over .300 most of the year, and was as high as .363 in mid-May, trailing only Griffey (.369) in the American League. My on-base percentage was at .430, also second in the American League (to another teammate, Alvin Davis, at .442). At the end of May, I was actually leading the American League in hitting at .355—but I wasn't even on the All-Star ballot. That's because in those days, the team submitted the players they wanted on the All-Star ballot at each position. The Mariners had turned in Darnell Coles at third base, and it was too late to do anything about it. Lefebvre lobbied with American League manager Tony La Russa—under whom he had been a coach—to name me to the AL squad, but he chose Kelly Gruber and Brook Jacoby as the backups to Wade Boggs at third base.

I wasn't concerned—I was just ecstatic to be playing every day. That was right around the time they traded Darnell to the Tigers, which made it official that the job was all mine. Darnell had a classy quote when he was traded: "Edgar came in and did a great job. He earned it, and I'm really happy for him. I mean that sincerely."

HAROLD REYNOLDS
Former Mariners Second Baseman

We made a lot of trades in those days, but we didn't trade Edgar, which tells you a lot about who he is, and how they valued him. Presley eventually got traded. Darnell got traded. Danny Tartabull got traded, you know what I mean? But not Edgar. Whoever could have stood in his way ended up getting moved. I think a lot of that was because of the person he was, but also that his upside was huge, which we obviously were finally able to see. I mean, for Hal Keller to trade Darnell Coles was like trading his son. Darnell was Hal Keller's firstborn. And that tells you the talent of Edgar Martínez.

One of the highlights of the season—really, of baseball history—occurred on September 14 in Anaheim. In the first inning, Ken Griffey Sr. hit a home run to center field off Angels starter Kirk McCaskill. And then Junior stepped up to the plate and, given the green light on a 3-0 pitch, hit one out to left field—back-to-back homers by father and son. What a special, poignant moment. As Lefebvre said, "It's like they should be written up for a Hollywood movie."

And when Senior hugged Kenny in the dugout, the first thing he said was, "It's about time."

On September 14, with the end of the season nearing, my average was at .296. I was tremendously motivated to finish above .300. It was driving me. I had always been a high-average hitter, and I felt to hit .300 in the major leagues over a full season would be a huge accomplishment, and a boost to my confidence. If I had hit .298, I would have felt the season was a failure. That's the way my mind worked: this is not a good year. I truly felt that way.

I then hit .371 over the final 12 games to bring my season average to .302 (with 11 homers, 27 doubles, 49 RBIs, and a .397 on-base percentage). On September 28, while hitting .300, I got a single and a walk and then was lifted for a pinch-runner. The Mariners shut me down for the final five games of the season because my knee was getting worse and worse. In early October, I had arthroscopic surgery to repair my meniscus. But the good news was that Dr. Larry Pedegana, the team surgeon, didn't have to scrape the underside of my kneecap like he expected. I was cleared to begin rehab right away and told that I'd be fine by spring training, which was reassuring.

It was very satisfying to hit .300. I felt good about my career, and unlike past years, I knew I was going to get another chance. The days of fighting for a job were over. What's more, I knew I could keep hitting .300 in the majors. But rather than settle for that, now I said to myself, "I can win a batting title in the big leagues." That became my new obsession, to hit for a high average and win a batting title.

I always needed something to drive me. As I look back on my career, "obsession" is the right word. Everything I would do from the morning when I got up until game time was geared toward the purpose of getting three or four hits that night. I wanted to succeed every at-bat. That's probably an obsession—healthy at times, not so much at other times.

One thing I needed to do was settle on a batting stance, and that was an evolution. At first, I would use all kinds of different stances. If I wasn't hitting well, I'd change. In the minor leagues, it kept changing, changing. At Triple-A, it changed again, and through my career in the big leagues, it changed at times. It was all about making adjustments after I settled into what became my basic stance: hands held high behind my right ear, with a leg kick as I stepped into the swing. The kick came from watching one of my childhood heroes, José Cruz Sr., as well as Kirby Puckett. I used to study great hitters to see what I could pick up. At times, I would hit like George Brett. When we played Kansas City, I'd watch him closely and emulate his style. Sometimes, I'd try Ryne Sandberg's stance. And sometimes, I would do Will Clark from the right side. My hips had a tendency to open too quickly, and Will's swing helped me stay closed longer. At the same time, the motion he used with his hands helped me get separation.

As I said, José Cruz was a guy I really admired. He had a great 19-year career, mostly with the Astros, making two All-Star teams, winning two Silver Slugger Awards, and banging out 2,251 hits. When José played in Puerto Rico, I would watch the way he held his hands high and eventually worked that into my game. My swing was kind of "inside out," so I had a little bit of a hole. I would make contact, but it would be a weak fly, or I'd miss it foul. I always could make contact with a fastball, even if I had two strikes, but I would clip it foul. So moving the hands higher, and working on the tee high, helped me get on top of the ball. I always felt it's easier to move your hands down to meet the ball than to move them up from a lower position. I remember watching Cruz, when I played against him in Puerto Rico, handle a ball that was high and away, and he would hit a line drive the other way. I said, "That could really help me." I emulated his approach.

JOSÉ CRUZ SR.
Former Major-League Outfielder, Cardinals, Astros, and Yankees

It makes me feel good to hear Edgar modeled his swing after mine. When I was in St. Louis, early in my career, I remember watching Vic Davalillo doing that, and then I started doing it. I'd watch a lot of good players and tried different styles. I used to hold my bat like I was shooting a rifle, with my front elbow. Bob Gibson, who was actually a great hitter himself, put the elbow down. Gibson, when he pitched, he'd put my name in the lineup. A lot of times our manager, Red Schoendienst, didn't put my name in the lineup. But Gibson said, "When I'm pitching, you're playing."

Then later I watched Vic Davalillo and I said, "Let me try that." I did it the rest of my career. Roberto Alomar used to imitate me. I think Edgar saw me playing in Puerto Rico. I got a chance to watch Roberto Clemente and Orlando Cepeda when I was younger. When it comes to how you hold your bat, I always say, it's not how you start, it's how you finish. I started like that to get the pitcher to think about it. When the pitcher was ready to throw, I'd put my hands in the position they were supposed to be to hit. Sometimes, you'd be a little late and have to make adjustments. When a guy throws harder, you'd have to put your hands down quicker. Nowadays, guys are throwing 98, 100 miles an hour. Some people say no one was throwing hard when we played, but I say, we had Seaver, J.R. Richard, Candelaria, Nolan Ryan. They all threw hard. There were a lot of Hall of Famers. That's what kept us hitting .280.

Whenever I see Edgar, I always give him a hug. He was a great hitter, great person, and a good teacher, too. My son, José Jr., said he always listened to Edgar when he played for the Mariners, and even after he played for the Mariners. Edgar was like a master hitter for me. I remember when I first saw him playing in the winter league for San Juan. He was playing third base. When I saw him swing the bat, I knew this guy was going to be a good player. He was a special hitter, with opposite-field power. He was one of those hitters, you don't see many guys like him. Watching José Altuve out here in Houston, he's like that, too.

I want to see Edgar in the Hall of Fame. He belongs in the Hall of Fame. To me, Edgar has got just as good numbers as Clemente. With those numbers, he's got to be in. You don't have to have 3,000 hits. He was a great hitter, and the Mariners loved him the same way Puerto Rico, including me, loves Edgar Martínez.

RICK GRIFFIN
Mariners Athletic Trainer, 1983–2017

When Edgar was 36, he had a really good year, and when he was 37, he had an ever better year. We were at spring training after that, all standing behind the batting cage. Edgar would always hit with Griffey and Buhner in the same group. It was always fun to watch because they were such fun hitters, and they'd always play little games with each other.

Edgar got done hitting, and Lou called him over. He said, "Edgar, when you're 37 years old, you can't hit with your hands up high. You've got to drop your hands lower, because as you get older, you lose some of your reflexes. You've got to get your hands lower so you get to the ball quicker." Edgar looked at Lou and says, "Lou, did you ever lift weights when you played?" Lou goes, "No, I never lifted a damned weight in my life." Edgar goes, "I lift weights every day. My hands are fine." Then he just kicked it that year. That was the year we won 116 games, and Edgar was a huge part of it.

Same thing with the leg kick—I felt it could really help me, so I eventually incorporated it into my swing. I used to do it all the time in batting practice and I'd hit the ball all over the place. I had more drive with the kick. I could hit the ball farther. But it took me a while to have the courage to say, "Okay, I'm going to stand up at the plate in an actual game with the high hands and the high leg kick."

It was my teammate at Triple-A in Calgary, Brick Smith, who finally goaded me into it. I would talk to Brick, who was a friend of mine, and tell him that when I used the high kick, I could hit the ball farther. He kept telling me, "Why don't you use it then? Do it in a game."

I'd say, "I don't know—I'm not a home run hitter."

He's like, "Oh, you're a chicken." He kept telling me that.

Finally, on the last day of the season, my last at-bat, I told him, "I'm going to do it. I'm going to hit like José Cruz my final at-bat."

"You don't have the balls," he said. "You're not going to do it." Well, I did it—and I hit a home run. I pulled it straight down the line. A no-doubter.

That's when I said, "I've got to try this."

BRICK SMITH
Teammate, Chattanooga, 1985–86; Calgary, 1987–88; and Mariners, 1987–88

I'm pretty sure it was the end of the year in 1987 in Calgary. We were in the last group in batting practice, near the end of the year. Edgar had been goofing around—you know how he was on the tee. I said, "Edgar, with your balance and hand-eye coordination, why don't you just try this?" Everyone tries to launch the last round of BP. The thing that amazed me about him—and I tell this to kids all the time—is how quiet he was at the plate. Him and Tony Gwynn, of all the hitters I saw—and most of my experience was in the minors—they had the quietest swing. Their head never moved. If you watch video of Edgar, it's incredible. Gwynn, same thing.

So anyway, I told him to just trust it. Crank it up and let it go. I said, "Edgar, you've got a lot more power than you think. Give it a shot. What have you got to lose? Let the big dog hunt." Yes, I did say, "You don't have the balls." So what did he do? Hit a bomb. I swear, it was on the next swing. Usually, Edgar's really reserved, but we were high-fiving. I said, "What did I tell you?" He didn't say a word, just smiling. I remember it vividly. I can't tell you how many countless times over the years I would watch him hit that way and think, "I know where that started."

107

Most people don't know this, and I feel bad for him, but Edgar was a fantastic third baseman before he started having leg issues. Accurate arm. He'd throw a light ball to first base. I mean, he was fantastic. Edgar was the guy you'd want them to hit it to in tight situations. In Double-A at Chattanooga, I was fortunate to win a batting title, and then at Triple-A, it was reversed. Edgar was incredible. I was like, "Edgar, what in the world happened? Now you need to help me." So he would help me.

In Chattanooga, he hit .250, but he wasn't physically developed. He was young. Then he got to Calgary and all of a sudden took a more focused approach. When he came back in 1987, it was phenomenal. From Chattanooga to Calgary was a complete reformation. I don't know how else to put it. His swing was fluid, it was smooth. We didn't keep track of swing-and-miss ratio back then, but it was incredible. That's when he won his first batting title, and we all said, he's for real.

I know Jim Presley had a big contract—and no disrespect to anyone—but I think people started realizing this guy can hit, and we have to find a place for him. Ask anyone that's played, and if they're honest, there are certain guys you play with, you know they have it, whatever "it" is. Lots of guys have it and never get the opportunity. With Edgar, we're thinking, "If this guy doesn't get a shot, what chance do I have?" Maybe they thought Presley had more power. But we were thinking, "This guy can pick it, and he can rake." History speaks for itself, and so do his numbers.

Edgar's a good soul. I love him to death. It has nothing to do with the Hall of Fame; he's just a good guy. I've never heard anyone say anything bad about him. When you leave the game and look back, you're more proud of the guys that weathered the storm. You feel better for the guys that were in the minors for years and then hit it big. You know the first-round choices are always going to get a chance. When someone like Edgar comes through, you think, "This is what it's all about." Maybe a lot of players who never made it are jealous, but I've never been that way, especially with Edgar. He's one of those guys you pull for. I've never known him not to do the right thing. He did it right, and he did it clean.

The leg kick became a big part of my repertoire. It wasn't always easy, because some pitchers could get you off your timing. I actually felt it was inconsistent, but I kept trying it and eventually I got used to it, so I started using it more and more. Sometimes I would feel, "It's not working for now," and so I'd stop using the high kick. But it was part of my swing. When I was doing well, I was doing the high kick.

A lot has been made about how I could (or should) have been playing regularly in the major leagues much earlier. I probably lost three prime years—age 24, 25, and 26—when I was a backup and shuttled between Seattle and Calgary. Obviously, my cumulative statistics, like the number of hits and home runs, would have been higher, and that might have helped me get to the Hall of Fame sooner. Sometimes I think about that, what would have happened if I was given a chance to play earlier. No question, it was frustrating at the time. But at the same time, there's nothing I can do about it now. I have no control over any of that. I choose just to think about how fortunate I was to be given the chance to play and build a career in the major leagues, even if it wasn't until I was 27.

I've never been one to dwell on the negative, or on things I can't change. I choose to focus on all the positive things that happened to me. And after my breakthrough year of 1990, many more of them lay ahead.

Chapter 5

The Mental Game

WHEN I MADE THOSE FOUR ERRORS in a game against the
Baltimore Orioles, I was at a critical point in my career, and as I said,
it shook me. After years of kicking around the minors, and yo-yoing
up and down between Triple-A and the majors, I finally had a chance
to stick with the Mariners for good that year. Jim Presley had been
traded, Darnell Coles had been moved to the outfield early in the
season. The third base job was mine. This is what I had been striving
for and yearning for, all these years. So not only was a game like that
embarrassing, but I feared that it might cause the Mariners to give up
on me once and for all.

They didn't, of course. Instead, it turned out to be a critical turning
point in which I learned how vital the mind is to success in baseball.
And beyond that, it was when I learned how to harness the power of
the mind and put it to work for you in a positive way, rather than
letting negativity and doubt fester and bring you down.

Because that's exactly what I was doing. I had always been a guy
who wanted the ball hit to him, because I knew I was going to make
the play. I had that kind of confidence. But after that game, that

feeling totally flipped. The errors played with my mind. I realized that I began to see myself making an error before the ball was hit to me. That would be the first thought that came into my head. You can't play baseball that way—it becomes a self-fulfilling prophecy. I learned through time and study that the mind does that to protect us. But for performance, it's not good.

That's when I realized I had the same tendency on offense. If I had a bad stretch of games, now I would see myself making outs. If I struck out two times in a game, before I got to the plate the next time, I would see myself striking out again. That's the first thing that came to my mind. No doubt it was holding back my career, especially with the pressure I was feeling to play well so I could finally hold on to the third-base job.

I said to myself, I can't play the game like this. I will have zero success if I keep doing this. I went to a bookstore—I can't remember whether it was in Seattle or on the road—and found the self-help section. I picked up a small book, really more like a pamphlet, that dealt with the mind. I can't even remember the name of the book, or the author. I carried it with me for a while, but it disappeared in one of our family's moves. Yet this little book had a profound effect on my career. It changed the way I approached baseball, changed my preparation, and ultimately, changed my results. I learned how to erase the negative image with a positive one.

The book taught me how the subconscious and conscious mind worked. When I had a negative event—whether I struck out three times or I made an error or we lost a game—I learned that this failure would have a negative effect on my confidence. Of course, I knew that intuitively, but this book helped me make sense of it. I learned that the next time I went to the plate, or took the field, my subconscious mind would bring that event back to the surface, and I would feel very low confidence in myself. I learned there were exercises I could do, such as repeating the opposite result over and over and over again, that would start changing that negative image in my mind. For example, if I struck out, before I went home I would visualize myself hitting the ball in the gap. Or I would say in my head, over and over, "I hit the ball really well."

All these exercises helped, little by little, to bring my confidence back. I would repeat these mantras on my way home, before I went to bed, and when I got up in the morning. In my mind, I would see myself getting hits. I took that book on road trips with me, studied it on the airplane or in the hotel room, until I had it down. When you learn how to do these exercises, you can master it. It helped me immensely on days I struggled. It helped get me out of slumps sooner. It helped me handle the stress and pressure of big moments in ball games. Very quickly, it became a part of my routine. Throughout my career, I worked on my mind just as much as I worked on my hitting. When I changed my thought to something positive, I would feel a positive energy. If I woke up tired, I'd have to say, "I feel good, I feel good." And the energy would come, and I'd feel better.

You might call it tricking my mind, but it worked for me. I got interested in reading and searching for more. When I'd find pieces I thought were helpful, I'd store it away. Eventually, I didn't need the pamphlet anymore. But I kept studying the subject, kept searching for any books I could get my hands on that dealt with mental preparation. In the minor leagues, we were given a book about mental training, and it had some good information, too. I had a lot of talks with Gary Mack, the Mariners' sports psychology consultant, who had written a book on the topic called *Mind Gym*. Sadly, Gary died in 2002. When the internet came around, I would search topics I felt would help me, like goal-setting, visualization, affirmation, controlling my self-talk, resiliency, awareness. I'd pore over the articles I found. In fact, I still do. Once you learn the basics, it's practice, practice, practice. Eventually, I focused on affirmations, visualization, and self-talk—the inner voice.

They worked for me. When I first came to the big leagues, I knew I had the skill to succeed. But I didn't feel I was performing to my capabilities, and it was very frustrating. I'd know the pitcher was going to throw the fastball, and he'd throw the fastball, and I'd take it. I wouldn't swing, even though I knew I should have ripped that pitch. I knew I was a good fielder, and I'd make an error. I wasn't as confident as I had been in the past. That's why I sought help.

I saw and felt improvement right away, within days. But I would still catch myself occasionally with a negative idea in my mind. It took me a little time to stop that. Seeing the clear picture of what I wanted, that took me a little time. Feeling the right emotion of confidence took me a little time and a lot of practice. Believing that this really helped me, also took me a little time. But when I started seeing consistent results, I hung onto it and kept practicing that technique over and over. I became convinced I was on the right track.

Eventually, I noticed that when I failed, I didn't feel the same frustration and doubt as when I struggled during that earlier period. It was a different feeling. I felt confident I was going to get out of it. That in itself gave me confidence. Even if I struggled, I said, "I'm going to get out of it. I know how to come out of it." It's amazing how powerful the mind is. I've always believed if players practiced this kind of mental training, it would be extremely beneficial. I've seen some quotes about it from Michael Jordan and Kobe Bryant, two of the best basketball players in history. Kobe is mostly in tune with mindfulness, which is a way of focusing on how to use your senses to stay in the present. So there are some players, great players, who are aware of the importance. But there are still so many players who are not maximizing their mental potential.

DAN WILSON
Former Mariners Catcher

On road trips, you couldn't help but go to the back of the plane and see what he was reading. It was a lot of those kinds of things. He really took the mental side of the game very seriously. He loves to talk about those kinds of things. I do think that was the separator for him. Gosh, if I was a young player, I would pick his brain incessantly. "What is it that you did between your ears when you were in those situations that helped you to be successful?" There's part of baseball where you trick yourself pretty much every day. But that's where the difference lies with him. There's a lot of players that have great swings. But it's what he did between the ears that made the difference.

Eventually, it became part of my daily routine to work on my mental skills. Let's say there was a situation that was key in the game, and in the past I made the play. I'd think about that time I made the play. I'd bring it in my mind and replay it. That's the one I want to recall, over and over and over, until the one where I made the mistake started being less and less visible in my mind. Basically, you erase it. What I learned is the subconscious mind is where all our history is. That's all memory, all your past, as you remember it. That doesn't mean it's real, or true. It's our own personal history. I learned that if you tell your subconscious mind what you want to happen, it becomes a belief. It becomes real, in your mind. That's all that is important.

115

You do that in large part by learning about affirmations and visualization, and controlling your self-talk. Those three tools, that's what I became good at, because I practiced it every day. My self-talk, the way I talk to myself in tough situations, that is key because those thoughts and conversations within myself create images and emotions. If the emotion is good, that's all that matters, because now it will be in my history, my subconscious mind, as something positive. So I kept working on changing those bad images, changing them to positive.

I'd do it before the game. Just a conversation with myself. I didn't have to say it out loud. I would do it sometimes in the on-deck circle. But the night before, and the morning of the game, those are the best times to do it. Your mind is completely at peace. It's why they call it the alpha state, right before you go to bed. That's when it stays in your mind the most. I'd see the images, do my affirmations. At the beginning, I had to do it for a long time, an hour. It became shorter and shorter over time. Sometimes, 10 or 15 minutes would be enough. But I was doing it so often, every day, it had already changed so much of my subconscious mind. My past history, it became very positive.

That's why the elite athletes like LeBron James, like Michael Jordan, like Ken Griffey Jr., never talk to themselves negatively. You never heard Junior say, "I don't feel good at the plate." It's not in their history. You never saw Junior walking with his head down saying, "How am I going to get out of this slump?" Because their subconscious mind is so full of positive things that there's no room for negativity in their thoughts. Even in Junior's final season, when he struggled at age 40, there may have been a realization that the end was getting close. But not because he couldn't perform.

One part of my game that I really took pride in was my batting eye—even though, as I discussed, I had to work so hard to control the eye condition I had, strabismus. The success I had in that regard, the .418 career on-base percentage—I credit my mind for that, too, in a way, because I became conditioned to study to overcome my deficiencies. I obsessed on learning how a guy pitches, his tendencies, and how his catcher calls the game. I had to do that.

If I didn't visualize a fastball in my mind first, I didn't know the velocity, I didn't know the movement. I struggled with it. But if I see the fastball first in my mind before I'm going to swing, I have a better chance to connect. The same way, if I see in my mind the breaking ball—the shape, the velocity—I have a better chance to hit it. It was almost like I saw the pitch before it was thrown. I believe my mind helped me see better. Before, when I didn't know what was coming, and it was a breaking ball, I would lose sight of it. I knew, "Okay, that's my condition." But because my mind wasn't connected, it wasn't helping me see it.

I learned that the mind has the ability to see an image and retain that image. When you take that pitch, already you know if you can hit that ball or not. So the next time, you're looking for that pitch. It gave me the confidence I could hit it. That helped me a lot. I would guess what the pitcher was going to throw, and I got good at it.

MIKE BLOWERS
Former Mariners Third Baseman
The longer Edgar was in the league, he was seeing pitchers more and more, and he used to talk to me all the time—he could set up pitchers. He knew what they were going to do, which I think freed him up to be more aggressive with his swing when he needed to be. I think all those things played together. He prepared as well and was as smart as anybody as far as studying pitchers and paying attention. If they were giving something away, Edgar could pick it up like nobody else. I think it's kind of a lost art. There

were times he'd pick things up for myself and other players, and he would share it with us. But if it was something that was really late, I couldn't use it. I had to pick the ball up earlier, where he could still stay in there and have a better idea, which was amazing. He was the best at that.

ALVIN DAVIS
Former Mariners First Baseman

Edgar became the guru. He became that player that every team has one or two of, that the others hitters went to to get fixed. All of us talk about plan and approach, but I'm talking about mechanics of the swing, and mental approach. Not just a plan, but what are we facing and how can we attack it that night? All wise young players are asking that question constantly: "Do you see anything in my swing?" There's a select group of players that other players come to. Edgar was that guy.

MIKE WISHNEVSKI
Teammate, Wausau, 1984; Chattanooga, 1986; Calgary, 1987–88

You didn't see Edgar walk back from the plate too often, but when he did, some people thought he had his head down. I think every time he was coming back, he was reviewing pitch selection. Edgar was a student of the game, even in the minor leagues.

RICK GRIFFIN
Mariners Athletic Trainer, 1983–2017

I was so lucky, because when he was DH, he sat by me on the bench. I sat by him on the bench for 10-plus years. We would always talk about baseball. We'd talk about hitting and situations. He would tell me things.

He would say, "Watch the second baseman on this next pitch. If he moves a little bit to the right, it's going to be a fastball. If he moves a little to the left, it's going to be a curveball." He would tell me that.

He would tell me sequences of pitches of what they were going to do. All the time, just arbitrarily, I'd say, "Edgar, what's he going to throw on this pitch?"

He'd say, "In this situation, because of this, he's going to throw a fastball away right here." He'd be right about 90 percent of the time.

The Mariners made that one commercial, where there was the bogeyman, and Dan Wilson, I think, said, "There's a guy that could tell the pitch that was coming." Every time I saw that, I would laugh, because Edgar would sit on the bench all the time with me and do exactly that. Robbie [Cano] told me that most of the time when he goes to the plate to hit, he'll ask Edgar what he thinks will be the sequence of pitches the guy's going to throw. He'll use Edgar to prepare him to watch for sequences.

Edgar would pick things up. Pitchers would do things with their glove. Bobby Tolan was the very best I ever saw, but Edgar learned how to do that. Edgar would see things and he would tell the guys. In 2001, we had some guys that could hit. It seemed like they knew every pitch that was coming, because they knew what the pitchers were doing, and they'd keep little books on it. Edgar was front and center on that.

Edgar didn't let outside events cloud what he was doing. They always talk about how you don't want to hear the noise. Edgar didn't hear the noise. Edgar was funneled—funneled into hitting, funneled into being a good teammate. He had a real good, funny personality, but it didn't come out too much. Some of the players were kind of afraid of him, because he was quiet; they didn't think they should talk to him. I'd say, no, he's not like that.

I studied the catcher as well, how he called a game, his tendencies and mannerisms. If the pitcher shook off a sign from the catcher, I'd try to think along with him. It's a mental game between the pitcher and the hitter, and even the catcher and hitter. Even with my eye condition, I got really good at outthinking the opposition, or more accurately, thinking along with them. All that helped me not only to hit for a high average, but achieve a high on-base percentage through walks.

Thinking back, I realize now that I actually started using visualization when I was 10 or 11 back in Puerto Rico. I would go in the backyard after watching Roberto Clemente play in the World Series in 1971. I would get a broomstick and just hit rocks. I was playing out in my mind that I was in a stadium full of people, and I was coming up in a big situation, and I would get the winning hit—a double or home run.

All this visualization I was doing for years as a kid, it did a few things for me. One, it developed my hand-eye coordination, so when I started playing Little League, I already had that ability. It made it easier for me to adapt to the game very quickly.

But the other thing it did, it developed in my mind that I saw myself doing well. When I was hitting rocks, I was always triumphing. Unconsciously, it built my confidence. I was seeing myself as one day being a major-league ballplayer and having success. To me, it was very amazing that many years later I was able to play in the big leagues and do well. Not only that, but out of Puerto Rico, only two players have won batting titles. Roberto Clemente won four, and I won two. After I retired, they gave me the Roberto Clemente Award, one of the greatest honors of my life.

What I'm saying is that through visualization I was seeing myself in the future, and it became reality. If we're aware of this power, we can use it to help get where we want to be, five, 10, 15 years from now. Make the time to just imagine yourself doing something that you aspire to. This can help you achieve your goals. As a child, I wasn't aware of what was happening in my mind. But now I believe all that visualization, seeing myself in the big leagues one day, hitting rocks, all those pictures in my mind translated into giving me a lot of confidence. It almost was like painting my future.

And I think it helped a lot in my early years, all the amateur leagues I played in, semipro ball, through the minors. I believe it helped me, in that sense, to reach the major leagues and have success in the major leagues, because I had innate confidence I had developed early. That didn't mean I was perfect, though. The confidence wavered at times. Early on with the Mariners, especially after that four-error game, I needed the extra tools.

Losing confidence is what really contributes to long slumps. You have to reverse it. You have to change negative thoughts to positive thoughts. Baseball can be a frustrating game—sometimes, you do everything right, hit a line drive, and the guy makes a great play. You can hit the ball on the nose four times and go 0-for-4. To me, in that situation, I concentrated on the positive. The positive was, it felt good to hit the ball hard. I stayed with that feeling, and didn't dwell too much on the negative side, the 0-for-4.

In our sport, we fail so often, it's very easy to get negative. I had this constant battle with myself to change any negative thought and turn it into positive. And if I hit a bloop single, a ball I mis-hit that somehow dropped in safely, or a well-placed dribbler that accidentally became an infield hit? That was positive, too. Very positive. Those are savers. When you don't feel the swing is that great, bloop singles are great. It gets you back on track.

I grew to feel very comfortable in pressure situations. Again, the tendency of the mind is to flash on what could go wrong. What I

121

used to do was simply focus on what I wanted to do in that situation. That is something really hard to master. The mind has a tendency to go back and forth. For example, if there's man on third base and it's a big run, it's very easy for me to say, "I don't want to hit a ground ball to third base." If I do that, I'm concentrating on the negative. And more often than not, that's what I'm going to do—hit a grounder to third, and the run doesn't score. If I eliminate those thoughts, and concentrate only on, "I'm going to hit this ball up the middle," and focus on that, I have a higher percentage chance of achieving that goal. The key in that situation is to not focus on what you don't want to do, but on what you want to do. The more you master that, the more consistent you're going to be.

Of course, it's one thing to do that in April, when the stakes aren't nearly so high. It's another to do it in the postseason, with 50,000 people in the stands, a national television audience, and the fate of your team hanging in the balance. As an older player, it gets easier, because you've been in so many high-leverage situations. But as a young player, you have to prepare for that type of pressure. You have to visualize yourself doing well. You have to always anticipate a situation, and focus on the positive. That's the only way you can feel more confidence. Use words like "I can do this." "I will do this." Not words like "I wonder if..." or "maybe I will." Affirmation has to do with strong, positive words that imply you will succeed.

Doubt is not a good thing in sports. We have to be aware when the mind goes there, and we use that kind of language. Negativity creates a lot of doubt. It's like going to the plate and wondering, "Will he throw me a slider or will he throw me a fastball?" When you're so confident, you know he's going to throw you a fastball. When the fastball comes, you're right on it. When he throws a slider, you take it, because you're so confident that's the pitch he's going to throw. You want to avoid doubt. I think when it comes to how we talk to ourselves, what language we use is very important, very powerful. Sometimes, we're not aware of what's happening upstairs to subtly take us out of our game. We have to learn to listen to our mind talking to us.

One trick I'd use was to watch video of myself getting hits, and hitting the ball hard. Some guys look at their poor performances to try to figure out what they're doing wrong. I preferred to look at my good performances to see what I was doing right when I had success. Our video man, Carl Hamilton, would compile something like a highlights video. I would find the things I was doing right during the times I was hitting well, and then I'd go outside and practice. It put me in the right frame of mind.

HAROLD REYNOLDS
Former Mariners Second Baseman

I think Carl Hamilton was big for Edgar. When you have a hunger and a thirst for knowledge, you're looking everywhere for it, and here comes Carl Hamilton with his videos when no one was doing it. Edgar was into all of that. He was the American League Tony Gwynn. What I remember, more vivid than anything else, was him constantly going back and looking at his swing. We had these Etch-A-Sketch type things, compared to today, and it would print off almost like a computer, print off frame-by-frame, when you're hitting. I remember Edgar always going back and looking—"Oh, I didn't get my hands where I wanted to." With today's technology, I can't even imagine.

I was also big on goal-setting. There's something in sports called the "comfort zone." We hear it all the time—"He's in a comfort zone." But that can be a bad thing, too, if you allow yourself to get too comfortable. I feel that not enough players set high goals, high expectations, for themselves. I'll talk to players and I ask, "What is your goal for this year? What do you want to hit?" Too many players say, well, "If I could hit .270, 15 homers, 70 RBIs, I think it would be a good season for me."

The way the mind works, that's what they expect for themselves, so they're shutting themselves out of higher achievement. When they raise their average to about .270, they tend to relax. When they relax, they stop doing the little things that got them to .270. So now he goes back down to .250, and he gets anxious. And the player once again does extra batting practice, he gets up early and stretches and exercises, he goes to bed early—all those little things he did to get to .270. And he does it again. If he raises his average above .270, though, he feels outside that comfort zone. He relaxes even more, and naturally, he will be back to .270. He will always be between .280 and .250. That will be the range.

That is why you see other players that work really, really hard and they're very, very disciplined. That is because their goals are so much higher, and it requires stricter discipline. The mindset is, "Well, if I'm going to hit .350, I have to do all these things. I have to work extra, train extra, get my rest. I have to come at this time to the stadium. I have to leave at this time." Their routine is shaped by that high a standard.

We had it here in Seattle with Ichiro. He came to the ballpark at the same time every day. He was very disciplined about his routine. He went to the training table at the same time to get his massage. He went at the same time to do his workout. Everything is very disciplined, because he has high standards, and he doesn't feel confident to reach his goal unless he does all that. So that's what it takes.

If someone is hitting .270 and wants to hit .320 or .330, he needs to reassess his goals and apply all that discipline. My obsession was to hit .350. I hit .350 just once in my career. But I learned it's okay to not meet your goal. It's more the journey you went through, and not the result. So I didn't look at my number anymore. I looked at the work I put into it, how I handled it, how I contributed to the team. The number, I can't control, so I'm not worried about it anymore.

I truly believe that what makes one player hit .350 and another player hit .315 is that they believe they can do it. If they believe they can only hit .315, that's what they're going to hit. But if they alter their thinking and say, I'm going to hit .350, and they repeat this with emotion and they expect to do that, their whole routine changes. They start doing all the things, simple things, it takes to raise their game. If they don't feel good with their swing, they go to someone who is doing really well. "Do you see my swing? What am I doing wrong?" Those are the things that people who always hit .230—they never do that kind of stuff. It's a lot of these pieces missing. It just takes a stricter discipline. Everyone has talent, or they wouldn't be in the major leagues. It's what they do with it that determines how high they go.

For me, all my mental preparation came together in the biggest at-bat of my career, at the most pressure-packed moment I would ever face, in Game 5 of the American League Division Series against the Yankees in 1995. To recap, we were down 5–4 in the 11th inning, with runners on first and third, and Jack McDowell on the mound for the Yankees. If we lost, our magical season would be over. In my previous at-bat in the ninth inning, I struck out on a split-fingered fastball against McDowell when a hit could have won the game. I came to the dugout, and obviously I was very disappointed about it. Norm Charlton, our relief pitcher, told me not to worry, I was going to be up again in a big situation. I was preparing myself for that moment. As a DH, I had plenty of time to do that, because I don't go out on the field to play defense. I went through a series of visualization exercises mentally, and I stayed very positive.

One thing I knew, McDowell was going to try to get me out with the split-fingered pitch again. He had struck me out with that. He wasn't throwing hard, like he used to in his prime. His fastball wasn't that fast anymore. The split was his out pitch. When I came up in the 11th, the crowd at the Kingdome was going crazy. It was bedlam, but I felt calm. I took a fastball for a strike, but I didn't care. I knew I was going to get split, split, split. I knew it with all my heart. That's what those mental exercises did—took out the doubt. Once I saw the fastball on the first pitch, I knew he was going to throw the split. It gave me that confidence.

That was my mental process. I did the visualization, and I saw myself hitting the ball hard. I envisioned the shape and texture of his split-fingered pitch. What I actually wanted to think in that moment was hitting the ball solid. It wasn't "hit the ball hard." That's different. When you say, "hit the ball hard," you swing harder. You overswing. But when you say, "hit the ball solid," you actually quiet everything down so you can make solid contact. That's what I was trying to keep in my mind: just hit the ball solid somewhere. I was able to not overswing. I tried to make it simple.

And, of course, I got the split, just as I knew I would, and I hit a double into the left-field corner that scored both runs. We won the game and won the series. It's the at-bat that defined my career, but in a weird way, I felt like I had already experienced it. Because in my mind, I had.

I believe my mental preparation, dating back to that little pamphlet I picked up at the bookstore, dating back even farther to hitting rocks in the backyard when I was 10 or 11 and pretending I was Roberto Clemente in the World Series, had led me directly to that moment. It's a very powerful feeling to be clearheaded and positive in the tensest situations. As an athlete, we practice mechanics, we practice training our bodies, all these things that require a lot of discipline. But the mental side is hugely important, too. There are tools and exercises we can use to train the mind, and they all came together for me in the 11th inning that day.

Yes, it's true that some people are simply faster and stronger. But the mind is a great equalizer. How much do you want it? That's the key. For years, I watched the kid in Boston, Dustin Pedroia. He's a little guy, but he put up numbers like a big guy. I think it's all those things a person has within himself, what he believes he can achieve, how badly he wants it, and whether he has the discipline to work for it. All those things make regular players become very good players. Conversely, I've seen guys who had all the talent in the world, superstar ability, but they just lack the discipline and the desire. They lack that focus, and they never make it. That's what it takes to reach your goals. It takes a lot of discipline.

I honestly believe that the epiphany I had, that I needed to train my mind, was a major part of my success. Because the game is confidence. We as players have the talent. That's why we made it to the big leagues. But how we use those skills, it's all in the head. When you have the image in your mind that you see yourself succeeding, the game becomes easy, like you're a kid playing in the backyard. When you see yourself not performing and making mistakes and striking out, it becomes the toughest game in the world to play.

It's how you switch from those negative images to the positive ones that makes all the difference in the world. That takes work and practice. But it's what makes great players great.

Chapter 6

Batting Title

AFTER HITTING .300 IN MY FIRST full season in the major leagues in 1990, one good thing happened right away: during spring training of 1991, I signed a two-year contract for $850,000 guaranteed, with incentives that could bring it up to $1 million. That extra year eliminated a lot of worry and allowed me to just concentrate on getting better. It also cemented the fact that I was the Mariners' third baseman moving forward.

"It makes me feel like I have a future here," I told the media when my new contract was announced.

Not bad for a guy who had signed with the Mariners out of a tryout camp in Puerto Rico for $4,000 and was unsure if it was worth it to quit my night jobs to pursue a baseball career that might not succeed. My cousin, Carmelo, was right when he told me back then that the real money came when you made it to the major leagues. But the biggest reason I was happy to sign this contract, and an even larger contract the next season, is what I could now do for my grandparents. When I signed a three-year, $10-million extension in August of 1992, I described it as the most important day in my career. Sure, it was great to have security and financial freedom—something that I was never sure would happen in the struggling early days of my career. But the reason I said that is because I could now take care of all my grandparents' needs, which was tremendously gratifying.

They took me in when I was a baby, and they raised me. They gave me a great life, a happy childhood. I wanted to give something back to them. It felt really great to get to that point where I could ensure they didn't have to struggle any longer. My grandfather was always worried about his debts. I paid off all their debts, especially the medicine that both of them needed and which was extremely expensive. My grandmother was dealing with diabetes and high blood pressure. I bought the house from my grandfather so that he no longer had to pay off the loans, though they continued to live there. I still own that house, and it's always there for various family members who need a place to stay.

The other good thing about the spring of 1991 is that my knee felt good again after the surgery. I had a great spring. I hit over .400 (.414), and I felt my work with the new infield coach, Ron Clark, really helped my defense. As I told reporters that spring, I was embarrassed about leading the league in errors and determined to turn things around. It sure helped to be able to move without pain. The manager, Jim Lefebvre, noticed the difference. "A new leg, a new man," was his quote about me to the *Seattle Times*. Halfway through the Cactus League, I was hitting .540 (19-of-37) to lead all hitters in Arizona and Florida.

One change that had a huge positive affect on my career around that time was that I began serious weight training. At that time, I had never used weights, except maybe some dumbbells every once in a while, like a pitcher. In those days, I thought running was the proper conditioning routine for a baseball player. I would jog—not even sprint. But it was clear I needed to generate more power if I wanted to play regularly in the major leagues. When Ken Phelps suggested I lift weights, I said, "Hmmm, I better look into this."

I began to pump iron regularly, and did so the rest of my career. In fact, I would work out in some fashion after every game, whether it be riding an exercise bicycle or lifting weights. I gradually got stronger, and the power came around. That was another major turning point in my career. It wasn't like I went overnight from no power at all to suddenly being a power hitter. This was a change already happening as I matured physically and mentally and worked on honing my batting skills and techniques. But weight training was invaluable for me to take the next step.

I hit as many as 37 homers in a season, and slugged .515 for my career, with a high of .628 in 1995. I never considered myself a power hitter, per se—more of a gap-to-gap hitter—but as I got stronger I had the ability to hit 20 to 30 homers a year. My technique for weight training was to push hard and take workouts to the limit. It wasn't just maintenance. I pushed myself to build strength.

I'm in my fifties now, and I still lift weights. I have a multitask exercise machine at our house. Interestingly, I found out that my father was a fanatical weightlifter until he died. We didn't have a close relationship, so it wasn't something we ever talked about, but I know he worked out all the time. I guess it's in the Martínez genes.

RICK GRIFFIN
Mariners Athletic Trainer, 1983–2017

Edgar was like a nutritionist as a baseball player. He would not put bad stuff in his body. He knew what was good and what was bad and he would not put sugars in his body, he would not put certain things in there he knew were going to possibly put him in a bad situation. He always watched what he ate. I have not seen many players look at labels on things when you go to restaurants. He would look at Gatorade to see what the percentage of sugar was. He would not eat stuff that had a lot of sugar in it. I probably had 500 meals with Edgar, and he would read the labels on things. Or we would go to a visiting clubhouse and he would read the label of everything because he didn't want to have anything with x amount of sugar in it, or x amount of this in it. He knew all that stuff.

Another person who helped me a lot with my conditioning was Peter Shmock, the Mariners' strength coach in the early part of my career. Peter was a former shot-putter who competed at the University of Oregon under legendary coach Bill Bowerman and made it all the way to the Olympic trials in 1976. When I hurt my hamstring in 1993, I asked him to come with me to Puerto Rico during the off-season to help my rehab. He spent a week there with me. We worked on weights, but mostly we concentrated on getting my legs strong again, which turned out to be very helpful. Between that and a sports medicine clinic I went to in Puerto Rico that helped me strengthen my hamstring, it really helped me bounce back from that injury.

PETER SHMOCK
Mariners Strength and Conditioning Coach, 1983–94

That was a wonderful time for me in Puerto Rico, having the opportunity to work with Edgar. I liked him, and we got along. What was so amazing was how much he wanted to come back and play at a very high level. Every morning, maybe except Sunday, he'd pick me up at 8:00 in the morning. We'd grab coffee, then head down to the beach. It was warm and humid, and I brought a bungee cord that I put between two palm trees 20 feet apart.

He's jumping over that bungee cord, suspended 2½–3 feet off the ground, doing jumps off that and other agility moves and strides in the sand. I'd say, "Let's go in the ocean," which is a nice way to get the body to heal.

Then he'd run some errands. I was with him the whole day. We'd end up at his house, where he had weight-lifting equipment, and we'd lift for about an hour. Then his aunt would make us a meal, after which we'd run some more errands. People in Puerto Rico always wanted Edgar's time, and I'd just hang out with him. Then, finally, it's 2:00 or 3:00 in the afternoon, and we're at the ballpark and I'm stretching him. He'd play a game while I'd hang out and sit in the dugout with the rest of the players. Afterward, we'd drive home and then start over the next day.

Edgar was always self-motivated. I would kind of nudge him. If you do this, this will be the outcome, or do that, that will be the outcome. Edgar was always doing his thing, and always doing his own research and kind of looking. After a few years, we started connecting more, especially during spring training. Very early in Alex Rodriguez's career, I remember I helped set up the training area for the new complex in Peoria, and Edgar would let me lead the two of them. Whatever Edgar did, Alex did. Alex was smart that way—"Let's learn from the best."

At that time, we were doing really different movements. Someone took still photos of us training back then, and I looked at them recently. My reaction was, "My god, I had him doing that?" First of all, Edgar was doing the movement really well, and it was one that was hard to execute. I didn't recall getting him to do something that tricky, but evidently I did. He was doing what's called either an overhead squat or snatch squat. It's one of two movements in Olympic weightlifting.... It's as much about flexibility as strength. It was a time he was certainly getting stronger and bigger, but you can't do that movement without being loose and mobile. You just can't.

Edgar was as diligent as they came. I've been around athletes all my life, top-notch athletes way before the Mariners. You just observe tendencies after a while. Baseball loves to say "work ethic." He was just really consistent, and it reminded me of track-and-field athletes. They're a little different; they're individuals, not on a team, and they have to be self-motivated. I admired how Edgar took care of himself, admired the way he practiced, admired his consistency, his routine.... What I learned from Bowerman, which was counterculture, was that throwing hard, swinging hard, wasn't necessary. Sometimes it was, but mostly it was learning about rhythm and position and stance and posture.

Edgar understood that. Every time I'd watch Edgar, he'd start his day off hitting off the tee with his left hand, then his right hand, then both hands. Then batting practice, and the first ball you didn't think was hard enough to get out of the infield. No effort. This is very much how I trained, and how I learned from my mentors. There was consistency, but also, in my way of thinking, he knew how to take his skills to a consistent level to get better. And do it in way where it would not leave him often. If it did, he knew how to get back there. And to go with his consistency, the thing I would have loved, was this even-keelness with him. "Hey, I hit four home runs," or "I was 0-for-20"—which didn't happen often—and there wasn't a big sway one way or another emotionally.

He basically said, "I have to get stronger, and the only way to get stronger is to lift weights, and I have to do it in a way that's good for me." Edgar was willing to listen, but he also knew intuitively that strength from the center of the body out was the key, not only to be functionally stronger, but in a way that was athletically efficient. And so he did.

He put on some weight. He has a body type that's very easy if you feed it the right fuel, lift the right weight, employ the right movement reps and time off. He's a guy that can get pretty thick, with his body type. That's a plus to getting stronger but it can also be minus, because that body type can get tight as well. As we worked together in the later stages, he was getting strong, but I said, "We've got to keep you loose." Musculature that is hard and not supple is not very useful. In our time together, that never happened.

In my view, there are two applause points I give him. One is longevity, through a system that works. If you can't perform at a high level, you can't play. He matured, he grew, and he changed, because his training got more sophisticated. The other was his ability to come back every single day and make adjustments, also knowing how much was enough so he could play. Guys that don't do anything to take care of themselves either get real lucky and have a long career, or they don't get lucky. Guys who do too much, who are always training, that doesn't help them. He was a guy who found the middle ground. If you don't have enough self-esteem or self-confidence, you want to literally and figuratively pump yourself up. He didn't fall into that trap. I was gifted with my time with Edgar, and I'm appreciative of that.

RICK GRIFFIN
Mariners Athletic Trainer, 1983–2017

Pete Shmock was an innovator. We were the first team that ever had a strength and conditioning coach. I hired Pete Shmock because he was an Olympian, and I didn't want a football guy. I didn't want a football strength coach coming in and turning everyone into football players. They would have gotten too tight, and they wouldn't have been flexible. So we hired Pete, and Pete started developing programs for Jamie Moyer, Edgar, Dan Wilson, a lot of guys. He did a really good job with those guys for a long time.

Edgar, even when he was young, he would work out, probably more than any of the other players. That slowly evolved into kind of his mantra. After every game—and I've used him as an example hundreds, if not thousands, of times—for 20 minutes he would go in the weight room. He would do something. He would do different things according to what was supposed to be done that day. One day it might be cardio, one day it might be legs, one day it might be upper body, it might be core. Whatever it was, he did it every day for 20 minutes. He could have gone 4-for-4 or 0-for-4, it didn't matter, that was his routine and he stuck to it. I used to always tell players, even pitchers, if you're going to be successful and have a long career, you have to have a routine, and you have to stick with it, whether you win, whether you lose.

And he was the example. The pitching example was Moyer. We had these two older guys who were outworking every single person on the team, and all the young players were embarrassed. Those two guys brought everyone to their level. They all respected them. The fact they had long, successful careers, they were the perfect example for a young player for me to say, just look. Look at this.

I always felt that the legs were the key to hitting. In the 1980s, when I was pretty much a singles and doubles hitter, I wasn't using my legs properly. I could use the whole field, but when I focused on strengthening my legs, I started driving the ball more, and that made a big difference in advancing my career. In 2018, I went on the *MLB Central* show on the MLB Network to talk with Eric Byrnes and Robert Flores about how I used my legs to generate power. Byrnes talked about how he used to study my tapes when he played for the Oakland A's and was struck by how my back leg would slide out whenever I hit. Byrnes mentioned how José Altuve and Miguel Cabrera both hit the same way and said they picked that style up at least partially from me. In the studio, I showed them some drills I did on the tee to help facilitate that technique, such as moving the tee way back and working on staying in the zone. If you don't release your back side, you're liable to roll over on the pitch. Players I've watched that have opposite-field power, they stay in the zone and they drive with their legs.

On Opening Day of 1991, I hit second in the batting order, right in front of Ken Griffey Jr. But a week later, Jim Lefebvre put me at cleanup for the first time in my career—the day after I hit a three-run homer to lead us to our first win of the season. Yes, I was working hard on my strength, but at that point it raised a lot of eyebrows that I was hitting fourth. I was still regarded as being light on power. With six straight losses to open the season, Jim was trying to shake things up. He explained it by saying, "We're not a home run–hitting ballclub. What I try to do is put our best hitters together to create a situation for us, then hope our big hitter can come up with the key hit. Edgar is not there to hit home runs. He's there to make contact."

I did get a two-run single that propelled us to a 3–0 win behind Brian Holman's shutout. Over the next two weeks, I stayed at cleanup and hit .438, although I didn't hit any home runs. After that, I moved all around the batting order that season. I hit second 12 times, third 15 times, cleanup 20 times, fifth 20 times, and sixth 11 times. Believe it or not, I was our leadoff hitter more times than any other spot in the batting order—67 times, with Lefebvre saying he wanted to take advantage of my high on-base percentage (certainly not my speed).

By 1993, when Piniella became manager, I settled mostly into the No. 2 spot in the order—right ahead of Griffey—and then in 1995, Lou more or less made me the cleanup hitter, right behind Griffey (although I batted third while Junior was on the disabled list for nearly three months). I hit predominantly cleanup the rest of my career, except for 2001, when Lou moved me up to the No. 3 spot in front of John Olerud and Bret Boone. We led the major leagues in runs, so I guess it worked out all right. I also hit fifth from time to time, but mostly I was penciled into the four-hole for the final 10 seasons of my career.

Early on, each manager had different thoughts about where to hit me. I actually liked hitting second, because I was the type of hitter that would get on base and use the whole field, which I thought was conducive to the two-hole—especially on the carpet at the Kingdome. For sure, I never thought I was going to be a cleanup hitter. But Lou had a good idea about what he wanted in the cleanup hitter spot. He wanted an all-around hitter, not necessarily a power guy. He wanted someone who could use the whole field and could hit well with men in scoring position. I don't think any other manager saw me as a cleanup hitter. At the beginning, I didn't feel that way, either. I'd think to myself, "I'm not a cleanup hitter." But over time, I got used to that and I didn't feel like I had to hit home runs. Just be myself.

When I was hitting in front of Griffey, I knew I was going to get pitched to, and I knew I was going to see good pitches to hit. That's another reason I liked the two-hole. I knew I could be aggressive the whole at-bat, because they didn't want to pitch around me. They didn't want to face Junior with a runner on base. When I hit behind Junior, it was an interesting dynamic. I think the opposing manager never wanted to give in to Junior.

Still, I think that over time, as I became better at driving in runs and being productive, pitchers might be more apt to challenge Junior. Or they might have a preference, depending on the situation. Sometimes, they simply would not pitch to Junior. They'd rather pitch to me. But I sensed that sometimes, especially if it was a left-handed pitcher, they would pitch to Junior. It went back and forth. In reality, with the game on the line in the late innings—especially one-run games—they didn't want to face Junior. I didn't take that personally, but I loved those situations. In my career, I hit .312 in what they call "late and close" situations—seventh inning or later with the batting team tied, ahead by one, or the tying run at least on deck. Lou once said, "Edgar gets his dander up a little when they walk Junior"—and I suppose that was true, too.

MIKE BLOWERS
Former Mariners Third Baseman

The thing I talk about all the time with Gar that was interesting, I can remember in '92 when he won his first batting title, he hit second in the lineup most of the time. We had Junior hitting behind him. There were a lot of people saying, well, he's just getting fastballs to hit because nobody wants to pitch to Junior. Then when he wins his second batting title in '95, he was the one hitting behind Junior. He's hitting cleanup. I thought that was so awesome. It just put a lot of those things to rest. At that point, he was a great hitter and everybody knew that. But it was pretty cool to do that with a guy like Griffey, someone who has the most votes in the history of the Hall of Fame, and Edgar hit both in front of and behind him. I'm not sure there was anybody in the game who could have protected Junior like Edgar did. He was the perfect guy to be there, because he could beat you so many ways at the plate.

In a game against the A's on April 20, 1991, a sign appeared in the stands at the Kingdome that said—for the first time, as far as anyone knows—"Edgar esta caliente." In English that's "Edgar is hot," a phrase that caught on, for some reason. It stayed around the rest of my career, in fact. In an article in the *Seattle Times* by Tom Farrey in July 1991, the creator of the sign was identified as Mary Harder, a 38-year-old season-ticket holder, who would set the blue felt banner reading "Edgar esta caliente" over the railing at every single game she attended. Farrey wrote: "After back surgery and her father's death last year, she went looking for model of stability. She picked Edgar Martínez. 'I was at a time when I really needed a hero,' Harder said. 'I've come to admire Edgar so much.'"

I got used to seeing those signs over the years—even when we moved to Safeco—and I got used to the drawn-out chant of "Eddddgarrrr" when I came to the plate. It makes you feel good to hear you've touched fans like that. It also makes you feel good to hear your manager admit the Mariners blew it by not giving me a full-time job earlier. That's what Lefebvre told Steve Kelley of the *Seattle Times* when I ended April with my average over .400.

"We made a mistake with him," Lefebvre said. "We thought we needed a power guy at third base, so at the beginning of last year, we gave the job to Darnell Coles. You have a tendency to do that—think you need a guy who will hit you 20-plus homers at third base.

"But we switched to Edgar in a series at Oakland last year, and he started hitting and never stopped. We're not a home run-hitting team. We realize that now. We're a team that's got to put men on base and then move them around."

In mid-May, we made what seemed to be a minor trade. We sent a minor-league pitcher named Jim Blueberg and cash to the Yankees for third baseman Mike Blowers. Blueberg never made the major leagues, but Blowers became an important player for us, especially in 1995 when we had our magical run to the first playoff berth in club history. But right then in 1991, we had more modest goals. The Mariners, who began as an expansion team in 1977, were still trying for the first winning season in our history. That pursuit meant everything to our veterans—especially to the guys who had been around the longest like Alvin Davis, Harold Reynolds, and Dave Valle.

The best record in franchise history to that point was 78–84 in 1987, the year I broke into the big leagues. But we were developing the core of a pretty good team. Griffey, at age 21, was emerging as the star everyone knew he was destined to be. Randy Johnson was still harnessing his control, but you could tell he was going to be a dominating pitcher. Jay Buhner, Omar Vizquel, and myself were starting to make our name. And those core veterans like Alvin, Harold, and Dave were still productive.

On August 16, we stood at 10 games over .500 (63–53), and it looked like a winning season was finally going to happen. But then we went into a tailspin, losing 16 of 21 games to fall back under .500 at 68–69 on September 8. With 25 games remaining, it could go either way. And we made it tense, believe me. We'd go on a little bit of a spurt, and then immediately go into a slide. We lost five out of six to drop to .500 (77–77) on September 28. We needed to split our final eight games to avoid another losing season, and win at least five to achieve our primary goal, a winning record.

It was like our own version of a pennant race. Though some players, like Jay Buhner, made it clear that they had much higher aspirations than just .500, it was still a huge satisfaction when we came from behind to beat Texas in Arlington, 4–3, on October 2, for our 81st win. That assured at least a .500 season, and we celebrated almost like we had won a division title. Lefebvre said there was "a World Series feeling" in our dugout, and our longtime equipment manager, Henry Genzale, called it "my proudest day to be part of the Mariners."

And when we won our next game in Seattle on October 4 to clinch a winning record, beating the White Sox 6–4 at the Kingdome, an emotional Alvin Davis told Bob Finnigan of the *Seattle Times*, "Winners… we're winners. It means so much to those of us who've been here. The young guys look at our happiness and ask, 'What's the big deal?' But this means more than winning a pennant. That kind of joy is in the heart. This emotion comes deeper in the body, in the gut. You have to come back the next year and win a pennant over again."

As one of those young players, I'll admit it seemed a little unusual to be celebrating just for winning 82 games. We wound up the year with one more victory for a final record of 83–79—12 games behind the division champion Twins. But I understood that for this organization, it was a big accomplishment, especially to someone like Alvin Davis, who knew that his time with the Mariners was winding down. Still known to this day as "Mr. Mariner," Alvin signed as a free agent with the Angels the following February, so this was his final chance to leave his mark in Seattle as a winner. Alvin had been in the organization since 1982, Harold since 1980, and Valle since 1978. For them, it was the culmination of a long quest for respectability. The rest of us hoped it was just the beginning.

ALVIN DAVIS
Former Mariners First Baseman

There were a lot of tears that night. I think in some ways, if you didn't understand the whole story, you might be going, "What's going on here?" We didn't have champagne, but as far as congratulations and tears of joy and relief, I remember [Mariners announcer] Dave Niehaus saying, "What's the big deal? We didn't clinch the division." The word that comes to mind is relief; a sense of relief. We finally won our 82nd game. We had been in the mid-70s, 78, but we couldn't get over the hump. Because it took so long to get there, you feel like second-class citizens.

It's one thing if the club is 50 years old or 100 years old and has won a couple of championships and is going through a dry spell. We had never won, never figured out a way to win more than we lost. We probably had more 100- or 95-loss seasons than 75-win seasons. It was really hard to describe. Around us were teams like the Twins, who went from near the bottom in '86 to winning the World Series in '87, and did it again in 1991. You're like, how does that happen? In our minds, you had to win first before you could win big.

Alvin's departure was just one of many major changes for the Mariners after the 1991 season. For one thing, Lefebvre was fired just a couple of days after leading us to our first winning season, reportedly because of a rift with the front office. The new manager was Bill Plummer, who had been Lefebvre's third-base coach for the previous three seasons.

I had a huge comfort level with Bill. He was my manager in Double-A Chattanooga in 1985 and for three seasons at Triple-A Calgary in 1987–89, in addition to being with me in Seattle as a coach the previous three years. He believed in me. I had won a batting title under Bill in the PCL. There was a confidence in the relationship. I didn't feel I needed to prove to my manager I could hit. The trust was already there. That really helped. And speaking of trust, Plummer named Marty Martínez as his third-base coach, which delighted me as well. It was great to reconnect with the scout that signed me and a man who had been an important confidante for me throughout the minor leagues.

The best thing by far to happen to me in 1991, though, was meeting Holli Beeler. I was at the hotel, waiting to meet outfielder Henry Cotto to get something to eat. Jim Street, one of our beat writers (for the *Seattle Post-Intelligencer*) had his girlfriend, Elaine, with him, and she came up to me and said, "I see you by yourself all the time. I know someone you would really like." After we finished our conversation, I asked her to give me Holli's number. But Elaine said she had to talk to her first. She didn't give me the number. I kept persisting, though, and finally got it.

When I called Holli to ask her out, she didn't want to go. She basically said, "No, I have to study." Whether that was an excuse or not, I didn't know. But she didn't want to go out. I persisted and kept calling, and finally Holli said, "Okay, we can go out." We went out to dinner and I knew right away I wanted to keep up the relationship. It was a blind date that worked. Holli once told *Sports Illustrated* that my persistence was "typical Edgar. Whatever he decides to do, he is determined to be successful at it. The man has an iron will."

Why was I so persistent? Curiosity, at first. And then once I saw her, I knew how beautiful she was. That was my first reaction—what a beautiful girl. But once I met her, I knew the relationship could go a long way, because of her personality, and her mind. Holli grew up here—she went to Bellevue High School and Seattle Pacific University.

We dated for a year and a half, got married in October of 1992, and now we've been married for 25 years. We still get along great, and love to be around each other. Holli likes to be productive; her mind is very active and sharp. She decided she wanted to go back to school, so she got her master's at the University of Washington, and was very involved with our foundation. And then she pursued a corporate job as a vice president of diversity and inclusion. She loves that and has accomplished a lot. I'm proud of her. Beyond all that, she's a great mother to our three kids. It's not always easy being a baseball wife, but she has handled it wonderfully. I'm thankful every day I kept pushing for that phone number.

In December, the Mariners made a major trade, sending three pitchers—Bill Swift, Mike Jackson, and Dave Burba—to the Giants for outfielder Kevin Mitchell, who had been the National League Most Valuable Player in 1989. With Griffey, Mitchell, and Buhner in the outfield, and Tino Martínez ready to break out at first base, we thought we were poised to be contenders for a division title, not just for a .500 record.

I was coming off a solid season in 1991. My error total had dropped from 27 to 15 (with a 31-game errorless streak in June) and my fielding percentage rose from .928 to .962—fifth-best in the American League. Ron Clark, the coach who worked so hard with me on my defense, told a reporter I was as good a defensive third baseman as there was in the American League. I hit .307, the second year in a row over .300, which was an accomplishment. I had 14 homers, 35 doubles, and 52 RBIs, all of which were an improvement over 1990, but I felt I still needed more production. For the second year in a row, injuries marred my season. In 1990, when my knee began to bother me, I dropped from a league-leading .355 in May to finish at .302. In 1991, I was hitting .350 in June, but then I had groin and back problems that led to me hitting barely over .200 for the next month.

I was hoping for a fully healthy season in 1992. I turned 29 in January, and with two full seasons under my belt, I felt like I was just entering my prime. My confidence was growing after hitting .302 in 1990 and .307 in 1991. In my mind, I felt I was poised to go well over .300 rather than just straddle the borderline. That's what was driving me. I wasn't satisfied just hitting .300.

I met one goal in 1992. After a slow start—I hit just .224 in April—I caught fire and ended the season with a .343 average to lead the American League. Winning the batting title was a tremendous accomplishment. But unfortunately, our team didn't come close to meeting expectations. In fact, we ended up with the worst record in the American League, losing 98 games. I was just the second American League player in history to win a batting title with a last-place team, and the first since Dale Alexander in 1932 with the Red Sox. That actually made it tough, in a weird way. I couldn't really savor my success. In fact, it was almost like I didn't want to talk about hitting. It didn't feel right when the team was struggling so much. It felt bad to get three hits, and your pitcher gives up five runs, or something like that. I said at one point I would sacrifice hits if it meant more wins, and I meant it. When people—reporters, or even players—wanted to talk about my hitting, I tried to avoid it. It was just an awkward year—doing so well and yet feeling uncomfortable.

I was also literally feeling uncomfortable most of the year, from a nagging shoulder injury that was diagnosed as "impingement syndrome" with some tendinitis thrown in. So much for my hopes of staying healthy. I had to change my throwing angle, because anything over the top, I felt discomfort. I was more or less throwing sidearm. And instead of hitting with my hands held high, I had to bring them down in order to manage my swing with the discomfort. Whenever I dived, my shoulder would get inflamed. I took a cortisone shot in May, the first of three I would receive that season, but that only helped so much, and the relief was temporary.

Yet I figured out a way to make it work. Despite playing in just 135 games, I tied Frank Thomas for the most doubles in the majors, 46, to go with 18 homers. My slugging percentage of .544 was nearly 100 points higher than 1991 and was second only to Mark McGwire in the American League. The doubles total and slugging percentage were both Mariners' records, surpassing Ken Griffey Jr. from the previous year. Here's how I explained my rise in power to the *Seattle Times*: "You get some key hits and pretty soon you are seeing the ball better and making better swings. With Kevin [Mitchell] and Ken Griffey batting behind me, I'm getting better pitches to hit. I know if I wait, I'll get what I want."

In the same article, Harold Reynolds said that the Mariners players called me "The Maestro." I don't know about that. Griffey always teased me by calling me "Héctor," of all things. That dated back to Lou Piniella's arrival as manager, when he mixed me up with a former teammate of his named Héctor Martínez. Lou was famous for mangling names, and when he called me "Héctor," Junior thought it was hilarious. From then on, he would needle me by calling me "Héctor."

Mostly, my teammates called me "Gar," a shortening of my first name, or "Papa," or "Papi," which really caught on later in my career. I think it stemmed from the fact I used "Papi" a lot myself. That's what my grandfather called me—and I called him "Papa." I had that habit of calling people that. Even my son, Alex—that's what I call him. Papi's a term of respect but mainly of affection and friendship. When we call someone that, it's out of the closeness of the relationship. The players that felt we had a closer relationship would call me that—Jay, Dan, Dave Valle, Bret Boone, Alvin Davis, and a few others.

BRET BOONE
Former Mariners Second Baseman
Everyone respected the hell out of Edgar because of what he had done, but he never let you know what he had done. He would walk around that clubhouse and you wouldn't know if he had a year in the bigs by the way he behaved. He took care of the young guys and never had that arrogance that comes with success, that pompous attitude.

He was just Papi, our buddy in the corner that could rake. All of us called him "Papi." Everyone knows David Ortiz as "Big Papi," but I'm like, "Edgar was Papi way before him." I'm sure Edgar is probably thinking the same thing—"I was Papi first," but of course, it's not like him to tell you that.

DAVID ORTIZ

Edgar was one of the greatest hitters that played the game. I first signed with the Seattle organization, and I remember being in the minor leagues, coming up through the Seattle system, and Edgar was the center of that powerhouse. He was an excellent right-handed hitter. He wasn't just a guy that could hit for power. He hit for a high batting average, too. He was beautiful to watch, the way he used to do things. I don't think there's going to be one person mad about him going into the Hall of Fame. You're talking about a guy who did the right thing during his playing time.

Early on in 1992, there was a lot of tension about our future in Seattle—and not for the last time. There were rumors that our owner, Jeff Smulyan, was going to move the team to St. Petersburg. This played some on our minds—you couldn't avoid hearing about it, because it was in the news every day. But in June, the sale of the Mariners from Smulyan to Baseball Club of Seattle, headed by Nintendo chairman Hiroshi Yamauchi, was approved by baseball's ownership committee. The ballclub was in Arlington, Texas, when the news came down, and everyone was relieved. We thought it might be what we needed to invigorate the franchise with new resources. My quote to the newspaper was, "Maybe we can afford some players now we couldn't think about getting before. We need something."

I guess I was one of the first ones to reap the rewards of the new ownership, because I signed my new three-year deal a month later.

In July, Tom Kelly, the Twins' manager, chose me for my first American League All-Star team—another tremendous thrill. I thought I had a shot the previous two years, but Tony La Russa, the AL manager, didn't select me. But this year I was hitting .314 with 13 homers and 42 RBIs while leading the American League with 41 extra-base hits— better numbers than any of the other third-base candidates, including Wade Boggs, who won the fan vote. I even had eight stolen bases (en route to a career-high 14) after having zero in 1991. I finished fifth in the voting, but it felt great to be going to San Diego for the game with Ken Griffey Jr., voted a starter for the third year in a row. Especially since my shoulder injury had led to some speculation that Kelly might bypass me to take someone healthier. To celebrate my selection, I hit a three-run homer in the first inning that night off Yankees starter Scott Kamieniecki, and later my 26th double.

When I got to San Diego, it was amazing to walk into the clubhouse with all those great players I had watched and admired—Cal Ripken Jr., Frank Thomas, Wade Boggs, Kirby Puckett, and so many more. Being there with Junior was very cool, too. And so was meeting the president, George H.W. Bush, who threw out the first pitch with Ted Williams. President Bush went through the clubhouse shaking our hands. Holli had been studying in Spain, and she flew in for the game. She came all that way, and I got one pitch! Tom Kelly put me in as a pinch-hitter for pitcher Jack McDowell in the third inning to face Greg Maddux. Two batters earlier, Griffey had hit a home run off Maddux. In fact, Junior told me before the game he was going to hit a home run, and then, being Junior, lived up to his prediction. Junior went on to go 3-for-3 in the AL's 13–6 victory and won a car as the game's Most Valuable Player.

When I stepped to the plate against Maddux, I knew he threw a lot of sinkers. So I went up looking for a sinker, which is what I got. I swung at the first pitch and grounded out to second base. That was the end of my night—about 10 seconds worth of action. But Holli said it was worth it. I felt the same way.

By the way, I got revenge against Maddux in the 1997 All-Star Game at Cleveland's Jacobs Field, when I hit a home run against him. I played in seven All-Star Games, starting four of them at DH, and despite going just 2-for-12, I loved every minute of it. The AL had a 5–2 record in those games I played in. When the game was played in a National League park, there was no DH, so I was relegated to pinch-hitting duties, which is not easy against that caliber of pitchers.

In 1992, I put myself in position to win the batting title by hitting .388 in July, lifting my overall average to .335, just barely ahead of Kirby Puckett (whom I surpassed on July 31) and Frank Thomas. August was even better. I hit .395 with 16 doubles to open up my lead in the batting race to 21 points over Puckett, .349 to .328. I told a reporter, "I feel so confident, I know I can hit whatever they're throwing."

And when the *Seattle Times* asked Puckett about me, he said, "He's a great hitter. He can hit, hit, hit. You can save a lot of room in your column just by saying three words—hit, hit, hit." I was named the American League Player of the Month in both July and August, just the third player to win back-to-back monthly awards.

Everything was clicking. I was setting my sights on a .350 average, 200 hits, and 50 doubles. I needed goals like that to push myself. But in early September, my shoulder flared up again, causing me to miss a game in Cleveland. There began to be a discussion about shutting me down for the rest of the season, because I already had enough plate appearances to qualify for the batting title. I fought back against that idea. I really wanted to finish the season—even though it was falling apart for the Mariners. We lost 14 games in a row, and 17 out of 18, at the beginning of September, and were battling just to keep from losing 100 games.

I felt it was important to ride it out and be there for the team. But not only was it hurting to throw, it was now also starting to hurt when I swung, especially decelerating at the finish of my swing. The pain was in the back of the shoulder, as well as some discomfort and stiffness in the front. My power was sapped—I had 14 homers at the All-Star break, but just four in the second half. After 125 games, I was on pace for 56 doubles, but I ended up with 46.

Finally, on September 15, I consulted with our surgeon, Dr. Larry Pedegana, and our trainer, Rick Griffin, and we decided it was best to undergo an operation right away. It was an arthroscopic procedure on the right acromioclavicular (AC) joint at the top of the shoulder. Griffin explained that the injury developed from diving to make plays at third base and throwing my bare hand down to the ground to lever myself back up into throwing position. Weightlifting probably made it worse. The medical people felt that the sooner I got the operation done, the better my chances of being ready for 1993.

The operation—the third of my career already—took an hour, and Dr. Pedegana removed two bone chips from the AC joint. But other than that, he said the shoulder "looked great" and that I could begin a six-to-eight-week rehabilitation program in a week. The message from the doctor was that I'd be fully available for spring training, which was a big relief.

When my season ended for surgery, I was leading the batting race over Puckett, .343 to .333, which ended up being the final numbers. Interestingly, it was the first time in MLB history that five right-handed hitters finished in the top five in the batting race—myself,

Puckett, Frank Thomas (.323), Paul Molitor (.320), and Shane Mack (.315).

All my life I had dreamed of winning a batting title, but when I finally did it, I had an oddly empty feeling. And not just because we finished 32 games out of first place. I felt like I should have been on the field playing. Because I sat out the last three weeks, the satisfaction was lessened. I didn't feel like I proved I could go all the way. Don't get me wrong—it was fantastic to be the batting champion. But it almost felt like winning a race by disqualification. I wanted to run the entire race and get to the finish line. I struggled with that for a while. That's why when I won my second batting title in 1995, and played all year from beginning to end, it felt so much better. I made it all the way to the finish line.

At the end of the year, the Seattle chapter of the Baseball Writers' Association of America named me the Mariners' Most Valuable Player. But our hitting coach, Gene Clines, had to accept for me. I had flown to Puerto Rico to be with my grandfather, who was in failing health. Despite my success on the field, a tumultuous season lay ahead for me in 1993.

Chapter 7

The Hamstring

WHEN WE REPORTED FOR SPRING TRAINING in 1993, we had a new manager: Lou Piniella. Nothing would ever be the same for the Mariners.

Nothing would be the same for me, either. Holli and I got married right after the season and went on a honeymoon cruise to Jamaica and the Cayman Islands. That was wonderful. Shortly afterward, though, we were in Florida on another trip when I got a call that my grandfather had passed away. He had been having health issues and had not been well enough to come to the wedding. But it was still a shock, with more to come. We flew to Puerto Rico for the funeral, and the day we were burying my grandfather, my grandmother had a massive stroke. She never recovered and was bedridden the rest of her life, needing to be cared for, until she, too, passed away a few years later. My grandparents were married for 40 years, and she had been dealing with high blood pressure. I believe that when he died and she pondered the loneliness of life without him, her blood pressure just spiked.

So it was an off-season tinged with sadness and spent dealing with the logistics of taking care of my grandfather's estate and my grandmother's long-term care. I did my best to rehab my shoulder. By the time we reported for camp at our new complex in Peoria in February, I felt like I was almost back to normal, health wise.

I felt bad for Bill Plummer, who was fired right after the season. He didn't get much of an opportunity to prove himself as a major-league manager—one year—but baseball is a business. After losing 98 games, the Mariners felt they had to make a change, especially with a new ownership group in charge. It was apparent right from the start that things were going to be different under Lou Piniella. He burned with intensity, and transferred that energy to the players.

We got a taste right away that there was going to be a new attitude. We dropped six games in a row at the start of the Cactus League season. We played all our exhibition games on the road that year because the stadium at our new complex wasn't finished yet. We were driving back in the bus after another loss, inching along in gridlocked traffic, when Lou saw a bunch of Little Leaguers playing a game at a school field. He ordered the bus driver to pull over. He stood up and said to us, "Even these guys would kick your ass."

It was funny and broke the tension, but there was also a purpose behind his message. Oh, yeah—we won 15 of our next 19 games before Opening Day, including the last eight in a row. We were a young team with a lot of talent, and he brought much-needed focus to us. He brought high standards and an unwillingness to accept anything but 100 percent effort and commitment. A lot of people had told Lou not to take the job in Seattle because it was impossible to win there. He refused to believe that, and he refused to let us believe that.

He knew his job was to teach us how to win. That didn't come overnight for a team that had just one winning season in its history.

But when you have Ken Griffey Jr. and Randy Johnson on the verge of superstardom, it's a good place to start. Lou led the Mariners to their second winning season in 1993—just barely. We finished 82–80, an improvement of 18 games. Most importantly, we were learning how to win.

That's the good news. The bad news for me is that I wasn't around for very much of it.

Oh, the spring got off to a good start. The Mariners had signed my cousin, Carmelo, to a minor-league contract with a major-league invitation, and it was great having him in camp and in the same clubhouse again. Lou had Carmelo in Cincinnati and liked him, so he had a hand in bringing him to Seattle. Carmelo is like a brother to me, so it felt like I had my brother playing on the same team. Carmelo didn't make the team and ended up playing that year in Triple-A Calgary, but it was still a good experience for both of us.

I was excited about all the changes to the team, including not just Lou, but a bunch of new players. That included our big free-agent pickup, pitcher Chris Bosio from Milwaukee, and outfielder Mike Felder to replace Kevin Mitchell, who had been traded to the Reds for Norm Charlton. Norm, who had won a World Series with Piniella in Cincinnati, was another big addition to our clubhouse, as well as our bullpen. Second baseman Bret Boone was a highly touted rookie trying to make the team. Omar Vizquel was rapidly developing into one of the best shortstops in the league. Jay was getting better each season. I was so excited that I reported to camp a couple of days early. In fact, I woke up at 5:00 AM and couldn't go back to sleep, so I just headed to the complex.

I hit .343 that spring and felt like I was finally healthy again. My surgically repaired shoulder felt good. So did my knees. I couldn't wait for the season to start so I could try to build on the batting title I won in 1992. One perk of hitting .300 a couple of times and then being a batting champion is that the bat companies started shipping me the best wood—the ones with the straight, wide grain. Of course, I could have used those when I was struggling early in my career, but better late than never. There's no doubt, the high-quality wood helps the ball jump off the bat. In 1992, I remember I used one bat that I really liked for a long time. When it finally broke, I was really upset.

A quick word about me and bats, since they were the implement by which I made my living for two decades. Bats were vital to me, and I treated them with great care and attentiveness. Jay Buhner told a reporter once that I always carried a bat around—"It's like a security blanket for him." I can't argue with that. I looked for three things in bats—balance, feel, and the grain. Joey Cora used to marvel that I would change bats even after a home run if it didn't feel right.

I was a Louisville Slugger guy, although sometimes I would use Rawlings. To be honest, if I was in a slump, I'd try anything, including borrowing a teammate's bat. I went through a lot of Harold Reynolds's bats one year. But the model I used the most in my career was the M356 by Louisville Slugger. It was a combination of the C243 from Louisville Slugger and another model from Rawlings—kind of the best of both worlds. I told Louisville I wanted the head of the C243, but a little smaller, and the thin handle of the Rawlings bat. It was a hybrid they made especially for me. The name—M356—came from the first initial of my last name and my average when I won the batting title in 1995. Having a bat named after you is kind of cool, I've got to admit. I heard that some other players used my model, including Jorge Posada of the Yankees. There was also an M343 model named for my 1992 batting title, but the M356 is the one I used the rest of my career.

I was an ash guy, too. Nowadays, almost everyone uses maple bats, but I didn't like the way it felt at contact. They say maple is harder, and I believe that. But maple doesn't flex, and that didn't feel right to me. With ash, you have more flex, and because of that, I felt like the ball jumped off the bat better with ash than maple. I also didn't like the way maple bats became like a sharp knife in the air when they broke. That was scary.

At the beginning of the year, I wanted my bats to be 31 ounces, but if it was slightly heavier, I was fine with it, because at that point I was rested and strong. Towards the middle of the season, as I'd start to wear down a little, I'd switch to 30.5 ounces. And at the end of the season, when I was most tired, I wanted them to be 30 ounces.

The length—34 inches—never changed. It was the weight that was vital to me. I believed that if I was seeing the ball well, the critical element was how quickly I got my swing from point A to point B. If I had a bat that was a little too heavy, I was going to be slow to reach the contact point. And I was not going to hit it squarely. So as soon as I started hitting foul balls with a bat, I'd go and change it. I felt if I was seeing the ball well, I should be able to square it up.

That's why the weight of the bats became almost like an obsession to me. I was famous for the little kitchen scale I kept in my locker. Every time a new shipment of bats came in, I'd weigh each one and carefully write the weight, in ounces, on the knob. If it wasn't the right weight, I'd toss it out—or give it to a teammate. You'd be surprised how often the bats weren't the weight they were supposed to be. It happened all the time. For most players, it doesn't make a difference. For me, at least in my mind, it made a big difference. That's why I started weighing all my bats. I felt like a slight discrepancy could throw me off my rhythm. Early on in my career, I got a bat that was supposed to be 31 ounces, but it didn't feel right. That's when I acquired the kitchen scale to check it out—and it was a full ounce off, the worst I ever had. If you want to know the truth, I didn't really need the scale. I could tell by feel if they were slightly off. I just weighed them because I like to know for sure—and I was usually right.

MIKE BLOWERS
Former Mariners Third Baseman

Edgar's the first person I ever saw weigh his bats—and I've never seen anyone do it since, other than guys in our clubhouse that were copying him. He'd put it in a Dixie or Styrofoam cup so it would stand up, and then put it on the scale and weigh it. No one had ever seen that, but after he did it, everyone was walking by his locker and weighing their bats. I just assumed if I ordered a bat, 34/32, that's what it's going to be. I never thought otherwise. Sometimes, I looked at the grain and I didn't like it. And sometimes it didn't feel right, maybe the handle was too thick or something like that. But to actually weigh them and see on a dozen bats how different they were, and for him to understand that half an ounce makes a big difference, if nothing else psychologically, was amazing. If they were off, he'd use them for batting practice. But his gamers were right on the button.

In 2011, Carlos Beltrán told a story to the *New York Times* about a time we were chatting about our bats at the cage. He had a C243, I had my usual M356. The article went on to explain that I held the bat to my ear and hit it with my fist. Beltrán asked what I was doing and I explained that "I just like to hear the pitch of the sound of the bat." He asked why and I told him: "The higher the pitch, the better the wood."

Like I said, bats were important to me, and I tried to learn every little nuance that I could. When I retired, I got a signed photo from the rep from Louisville Slugger who handled my bat orders. He wrote, "I'm sorry about the weight of the bat."

Back to 1993—after breaking camp in Arizona, we headed to Vancouver, B.C., for a couple of exhibition games prior to Opening Day at the Kingdome. The Mariners were trying to build their profile in Canada, so they took part, along with the Brewers, Blue Jays, and Tigers, in what was called "The Baseball Classic" at B.C. Place, an enclosed stadium. They hadn't played much baseball there, and there was a lot of concern about the condition of the field. The concern, it turned out, was warranted.

JOHN McLAREN
Mariners Coach, 1993–2002, and Manager, 2007–08
I was sent up to Vancouver early. They wanted me to check out the field. I mentioned that the dirt part was really soft.

In the fourth inning of our exhibition game against Milwaukee, I reached first base. Lou put on the hit-and-run. While I was sprinting for second base, I felt a pop in my left leg—a pop that had far-reaching implications, both short- and long-term. For starters, it pretty much ruined my 1993 season. Beyond that, it changed the course of my career, though I had no sense of that in the moment. All I felt was pain and concern.

I thought initially it was my knee, and not my hamstring, as it turned out to be. But whatever it was, I knew instantly that it was very,

very bad. I didn't have any stability in my knee. I had no illusions it was going to be a two-week thing, maybe a brief stint on the disabled list and then I'd be back good as new. No, I knew right away it was going to be a long time before I would play again. My left leg—never my right one—had given me occasional problems over the years, mainly tightening up now and then, but it was always something I could play with. This time, I felt like something was completely wrong. I hobbled into second base and then collapsed. I needed our two trainers, Rick Griffin and Tom Newberg, to help me off the field with my arms draped over their shoulders. The fact that it happened in a meaningless exhibition game, just two days before the start of the season, was extremely frustrating.

The injury was initially diagnosed by Dr. Pedegana as a moderate hamstring strain that would put me out of action for six weeks. But he added, ominously (and accurately): "It is a pretty nasty injury that can easily reoccur." Although I would eventually get to the point in my career where I overcame the injury—which took a lot longer than I hoped, or expected—I had little relapses almost my entire career. The injury certainly played a role in my switch from third base to designated hitter in 1995. I was constantly needing treatment that allowed me to play through the strains and tightness, until 2002, when I blew out the hammy again and needed surgery.

I made several attempts to return to action over the course of the 1993 season, but it never really healed completely, and I was limited to just 42 games. I hit .237 with four homers and 13 RBIs—quite a comedown after winning the batting title and making the All-Star team.

Making it even more maddening was the subpar condition of the field at B.C. Place that led to the injury. The infield dirt in the cutout around first base was very soft and wet, as was the dirt at home plate. It looked like they sprayed a lot of water on the whole field. It didn't feel like a major-league stadium, and I think that definitely contributed. I just felt the hamstring pop right away when I took off on the squishy dirt. In the same game, Milwaukee lost two players to leg injuries, second baseman Bill Spiers with a strained left quadriceps and outfielder Darryl Hamilton with a strained right groin. Eventually, the two managers got together and agreed that each team would shelf their running game.

We later found out that four days earlier there had been a Guns N' Roses concert at the stadium, which didn't leave enough time for them to put in the turf properly. The dirt around home plate and the bases was sandy, too loose, and missing the clay that provides grip on the cleats. They watered it down to try to make it hold together. One of the groundskeepers told the *Seattle Times* that because of the concert, they had run out of time to fix up the field properly. The dirt was brought in from Portland and was supposed to be the same as what we used in the Kingdome infield. Groundskeepers from Vancouver had made several trips to Seattle to examine our dirt and take samples for their own infield. But because of the concert, they had just two days to get it installed.

"They said they used the same mixture, including clay," Tony Pereira, the Mariners' director of stadium operations for the Kingdome, told the *Seattle Times*. "The problem was the time, not the composition of the dirt. It has to be watered a lot to make it compact. The dirt mix was dried out."

"The turf took two days to cut and shape," John Sutherland, director of operations for the Vancouver stadium, said in a press release. "By the time it was ready, the crew had little opportunity to prepare the mounds and bases the way we wanted to."

In the end, it didn't really matter *how* it happened. The damage had been done. Our catcher, Dave Valle, told reporters: "It was absolutely awful. There was a hole eight inches deep in the sand where the batters were. I'm just glad we didn't get anyone else hurt."

Lou was incensed. "Injuries are part of the game. But they shouldn't happen when playing conditions aren't what they should be," he said after the game. "It was like playing in a sandbox, like playing on a beach. The batter's box was a joke."

The Mariners had been planning to play six games a year in Vancouver beginning in 1995, but Piniella fumed, "The only game the Mariners will be here for is volleyball."

I wasn't too happy, either, although it wasn't in my nature to express it as vehemently as Lou. Not publicly, anyway.

LOU PINIELLA
Former Mariners Manager

I felt terrible about that. It was a cool day in Vancouver, playing on that makeshift-Astroturf infield indoors. We had talked about possibly not playing some of our players, but going up to Vancouver, we were under the scrutiny of playing our lineup. Edgar pulled his leg running to second base, and that started the process with his leg problems. He was basically out the whole year. Talking to Rick Griffin, our trainer, he said he had never seen such a severe injury to a hamstring. I thought, "Usually hamstrings take six weeks to two months and you're healthy again." Rick said, "I don't think so. This is really bad, as bad as I've ever seen."

RICK GRIFFIN
Mariners Athletic Trainer, 1983–2017

Edgar got really mad because the field was in bad shape. He really didn't want to play. He almost said he wasn't going to play because he didn't want to take any chances. Then he had to steal a base. When he stole the base, he tore his hammy, and he was out for quite a bit.

He was supposed to be out four to six weeks. Well, after about three weeks, he was hitting the ball really, really well in batting practice. He was crushing the ball. And Lou came up to me, and he goes, "You watching Edgar hit?"

I said, "Yeah, he's crushing it."

"I've got an idea," Lou said. "Let's activate him, and we'll just pinch-hit him in the ninth inning if it's a winning situation."

"Lou, he hasn't even run yet. He hasn't even jogged. I'm not comfortable with that. He's supposed to start jogging next week, and then I think he'll be okay. But I think that's kind of risky."

"No," Lou said, "I think we ought to try it."

I said, "Let's talk to the doctors."

So we talked to the doctors and decided we'd wait a week and see where he was at. He at least jogged a little bit. We were going to Texas, and Lou said, "It's 95 degrees, he'll be warm, we'll just use him off the bench and if he hits it, he jogs to first, and if he doesn't, that's okay."

The first game, we were down 2–1, there's a guy on first, it was the top of the ninth, and Edgar comes up and he hits a home run. Lou comes down, he's high-fiving, and he says, "I told you! I told you! That's great. It's going to be good."

Two days later, same exact situation, Edgar hits a ground ball to short, and he jogs to first, and he's out by 50 feet. Then Lou gets really pissed off and he starts screaming, "That's embarrassing. The reporters are all going to ask me how you can play a guy when he can't even run."

"Lou," I said, "this was your idea. Don't yell at me."

He was yelling at Edgar, and Edgar went up to Lou, and he goes, "It's okay. Tomorrow I will hit a home run, Lou, and I won't have to run."

We were lucky to have a good third baseman on the roster in Mike Blowers to step in for me. He'd come to camp as a non-roster invitee, but everyone knew Mike had talent. He ended up hitting .280 with 15 homers and 23 doubles in 127 games that year. The Mariners also picked up veteran Wally Backman from the Braves' Triple-A roster to provide depth. As soon as the swelling subsided, I set about rehabbing my hamstring so I could get back as soon as possible, but it was hard not being with the team when we opened the season three days later at the sold-out Kingdome against the defending World Series champion Toronto Blue Jays. I received a Silver Bat for winning the batting title, and a standing ovation, but it was small consolation.

"I am very disappointed," I told the *Seattle Times*. "I came out of spring training in great shape. My shoulder felt wonderful. My legs were strong. I was so excited… then here we go again. I get frustrated at all these injuries. Missing a chance at defending the batting title hurts me, yes. But most of all, I wanted to be with the team. We have been playing so good with so much to look forward to… now this. I am so disappointed."

"It's a damn shame," added Piniella, who was still upset.

Just two weeks into the season, I watched Chris Bosio pitch the second no-hitter in Mariners' history at the Kingdome against the Red Sox. That game is famous for the play shortstop Omar Vizquel made for the final out, bare-handing a grounder over the mound by

Ernest Riles and throwing him out. Unbelievably, in his very next start against Cleveland, Bosio collided with the Indians' Jeff Treadway during a play at first base and broke his left shoulder blade. He was out of action for a month.

It was shaping up as that kind of season, with Ken Griffey Jr. (sprained wrist), catcher Mackey Sasser (broken collarbone), and pitcher Dave Fleming (sore elbow) all missing time in the first two months. Still, we hovered around the .500 mark. Griffey said, "What we're doing right now is holding on until Edgar gets back."

Lou was getting antsy. "We need Edgar back in the lineup," he said. "These other teams can do anything they want to us and they've done it."

I finally made my 1993 debut in Texas on May 19, 40 games into the season, even though I admitted to reporters I was only 70 to 80 percent of full strength. I hit a double off Kevin Brown in my first game and a pinch-hit home run in my second game.

"He misses six weeks and comes back and hits a nasty Brown slider on a 3-2 count that I think maybe six players in the game could have hit. Then he goes up tonight and hits the first pitch he sees for a huge homer. It's not supposed to be that easy," Piniella said.

But it wasn't easy. In fact, it was too soon. I had a three-hit game against Kansas City in my fourth start, but that was pretty much my final highlight. I was wearing a bulky brace and I couldn't get untracked. On June 15, with my average at .213 after 19 games, with just four extra-base-hits in 61 at-bats, I went back on the disabled list. Opposing pitchers realized I wasn't at my best and began pitching around Griffey. In one game against Detroit, Junior walked four times, and the Tigers' manager, Sparky Anderson, admitted that their strategy was not to give Junior anything good to hit.

The year before, I'd made teams pay for that strategy, but as Piniella told reporters, I was not able to drive off my leg. I was swinging only with my upper body. In addition, my hamstring was starting to tighten up again, and my tendon was sore. I was running half speed on the bases. I finally aggravated the muscle during a hard swing against Kansas City on June 14, which sent me back on the DL. I had another MRI that showed inflammation but no further damage.

"I didn't feel like I tore it, but I felt a sharp pain that bothered me for a little bit," I said. "I knew it was going to be risky [to return before my leg was healed], but I wanted to help the team."

This time, I was out five weeks, returning on July 21—though the original prognosis was that I would be out until at least August 1. Once again, I probably rushed it. The Mariners used six players to fill in at third base, with Blowers getting the bulk of the time, in addition to Backman (who was released the first time I came off the DL), Rich Amaral, Greg Litton, Mike Felder, and Dave Magadan. It's a credit to Lou and the guys that when I came off the DL the second time we were still just one game under .500 and within four games of the division lead.

But my second try, which came after a four-game rehab stint with our Double-A team in Jacksonville (where I hit .357), didn't go much better than my first stint. I never was able to fully shake the injury. It was very frustrating, because each time I returned, I felt I was ready, but my hamstring just wasn't strong enough, and I kept relapsing. Playing 23 games in this next stint—all but two at DH—I hit .257 with just seven extra-base hits in 74 at-bats.

I had started off well enough this time, with a .293 average, two homers, and three doubles in my first 11 games back. But like last time, the hamstring got worse and worse. Before a game with Oakland, my leg collapsed during fielding drills. I recovered from that well enough to return to the lineup, but two weeks later, in mid-August, it collapsed again during a swing that resulted in a foul ball. The doctors decided it was time to shut me down for good, although I fought to stay active. The team was still alive in the division race and I was anxious to contribute as much as I could. But they convinced me that I risked a more serious tear if I kept playing. Dr. Mitch Storey, one of our team physicians, said it would take three or four months to fully heal properly. Doctors discovered I had pulled a calf muscle, too, probably compensating for the hamstring.

It had been a painful, frustrating season—one I never wanted to experience again. I would watch games with a bat in my hands—the good old security blanket—but I wasn't able to help the team. It turned out that my final batting average of .237 (which stood up as the worst of my career) was the second-lowest follow-up average ever by a batting champion. And my drop of 106 points from .343 to .237 was the fourth-largest decline by a batting champion since the turn of the century. That's not the kind of history you want to make.

"And I think I felt every one of those 106 points, too," I said to Bob Finnigan of the *Seattle Times*. "It hurt."

During the off-season, when I reflected on what went wrong, I determined that there was more to it than just some bad infield dirt in Vancouver. So much happened the previous off-season, both good and bad—I got married, my grandfather died, my grandmother had a stroke, I got the flu for a long time. Because of the circumstances, I was unable to prepare as diligently as I normally did. I wasn't working out three, four hours a day as I had other winters. I felt I was behind from the moment I got to spring training—and then, because every spring game was a road trip, we had to rush through workouts every day in order to hop on the bus. I truly believed I got hurt because I wasn't in good enough shape, and I vowed to never let that happen again.

RANDY ADAMACK
Mariners Senior Vice President (to the *Seattle Times*)

I can recall two years I came to the office the day before Christmas. The parking lot was empty except for one other car—Edgar's.

RICK GRIFFIN
Mariners Athletic Trainer, 1983–2017

We used to always do inventory on the first few days after the season ended. When Edgar was 40, on the second day, which was on a Tuesday, he came into the training room and said hello, and he had on his workout clothes. I go, "What are you doing?"

He said, "I'm starting to work out."

"You're taking one day off?" I said.

"Yeah, I'm only going to take one day off because I don't want to get out of shape. If I never get out of shape, I don't have to get in shape." He went down to the cage and he started working out. He took *one day off.*

It wasn't until I went back to Puerto Rico after the season that I was able to fully heal. I went to the sports clinic that I had used for years while playing winter ball. I called them and said I wanted them to look at my leg. Right away, they said, "You're just weak. Your leg needs to work." So they put me on this machine and ran me through a barrage of heavy workouts, up and down. The doctor—Dr. Dwight Santiago Pérez—said that even if it hurts, to keep working. This machine, it was tough. It did hurt at the beginning. But after a few sessions, I felt, "Okay, the pain is going away. I'm getting strong." I could tell. And I noticed that I got better and better. I was able to get back on the field for San Juan during winter ball, playing DH and some third base. With Carmelo winning the MVP award, we put up the best record in the league at 35–13 and then won the best-of-nine championship series over Santurce. During that time, I worked out with the Mariners' strength coach, Pete Shmock, who came to Puerto Rico to train me. I needed the hard work. Basically, they put me back on the field.

Once again, I was optimistic when spring training rolled around in 1994. Surely, I wasn't going to get hurt again. I was hoping my bad luck had finally run out. I felt I had worked hard enough this time to prepare myself for the year. There was some tension in the air, because our union was at odds with the owners and many people feared a work stoppage at some point during the season. In addition, the Mariners were under orders from ownership to trim their budget and so once again trade rumors flew all winter revolving around Randy, Tino, Omar, Jay, and myself—basically, everyone but Junior. No way were they going to move Griffey, who was rapidly becoming the face of baseball. In 1993, Junior had tied a major-league record by hitting home runs in eight straight games, on the way to hitting 45 of them— at age 23.

Happily, Randy signed a new four-year contract with the Mariners in December, so he wasn't going anywhere. With a league-leading 308 strikeouts in 1993, the Big Unit was on the verge of becoming the unhittable ace that eventually won 303 games, five Cy Young Awards, struck out more batters than anyone in history except Nolan Ryan, and was a first-ballot Hall of Fame honoree in 2015.

But less than two weeks later, we did trade Omar Vizquel, who had won the first of his 11 Gold Gloves the previous season. The Mariners sent Omar to the Indians for another shortstop, Felix Fermin, in a cost-cutting move. That one hurt. But we made another significant trade over the winter—pitcher Erik Hanson and second baseman Bret Boone going to Cincinnati for pitcher Bobby Ayala and a young catcher just breaking into the big leagues named Dan Wilson. No one realized it at the time, but in Danny we had just acquired one of the foundational pieces that would help us to four playoff berths in a seven-year span.

When camp opened, it felt great to feel part of the team again. As I said during a spring-training interview with Bob Finnigan, "It's a strange thing when you are injured. You are with the team, spend time in the clubhouse, maybe you practice and travel with them. But you're not really part of them. Omar [Vizquel] and the guys were supportive to me and tried to keep me up, but the players have to concentrate on doing their jobs every day. No one can have a lot of time for someone else."

In that article, I pointed out how lucky I was to be a newlywed and have Holli to bring some balance into my life. "I was very fortunate to have Holli last year," I said. "I don't even want to think what it would have been like to go home to an empty apartment every day. Even the year before when everything was so good, it was hard to go home and be alone. You want to share the good stuff as well as problems. But Holli helped me very much to get through last year."

I felt great in spring training. Lou even had me steal a base to see how my hamstring felt. Before one game, Griffey said he was going to give my leg a tryout. That day, I was on second base, and he hit a double. I raced around and scored. Once again, I was set to hit second in the order in front of Junior, which I loved. Once again, we headed to Vancouver for an exhibition game right before the season opener— which I didn't love so much. That meant I had to step back onto the field at B.C. Place, which had been my undoing the year before. But this time, the turf was in good condition, and I went 3-for-3, including a homer off Pat Hentgen—my fifth homer of the spring.

I was eager for the season opener on April 4 in Cleveland—the first game ever played at their brand-new stadium, Jacobs Field. I was full of excitement and optimism when I stepped to the plate in the first inning to face the Indians' Opening Day starter, veteran Dennis Martínez. The game had a playoff feel, with a jam-packed crowd to commemorate the new ballpark. President Bill Clinton was in attendance and threw out the first pitch. Rich Amaral, our leadoff hitter, grounded out to start the game. I worked the count to 2-2… and Martínez threw a pitch that ran in and thumped me on the right wrist.

As I mentioned earlier, maybe I lost sight of it because of my eye condition. Dennis was known for throwing tight—he would later hit me in a playoff game, as well. But whatever the reason, I couldn't believe it. I was hurt again—in my first at-bat of the season, one year and one day after I tore my hammy in Vancouver. My bad luck wasn't gone after all. It was continuing unchecked. I stayed in the game and came around to score on a sacrifice fly by our new left fielder, Eric Anthony. But after the inning, Blowers had to take over at third. I was experiencing sharp pains when I got to second base. I thought I had broken my wrist, which would have meant another long stint on the disabled list.

Fortunately, X-rays were negative, but I was in pain. I had a bone bruise, the doctors said. All I knew was that I couldn't throw, and I couldn't swing. Yes, the thought of, "Not again," went through my head. I was determined to get back in the lineup, but like last year, I probably came back too soon. I convinced Lou to start me five days later in a game in Toronto. But I struck out in my first at-bat, aggravated the wrist in the process, and then made three errors in the field that contributed to a loss. Obviously, I wasn't ready. That's the hard part about being hurt—I always felt that it's never 100 percent when you first come back. Because I missed so much time last year,

I was trying to push through the pain so I could help the team. This time, the doctors outfitted me in a splint and shut me down for three days. It improved somewhat, and I played one more game, going hitless in four at-bats as a designated hitter.

When I woke up the next morning, though, the wrist was sore, which I attributed to the long batting practice session I had prior to the game the night before. Dr. Pedegana ordered a bone scan to see if I had sustained any fractures that the X-rays had missed. Frankly, I was starting to get embarrassed about being hurt all the time. I was tired of having to answer questions every day. I felt like I still hadn't had a chance to show Lou my true ability. At that point, I had been available for just 46 of the 171 games he had managed in Seattle—and I wasn't at full strength for any of them. My talent was like a rumor to him, although he always made it clear that he still believed in me, for which I was grateful.

The bone scan came back clean, but the Mariners decided to put me back on the disabled list—my home away from home. They put my wrist in a cast to ensure total immobility. I finally returned to the lineup again on May 6 in Detroit, our 27th game of the year. At that point, we were 11–15, and Lou was looking for a boost. In my fifth game back, I had three hits against the White Sox, including my first home run since August 15 of last year. I was finally starting to feel better, and I had my average up to .300 by early June.

RICK GRIFFIN
Mariners Athletic Trainer, 1983–2017

It's funny—his wrist hurt so bad when he swung and missed. It was that way for two or three months. He would always tell me, "I only have one swing every at-bat and I have to hit it." He would always just wait until he got the pitch he needed or the pitch he wanted, and he would swing. Because if he swung and missed, he was done.

When Dennis [Martínez] came to pitch for the Mariners [in 1997], he would always talk about that. "I'm sorry I hit you, and blah blah." Edgar's wrist bothered him a lot that year. But I think in a way that may have helped him a little bit, because he realized he could really zone in on a pitch or a situation."

That was about the time that Griffey had an explosive interview with the *Tacoma News-Tribune* in which he said he wanted out of Seattle and expected to be traded before the end of the season. That was alarming, particularly since Junior was off to his best start ever, with 22 homers by the end of May, and was on pace to break Roger Maris's single-season home run record of 61. That record was 33 years old, but it was becoming increasingly clear that someone was going to break it very soon—and why not Junior?

That reason became crystalized on August 12, when the players and owners failed to reach a labor agreement, and we went out on strike. By that time, Holli was eight months pregnant, 18-year-old Alex Rodriguez had been called up and made his major-league debut on July 8 in Boston, Griffey had hit 40 homers in just 111 games (on pace for 58), and we were in Oakland on a road trip that had reached 20 games in 22 days. Yes, a 20-game road trip, with no end in sight if the strike hadn't hit. That's because four ceiling tiles, weighing 26 pounds each, had fallen into the stands at the Kingdome on July 19, while we were preparing for a game against the Orioles. The stadium was deemed unsafe to play in. Fortunately, no fans were around yet when the incident occurred at about 4:35 PM while the team was stretching, but two repair workers were killed on August 17 in a crane accident inside the Kingdome. The repair bill totaled $51 million, and the whole debacle helped convince people that the Kingdome needed to be replaced.

Meanwhile, we hit the road indefinitely while they worked on fixing the roof. The Mariners proposed playing at Cheney Stadium, home of our Triple-A team down the road in Tacoma, but the Players Association vetoed that. They also nixed other options that were proposed, such as playing at my house of horrors, B.C. Place in Vancouver, or at a neutral site such as Anaheim or Oakland. So instead, we headed out on a trip that took us to Boston, Detroit, Chicago, Anaheim, Kansas City, Arlington, and Oakland—with a quick excursion to Cooperstown for an exhibition game thrown in the middle between Chicago and Anaheim.

Once the strike hit, we never played again in 1994. On September 14, with the two sides still at an impasse, commissioner Bud Selig canceled the rest of the season, which meant no World Series for the first time since 1904. We finished the season with a 49–63 record, which was 14 games under .500. That sounds terrible (and it wasn't good), but when the season halted, we were actually on a roll. We had won six in a row and nine of our last 10 to pull within two games of division-leading Texas. The Rangers ended up "winning" the division with a record of 52–62. But everyone on our team was convinced we would have surpassed both Texas and Oakland (which finished second at 51–63) if not for the work stoppage.

I'll be honest—I was never too heavily involved in the strike issues. I knew the basics, but I let others, like our player rep, Dan Wilson, delve into the details. I had great faith in our union, led by Donald Fehr, and the unity of the players. I knew it was very, very strong. That took away all my worries of dealing with the complicated issues of the strike, because I knew it was being handled well. I guess, though,

Awaiting the pitch at third base in a 1990 game against the A's at the Coliseum.
(Otto Greule Jr/Getty Images)

Here I am in 1992—the first year I won the batting title—shattering my bat in an August game against the Rangers. *(Gary Stewart/AP Photo)*

The game-winning—series-winning—double in the 11th inning against the Yankees in Game 5 of the 1995 ALDS at the Kingdome. (Stephen Dunn/Getty Images)

Alex Rodriguez laughs as Luis Sojo douses me in the locker room after The Double.
(Stephen Dunn/Getty Images)

Me and Roberto Alomar playing for the San Juan Senators of the Puerto Rican Winter League in January 1996. He was also my teammate on our undefeated Puerto Rican Dream Team. (John McConnico/AP Photo)

Ken Griffey Jr. and Jay Buhner viciously attack me during 1997 Spring Training in Peoria, Arizona. (Elaine Thompson/AP Photo)

Getting congratulated by Ichiro Suzuki and Carlos Guillen after I drove them in with a grand slam during our historic 2001 season. (John Froschauer/AP Photo)

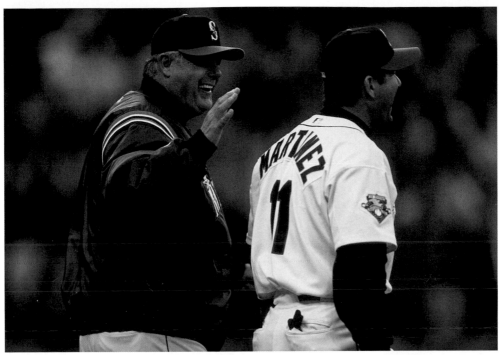

Me and Lou. (Otto Greule Jr./Allsport/Getty Images)

Here I am with my cousin Carmelo in a 2003 All-Star game between Puerto Rico and the Dominican Republic in San Juan. (GDA via AP Photo)

The fans and fireworks on Saturday, October 2, 2004, at the postgame ceremony they held for me. (Elaine Thompson/AP Images)

One of my prouder moments was receiving the Roberto Clemente Award here at a ceremony with Bud Selig before Game 3 of the 2004 World Series.

(Ron Vesely/MLB Photos via Getty Images)

Me and Holli watch as they unveil my No. 11 during the ceremony retiring it.
(Elaine Thompson/AP Photo)

Putting on the Hall of Fame jerseys with fellow inductees Mike Mussina and Mariano Rivera during the news conference on January 23, 2019, in New York. (Frank Franklin II/AP Photo)

Always a Mariner. (Otto Greule Jr/Getty Images)

that it was just another part of being consumed by my job and always focusing all my energy on what I needed to do to get better. I didn't really concern myself much with anything that didn't have to do with getting prepared and hitting .300. When asked for the *Sports Illustrated* article what I was thinking about when I woke up in the morning, Holli replied, "Home plate." There was a lot of truth in that.

I didn't quite make it to .300 in 1994, finishing at .285. I had my average at .300 on July 29 but hit .204 in the final 12 games before the strike. I'd like to think I would have made it back to .300 if we had played to the finish, but it was another frustrating, injury-marred year, disrupted by another long stint on the disabled list and then the work stoppage. I had played in just 131 games, combined, the previous two years. The good news was that I was able to head straight to Puerto Rico to visit my grandmother, still recovering from her stroke, and be back in time for the birth of our son, Alex, on September 14. That joyful event helped distract from the uncertainty that prevailed that winter.

I didn't know what 1995 would bring, or whether or not we would even play. It turned out to be the best year ever for me and the Mariners.

Chapter 8

The Year of Magic

I DON'T CALL THE 1995 SEASON the best of my career just because of the double—pardon me, The Double—that won the playoff series over the Yankees and remains to this day my signature achievement and an epic moment in Seattle sports history. It was so much more than that. It was just a magical combination of a fantastic group of guys, Hall of Famers and journeymen alike, who bonded together like no other team I was on; an incredible pennant race—the first in Mariners' history—in which we made one of the greatest comebacks in baseball history from 13 games behind the Angels on August 2; all played out against the backdrop of ownership's quest for a new stadium to replace the Kingdome, and the understanding that if that effort failed (as it appeared destined to do so many times), the Mariners would most likely be moving to Tampa Bay.

I firmly believe we saved baseball in Seattle in 1995. It was such an improbable, thrilling, roller-coaster ride that more than two decades later, I still can't quite believe we pulled it off. But every time I step foot in our beautiful ballpark, T-Mobile Park (formerly Safeco Field), I know it really did happen, and I am grateful and proud that I played a role in that feat. Heck, some people even say we helped save baseball, period. Remember, the players had gone on strike in August of 1994, causing the cancelation of the World Series that season for the first time since 1904. When spring training started in February of 1995, we were still on strike, and teams filled out their rosters with so-called "replacement players"—guys who were willing to cross the picket line for a chance to play big-league ball.

Not surprisingly, the anti-baseball sentiment was at a fever pitch when the strike finally ended on April 2—just a day before the season was to have started with replacement players. Many fans were furious at both ownership and players for all the years of labor unrest and repeated work stoppages that had culminated in a 232-day strike. It took our thrilling race with the Angels (which ended in a dead heat that forced an exciting one-game playoff), and especially our epic series with the Yankees, to remind people what a fundamentally beautiful and compelling sport baseball can be. Many analysts have pinpointed our postseason, along with Cal Ripken Jr.'s surpassing of Lou Gehrig's consecutive games record (which he achieved on September 6, 1995, with Game No. 2,131), as the beginning of the healing process.

It was by far my best year on the field, the only time I fulfilled my burning desire, my overriding goal each and every season, which was to hit .350 or higher and win the batting title. Even though I hit over .300 in 10 different seasons on the way to a career average of .312, and won the batting title with a .343 mark in 1992, if I didn't hit at least .350 for the season, I felt like I fell short. In some ways, I considered the year a disappointment, even when people were telling me how great I'd done.

That may seem crazy, and it may seem selfish, but that's what drove me. I was almost obsessive about my batting average and the belief that I could hit .350. For me, that's what it took to be focused

100 percent, to be disciplined, to maximize my work habits, and to avoid distractions. It controlled everything, that goal. And that year, 1995, was the only time I achieved that mark with a .356 average, the highest by a right-handed hitter since Joe DiMaggio hit .381 in 1939, and 23 points higher than the next-best hitter, Minnesota's Chuck Knoblauch (.333). It was as if, at age 32, everything came together, all the wisdom, strength, and perseverance I had gained through my struggles and triumphs. My confidence was as high as it had ever been, and for the first time in several years I stayed healthy the whole season. I think every player has a sweet spot in their career, and for me, that was it.

Here's the funny thing: I could have missed it all. The Mariners were trying to cut payroll, and there were a lot of rumors flying before the season that I was going to be traded—maybe to the Yankees, the team that was thrown out there most often as a trade partner. I heard talk of me hitting between Bernie Williams and Paul O'Neill. There was also talk that Randy Johnson might be dealt, too. Just imagine how different the fortunes of the Mariners—and my career—would have been if that had happened.

I didn't want to go anywhere, not even to New York, the city where I was born and where I still had relatives. I felt comfortable in Seattle. Our family, which now included my young son, Alex, was settled there. I was starting to think that I could be one of the rare athletes that would play his whole career in one city, like Tony Gwynn and Cal Ripken Jr. That was something that pushed me. At one point, I remember pulling aside our manager, Lou Piniella, and telling him that I was aware of the trade rumors and I wanted to stay in Seattle. I told him I thought we had built a very strong team that finally had a legitimate chance to contend, and I wanted to be a part of it. Lou listened, but he didn't offer any assurances.

Fortunately, Mariners management decided to keep all of us together even though they supposedly wanted to cut $5 million from payroll to offset losses of $40 million over the previous 2½ years, according to what was written in the newspaper. However, management also wanted to get funding for a new stadium, which was essential to keep the team in Seattle. The owners knew that the only way to do that was to win. So they gambled on keeping the team intact and trying to make the playoffs. They announced that Randy wasn't going to be traded, or anyone else. Jay had already been signed to a four-year extension over the winter when it looked like he might leave as a free agent. We learned later that Lou, in a meeting, had convinced the owners to keep the team intact. "I was there, but give Lou credit for his sales pitch to keep this team together," our general manager, Woody Woodward, told the *Seattle Times* in October. "He was very persuasive."

The owners hoped that their commitment would cause a groundswell of excitement among fans that enabled them to vote for a spending package that would finance the new stadium. But we had to win for that tact to work. It was really the only strategy they had, because with another losing season, no one would fight to keep the Mariners. I wouldn't say it put extra pressure on us, but every player knew what was at stake. No one—fans, media, politicians—ever let us forget. It was part of the reality of the 1995 season. The vote for funding was scheduled for late September, just before the end of the season. How well we played would likely make all the difference in how the vote went. You could say we were playing to save baseball in Seattle—at the very least to keep our talent-base together. It was hard not to think that, when our CEO, John Ellis, said just before Opening Day, "In many respects, it is the most important season in Mariner history. I'd be lying if I didn't say the performance of the team and the feeling of the community about the team don't go a long way toward making the stadium a reality."

Griffey expressed the players' feelings—and fears—when he said, "If we don't make it work this season, win the division and maybe go beyond that, the fire sale starts this winter."

I had waited out the strike in Puerto Rico, where we had one of the most memorable winter seasons in our country's history. The so-called "Dream Team," which I've already mentioned, won the Caribbean World Series, which is a huge deal in Latin America. All the best players from Puerto Rico were there, because we all knew the strike might last a while. My San Juan team won the regular-season championship, and then we filled out our roster with stars from other teams for the World Series. Our lineup was like a major-league All-Star team. My cousin, Carmelo, played first base. Roberto Alomar, who is in the Hall of Fame now, played second. Rey Sánchez, who had won the Winter League batting title, was at shortstop, Carlos Baerga was at third base, and Bernie Williams, Juan González, and Rubén Sierra were in the outfield. Carlos Delgado was at catcher; the talent pool was so strong that Delgado was chosen over another future Hall of Famer, Pudge Rodríguez. I was the designated hitter, and guys like Doug Brocail, Ricky Bones, and Roberto Hernández were on the pitching staff.

We rolled over the Dominican Republic, Mexico, and Venezuela to win the World Series without losing a single game. The tone was set in the very first game of the World Series against the Dominican Republic. We knocked out Pedro Martínez in the fourth inning. Juan González hit a grand slam, and we won 16–0 behind a three-hitter by Doug Brocail. The Dream Team is still legendary in Puerto Rico—you can find pictures of us hanging up in bars, restaurants, and even in some people's houses.

DOUG BROCAIL
Former Major-League Pitcher and Puerto Rican Dream Team Member

The lineup was ridiculous. The funny thing was, when I beat the Dominican Republic in the opener, I remember Pedro [Martínez] hit Sánchez. I said to my guys, "Hey, pick somebody," meaning, for me to hit. But Rubén [Sierra] said, "No. Go out and throw a no-hitter." I think I lost the no-hitter in the seventh. I felt unbeatable, because I figured, "Hell, if they put it in play, they're out." There's no better feeling than knowing all you have to do is let them make contact—and it's a guaranteed out—and shake hands at the end of the day.

Being there in Puerto Rico, you understood how important baseball was to the island. Everywhere you went, old men on the street corner were talking baseball. God, everywhere we went, it was baseball, baseball, baseball, baseball, baseball. You'd go out to eat, it was baseball, baseball.

Even though I couldn't understand the language, I'd be standing there with Roberto (Hernández) and say, "What are they talking about?"

He would say, "Oh, the old days. These guys remember watching Roberto as a kid."

I'm like, "Roberto Clemente?" He was my hero as a kid, growing up in Pennsylvania.

Hell, I'm playing with what, six Hall of Famers? Or guys who I perceived as Hall of Famers. Facing Delgado years prior, I knew what he could do with the bat. I wasn't sure how he was going to catch, but we were flawless. I lost the perfect game to a walk in late innings. I had shaken to a 3-2 curveball. And I asked the umpire, where was it? He said, it was probably a strike, but you fooled me.

We went out and ate that night. Oh my god. People knew who I was for the first time in my career. I think Bones started the next game and you couldn't hear yourself think. The stadium was ridiculously loud. Full? There were people standing in the street. It was unbelievable. If you would have had a stadium the size of a college football stadium, I think Puerto Rico would have packed it. The aura was just so unreal that you're like, "What the hell is going on here?" It was just baseball, baseball, baseball, baseball, baseball. And to have the greats on my side. When Igor (Juan González) hit the granny, it was all over. As soon as he hit the ball, the ball hadn't even gone through the infield yet, and, it sounded like a bomb went off, the roar. At that point, I knew we were going to win the Caribbean series. No matter what, seeing the people we had, I knew we were going to win.

I always look back and think, if I had that team in the big leagues, could I have been a 25-game winner? A 30-game winner? Around the horn, the amount of talent was unbelievable.

What I remember most about Edgar was the leadership and the poise. Nothing ever bothered Edgar. He was calm, cool, and collected. I remember I was in the dugout. Ricky Bones had gone through a little cold spot, and to watch Edgar walk up and put Ricky at ease. Just the professionalism.

It's unbelievable that such a small place turns out so many unbelievable players. Me and three other Americans lived together and drove to the games, and everywhere kids had broomsticks and taped balls and were out hitting. Baseball everywhere. You'd be getting ready for the game and run to your car because you forgot something, and kids are out in the parking lot smashing tapeballs with broom handles. No wonder they can hit.

After the series, we all stayed in Puerto Rico to work out together and wait for word that the strike was over so we could report for spring training. It was like a mini-spring training, something we did every year, but it got extended because of the strike. We stayed very active, so I felt sharp and ready when Sonia Sotomayor, then a judge of the United States District Court for the Southern District of New York, now a member of the U.S. Supreme Court, issued a preliminary injunction against the owners on March 31. When the Court of Appeals for the Second Circuit supported her ruling, the strike ended on April 2, 1995—one day before the season would have started with replacement players. Instead, they all went home, and the real major-leaguers headed for Arizona.

JOHN McLAREN
Mariners Coach, 1993–2002, and Manager, 2007–08

We had firemen, school teachers, guys who worked for Pepsi, guys from all walks of life in spring training. We did a lot of things for these players. The commissioner said you have to make it work. One thing I wasn't crazy about, we're working with these guys while the real players are striking. A couple of teams put their major-league staff down to work with the minor leaguers, and brought in their minor-league staff to work with the replacement players. If I had thought of that sooner, I would have done it. I was only doing what we were called upon to do.

It was a difficult spring. We didn't know any of these guys, but we were trying to make it work. I knew it wasn't going to be long. I kept thinking of our guys—"When are we going to get our guys?"

By the time we reported for the hastily arranged, two-week reset of spring training, I had a lot of excitement about our potential for 1995. Just look at all the talent on that team—Junior, Randy, Jay

Buhner, Dan Wilson, Mike Blowers, myself, and many others. We had a great core. We had experienced some growing pains, but that just made us stronger. All of us had a few years under our belt, good years, so we weren't wide-eyed rookies any more, yet we were still in our prime. I felt we had what we needed to actually make a push for the playoffs. Yes, at that point the Mariners had just two winning seasons in franchise history, finishing 83–79 in 1991 and 82–80 in 1993. And yes, we had finished 14 games under .500 at 49–63 the previous year.

It hardly seemed like the jumping-off point for a memorable season. But I felt like the foundation for our run was built in 1994, when we embarked on our massive 20-game road trip because of the falling ceiling tiles at the Kingdome. We all figured it was going to be miserable living out of a hotel for that long, but it turned out to be the best thing that ever happened to the Mariners. Being stuck on the road together so long, we bonded. It helped us learn more about our teammates. It made us care for and about each other. It helped us build deeper relationships. We talked a lot about our families, and we talked a lot of baseball. The laundry bills got out of hand, but the experience was invaluable.

Early in the trip, we lost seven games in row, but after a defeat in Chicago, the players had a meeting and agreed that we needed to make the best of the situation and stop feeling sorry for ourselves. We started having fun—and we started winning. Those two facts were not unrelated, in my mind. We had been having a pretty lousy season, but when the strike hit, we were on a roll, having won nine of our last 10 games and the last six in a row. No one in the AL West was having a good year, so that streak pulled us within two games of the first-place Rangers.

MIKE BLOWERS
Former Mariners Third Baseman

In this game, you spend so much time with each other, I think the tendency, especially when you're playing at home, is to get out of the clubhouse when the game's over. You have your family, you have your friends, that's what you go do. All of a sudden, that's taken away. And you're on the road. We started having dinner with each other instead of hightailing it out of there to go do what you have to do because of family commitments and things like that. So you get to know everybody on a different level. You think you know people, and our clubhouse was great. Everyone in there was great. All of a sudden you're spending all that time, you have to learn to coexist, get along, and you really find out what people are like and how they tick. So I think when someone is struggling in a period of time, it's easier to pick them up, to see what's happening and get them turned around quicker. That's what I think happened with that club.

Every single player on the team, myself included, was convinced that if the strike hadn't happened, we would have won the division and made the postseason in 1994. The strike was real, however. So our goal in 1995 was to recapture the mojo we had built on the road at the end of 1994, with a few key additions to the team like Joey Cora, Doug Strange, and Alex Diaz. Fortunately, we had the right leader in Lou Piniella.

As a team, we fed off Lou's intensity. When he took over as manager in 1993, following a 98-loss season, everything changed. Lou made it clear he wouldn't accept losing. He had the complete respect of all players, myself and everybody else. We knew Lou won as a player with the Yankees, and we knew the way he had played the game—hard-nosed and unrelenting. He had won as a manager, too, guiding the Reds to a World Series championship in 1990. We trusted all the information he gave us and the way he managed, the passion, that really helped our players to get focused and play consistently with winning in mind. In his first year in Seattle, the White Sox clinched the division against us at their ballpark. Lou got the team together for a meeting, and he broke down crying. He said, "You guys see that? You see what it's like to win over there? Remember that. That's what we're going to be doing before too long." That's the desire and passion he brought.

I loved to talk hitting with Lou. He had been a great hitter himself, with a .291 average for his 18-year career, and he really understood the craft. He was a great teacher, too. We'd talk—in Spanish—about hitting mechanics and also ideas about how to approach pitchers. One thing I can remember I used for years. He told me, "If you're having trouble with a pitcher, whether it's a slider or something else, just scoot up on the plate. Move on the plate." I tried that, and it worked. That's something I wouldn't have thought about. It's a simple thing, but it helped. There were just so many things about baseball he knew. It was always very helpful talking to him.

MIKE BLOWERS
Former Mariners Third Baseman
Lou loved all of his players, the guys who were around for a period of time. Lou loved all of those guys. But you could tell there was something special between he and Gar. I think in a large part it was because Edgar was a DH and he spoke Spanish. They had that thing going on in the dugout. In '97, when I came back as a part-time player, is when I saw it all the time. I saw

it here and there in the years before, but when I'm sitting on the bench every day, and I didn't know what they were talking about half the time, but it always felt like Lou was bouncing stuff off of Gar, because he respected him that much.

This was in the middle of the game. Just running scenarios and things past him, because Edgar was always walking around with that donut on his bat, and doing things, or sitting on the bench, and Lou would come down. He would always walk down there and say something to him. It was special. I think it was a little bit different, the two of them. Then you think about how many years they spent together. That was a very special relationship. I think Lou, too, being a right-handed hitter, really respected the hell out of him. Which was easy to see why.

LOU PINIELLA
Former Mariners Manager

His mechanics were very sound. He didn't over-stride, good plate coverage, and the ball jumped off his bat. I'd look at his swing carefully and ask myself, "How would I pitch him?" All those years, I never came up with an answer. His swing was short enough to get to the pitch inside, and he had the ability to wait on a ball and drive it to right-center when they changed speeds. To this day, I don't know how I'd pitch him.

And, of course, there were Lou's tantrums. Like the time he pulled out first base and threw it down the line after a call he didn't like, or the time he kicked dirt on the umpire… also after a call he didn't like. I could give you many, many more examples, of course. As players, we loved it. We absolutely loved it. Sometimes we had to stifle our laughter in the dugout, but we loved it. Over the years, we came to know how badly he wanted to win, his intensity. At the same time, we knew it would be over within an hour and he would be back to normal. It was great.

The best years in my career were playing with Lou. Some players, I'm sure, were intimidated by him. You could see that some of the guys, especially the young ones who hadn't gotten to know him yet, were very timid around Lou. In the beginning, I was too. But once you got past that, and realized his demeanor was all designed to help the team win, and to bring out the best in each player, you loved the guy. He wanted to see who was tough enough to handle the pressure of the major leagues.

Despite all the high hopes, we didn't get off to a particularly great start. We were barely above .500 at 15–12 on May 26 when disaster struck. Griffey—the one guy we could least afford to lose—broke his left wrist slamming into the Kingdome wall while making a sensational leaping catch to rob Baltimore's Kevin Bass of a home run. We had all seen him make spectacular catches like that many, many times, to the point that kind of play was almost routine for him. But this time, Junior didn't get up right away, and when he did, he came trotting in toward the infield. When you know Junior, you know he didn't complain about soreness or injuries. He wanted to be on the field, and he wanted to play. He didn't even want to DH; he never wanted to be a DH. He just wanted to be on the field and play every day. Once I saw him get up and kind of walk away, I knew this was bad.

We were all quite concerned, of course. When we found out the news—he had fractured his distal radius bone, which required surgery to install a steel plate and seven screws in his wrist—we were devastated. Junior was the best player in baseball, and the heart and soul of our team, and now he was going to be out for nearly three months. It was very frustrating to see him go down that way, because of what he meant to us. We didn't know how long he would be out, or how his game would be affected when he came back. The wrists are such a vital part of providing power, and Junior was a guy who had a great chance to break Roger Maris's single-season home run record every year. You just prayed that when he came back, he would be the same player.

MIKE BLOWERS
Former Mariners Third Baseman

When Junior went down, Lou's message was, "Okay, that's the news of the day. Now what are we going to do to fix it?" It was either feel sorry for yourself, or go out and make something happen, knowing that one day, we were going to get him back. That was kind of the goal. We're going to keep fighting, pick each other up, move along. Lou's coaching staff was exceptional as far as keeping us moving in that direction.

For us, it was just fun. It was fun to play. We looked forward to getting to the clubhouse at one o'clock in the afternoon, to play cards, to travel, to just go play the game. It was awesome. That was an awesome year. And then Junior comes back and the wrist still didn't look quite right. We knew he still had some plates and screws in there. And immediately he hits a home run, and we're like, "Okay, here we go." Then it got to be really fun after that.

I hit 23 home runs that year, so when Junior came back I think I was sitting on 18 or 19. He may have had six. I remember taking BP, and him giving me a hard time, saying, "Hey, Blow, you better go, because I'm going to catch you. I'm going to run you down."

I'm like, "Junior, we've got six weeks, you're not running me down." I think it came down to where it was really close. Junior wound up with 17. I thought it was funny.

I remember late that year, I was struggling a little in September, and he took my bat from me and handed me one of his and said, "Here you go, this has one more home run left in it." And I hit a home run that night with that bat, which I kept for years. He was great.

Meanwhile, we knew we had to rally together. We couldn't let Junior's injury derail our season. The goal was to just play our best and hang in there until Junior came back. As a team, we achieved that. We responded very well, and we had heroes emerge from the unlikeliest of players. I have images in my head of Alex Diaz making diving plays like Junior would make, saving runs for us. And getting big hits in clutch situations. Same with Rich Amaral and Doug Strange. When we needed a big hit, we executed and got it done. When we needed a walk, these guys would battle and get it done. And that's what it took. When you don't have your best player, you don't have much margin for error. Execution becomes the key. And that's what the team did.

Yet the Angels still looked uncatchable, at least to the outside world. When the July 31 trade deadline rolled around, we were one game under .500 and 11 games back of them. In past years, that would have meant waving the white flag and probably trading one of our veteran players to a contender to get back prospects and save money. But two things were different this year. One, the playoffs had been expanded to include a wild-card team for the first time The second-place ballclub with the best record would make the playoffs, and that gave us a chance to back-door our way into the postseason. We were hanging close enough in the wild-card standings to give us hope that we could make a run.

And secondly, the stadium issue was still a huge factor. There was going to be a vote on September 19 for a funding package that would finance the stadium. If the Mariners pulled the plug on the season by trading away key players, there was no way we would have mustered the support to win the election. Once again, ownership opted to go all in, just as they had when they decided not to trade Randy, pitcher Chris Bosio, and myself prior to the season. On July 31, we made a trade, alright—we acquired Andy Benes, an outstanding right-handed pitcher, for two of our top prospects, outfielder Marc Newfield and pitcher Ron Villone.

It was the type of trade we had never made before, taking on payroll and trading prospects to enhance the roster for the stretch drive. Two weeks later, we acquired Vince Coleman, a veteran outfielder who proved essential. And we had already signed reliever Norm Charlton after he got released by the Phillies. Norm had pitched for us in 1993 and we all loved his grit and fire—especially Lou, who had won a World Series with "The Sheriff" in Cincinnati. Those moves were a huge boost in the clubhouse. The feeling was, "Okay, guys, this is serious." It was a big motivation for everyone to push harder. The psychological lift was huge.

But on August 2, we fell 13 games behind the Angels. Only two teams in history had come from larger deficits to finish first—the 1914 Boston Braves, known as "The Miracle Braves," who were 15 games behind the New York Giants, and the 1978 New York Yankees, who were 14 games behind the Boston Red Sox. Lou Piniella was an outfielder on that '78 Yankees team, so there was no way he would let us give up hope.

We had a secret weapon, too. Well, not so secret. Ken Griffey Jr. might have been the biggest name in all of sports, not merely baseball. On August 15, after missing 73 games with his broken wrist, Junior came back. During his absence, I had one of the best stretches of my career, hitting .361 with a .505 on-base percentage and .627 slugging percentage, with 14 homers and 60 RBIs. In June, I hit .402, and I was fortunate to start at DH in the All-Star Game in Arlington, Texas—with Randy Johnson as the starting pitcher for the American League.

But I had plenty of help. Jay hit 40 homers and drove in 121 runs that year in just 126 games. Tino Martínez had a huge year with 31 homers and 111 RBIs (and pinch-hit for me in the All-Star Game). Blowers had his best year with 23 homers and 96 RBIs. Wilson, Joey Cora, Luis Sojo—they all had very good years, and Randy was absolutely dominant en route to his first (of five) Cy Young Awards.

In May we had called up a 19-year-old kid from the minors you might have heard of—Alex Rodriguez, who had been the No. 1 overall draft pick in 1993. Though he was still raw, and didn't play much, you could tell he was going to be a star. What I remember is that Alex was always asking questions, always watching and trying to learn. I remember he'd chase a lot of bad pitches, too. His stance was completely different in those days. But he was always trying to pick the brain of veteran players. You could tell he had that curiosity of learning—and then he would actually try whatever you told him.

After the 1994 season, Alex took home some hitting tapes of me at the plate and tried to imitate my approach and stance, which was flattering—and so was his quote in the paper: "Why not? Hasn't Scottie Pippen picked up pointers from Michael Jordan? When you're with the best, you learn from the best." Tony Gwynn said in spring training, "A-Rod does Edgar better than Edgar does." He just had the raw talent that was readily apparent. You could see, all this guy needs is to put some things together, and he was going to be a great player.

Junior was already great, of course. He was 25 in 1995, with six seasons already under his belt. He had that combination of being a transcendent talent, a five-tool player, and also having the attitude, the persona, and the makeup of a superstar. You could see that. It wasn't just that he was a superb hitter and had an amazing glove in center field. At the same time, his instincts, his makeup, his desire to win made him the best player in the game. That was another amazing thing about our team. We had the best pitcher, too.

If you had to choose which pitcher in all of major-league baseball you wanted to have on your side, no doubt you'd want Randy. We had him. The same thing with Junior. Who's the player in all of major-league baseball, from the defensive side, hitting side, from the makeup, from the stage of his career he was in—who was the best player? Who do you want? Junior. It was amazing to have both on our team. And Junior brought so much more than that. He brought his fun, relaxed personality to work every day. It never was a boring day in the Mariners clubhouse.

A quick word about Randy, the 6-foot-10 lefthander who was the most intimidating pitcher in the majors. He was the one where we thought, every five days with him on the mound, we were going to win. He gave us the swagger. He was the pitcher nobody wanted to face. He was that classic ace that when the team is down and needed a win, you have it right there. He was the guy where you can go into the playoffs, and know he was going to face the other team two or three times, and feel certain we had a good shot. He gave us that confidence.

Also, as a hitter, we knew if we got hit by the other pitcher, and it looked intentional, we were protected. Randy wouldn't say, "I'll take care of it." He'd just do it. And you knew. He was so intense. I'd leave him alone on the day he pitched, because he was getting himself into game mode. I'd let him be. You could tell. You could see it. I could recognize, "This is not the time to talk to Randy." It was just great to have a pitcher like that on your side. He played a huge role on that team.

Junior's return on August 15 was a huge boost—like picking up a superstar for the stretch drive. We had played nearly .500 ball without the best player in baseball (36–37), which is a tribute to the Stranges, Amarals, and Sojos, who really picked up the slack. When Junior left, we were 2½ games out of first place in the AL West. When he came back, we were 11½ games behind the Angels—but just one game out of the wild-card spot. We felt we were now a better team for having played without Griffey, because as Blowers said, "We know we can still win a ballgame without having Junior hit the big home run all the time."

But it sure was nice when he did. The game everyone remembers was against the Yankees on August 24, just nine days after Griffey came back from his broken wrist. No one knew how he was going to be, how quickly it would take him to get his stroke back. Well, we found out. With two outs in the bottom of the ninth inning, Junior hit a two-run home run off Yankees closer John Wetteland to give us a 9–7 win. Right before that game, I had called a players-only meeting to remind the guys that just because Junior was back, we couldn't expect him to do it all. We all still had to contribute. And then he goes out and wins the game with a two-out, ninth-inning home run. The lift that gave us was huge.

The next night, I hit two home runs and we beat the Yankees again. Our pitcher, Tim Belcher, had some nice words after the game: "What makes Edgar so tough is he has a presence and a makeup in the batter's box like a pitcher on the verge of a Cy Young. You look at Greg Maddux on the mound and he's just glowing, brimming with confidence. I witnessed it in 1988 with L.A. when Orel [Hershiser] threw that shutout-inning streak [59 consecutive shutout innings].

195

When he crossed the white line it was over. That's the same thing about Edgar. It's really fun to watch. I don't think anyone in the league considers him anything but the best right-handed hitter in the league."

Things were starting to happen—exhilarating things. The Angels were starting to slump. They lost their shortstop, Gary DiSarcina, to a thumb injury on August 3, and that seemed to take something out of them. From the day that Griffey hit his big homer until the rest of the season, the Angels went 12–23.

We couldn't believe it. We would see some of the Angels highlights, and the way they were losing—we're like, "We're going to catch them." We just felt nothing was working for them. It almost looked like it went from being a slump to turning mental. It kind of ignited our desire even more when we saw that.

One day, some workers at the Kingdome were putting up the wild-card standings on the wall and Jay went crazy, yelling at them to take them down. He didn't want us to go for the wild-card. We were out to win the division. That was Jay's leadership at play, but it also reflected the kind of attitude and confidence we had as a team. Jay was our outspoken leader, the guy who would say whatever needed to be said, when no one else wanted to say it. He would tell you straight what you needed to do, or what you shouldn't be doing. Every team needs leaders like that. Sometimes things need to be said, and you can't be afraid to be confrontational. Jay was our guy.

We started to push toward Jay's goal of grabbing the division. Junior's return had a ripple effect throughout the team, both in the clubhouse and on the field. With Vince Coleman—acquired the day after Junior came off the DL—getting on base ahead of him, Griffey was seeing more fastballs in the No. 2 hole. That's where Lou put Junior to take some of the pressure of hitting home runs off him. I certainly saw more fastballs hitting behind Griffey. And our confidence and comfort rose with Griffey back in the lineup. "It's outstanding to have your best friend back," Buhner said. "He was deeply missed by everyone. We showed a lot of composure, savvy, and unity until he came back."

We were winning crazy games, cutting the gap. I'd never experienced anything like that. We had such a great group of guys. In 1994 after the ceiling tiles fell, and then when Junior went down in May, we just got closer and closer. We bonded around the adversity. We enjoyed going to the stadium and spending time together early. The whole month of September was the most fun month I ever had in baseball. It was the right group of guys, and we were having a blast playing the game. For all of us, it was the first time gunning for a pennant or a playoff spot. We loved every minute of it.

MIKE BLOWERS
Former Mariners Third Baseman

First of all, it was the most fun I ever had playing the game. For me, personally, it was the best year I ever had playing the game. But it was just how close-knit that club was, which included everybody. It included Junior; even though he was the biggest star in the game, he was just one of us in that group. It was just so much fun to go out and be a part of that lineup. What I remember more than anything was when we got past the All-Star break, just having that feeling of, "We're going to score six runs every night." I know that didn't happen, but that's the way we felt, that we were never out of a ballgame. It didn't matter, to a man.

The Angels kept losing, and we kept winning. We started to think, "If we keep playing this way, we're going to catch them." We felt very confident. It was strange, but that's how we felt. We would talk about it that way: "We're going to catch them." We picked up a lot of confidence, especially when Junior came back. And the fans in Seattle started to pick up on it, too. Early in the season, the crowds weren't that great, but once we hit mid-September they started filling up the Kingdome, and we fed off their energy. It wasn't like the old days, when you could hear a single fan screaming at you. During our final homestand, we drew over 46,000 for five games in a row—over 50,000 in three of them. And in September we won 16 out of 19 games at home.

JOHN McLAREN
Mariners Coach, 1993–2002, and Manager, 2007–08
I remember one day, early in September, when they started packing the Kingdome, I saw a sign in the upper deck that read, "Refuse to Lose." I said, "Lou, that's kind of a cool deal."

Lou said, "I like that. It's got a little rhyme to it, a little poetry." That was our war theme, our calling. Refuse to Lose. We just ran with that.

On September 19, the day of the stadium vote, Doug Strange hit a game-tying, pinch-hit, two-run home run in the ninth inning against Texas, and then scored the winning run in the 11th on Griffey's two-out single. It was bedlam at the Kingdome. The Angels lost that night, so we pulled within a game of first place (and went one game up on the Yankees in the wild-card race). I remember Griffey's quote that night: "If I'm dreaming, I don't want to wake up." We all felt that way.

When we left the ballpark that night, everyone thought the ballot measure had passed, so there was jubilation about that, too. But a week later, when the absentee ballots came in, we found out it had actually lost by 1,082 votes. So there was still a huge issue whether we were going to get the new stadium or have to move out of town. John Ellis, the Mariners chairman, told King County executive Gary Locke that if the county didn't come up with a plan for the stadium within 30 days, the Mariners would go up for sale.

As a player, I tried to put it all out of my mind. It was hard, because it was on the news and in the paper all the time. Every once in a while, a politician would come into the clubhouse, or one of our players would be asked to go to the state capital in Olympia to speak. We'd get real estate brochures from Tampa Bay. But my thought was, we didn't have much control of that. The only thing we could control was how we played, and just trying not to get distracted with all the news and everything that was going on. Just go out and play. That's pretty much what we did. And if that helped us get a stadium, well, so much the better.

On September 22, we beat the A's 10–7 in front of 51,500 fans to move past the Angels into first place for the first time. It had taken us just 28 days to erase a double-digit lead by the Angels, who went through two nine-game losing streaks in the span of 35 days. We were down 7–6 going into the eighth, but just like we had done so many times, we rallied. My homer in the eighth tied it up, and then Alex Diaz's three-run homer gave us the win. Vince Coleman hit the first grand slam of his career in that game.

It was another of the wild, improbable wins that had become our trademark. Maybe the wildest and craziest came two days later, when we beat the A's 9–8 on Tino Martínez's two-run homer in the bottom of the ninth off Dennis Eckersley, the future Hall of Famer. A lot of people remember Dave Niehaus's call that afternoon on the radio:

"That was perhaps the most incredible game in their history! And 46,000 fans are losing their minds in Seattle! Tonight, I guarantee you, it will be sleepless in Seattle for everybody who was here today, including me!"

Said Lou, "It's in our destiny. It's in our control."

MIKE BLOWERS
Former Mariners Third Baseman (via the *Seattle Times*)

It would be interesting to find out what the Angels were thinking and how they felt, having such a big lead. That was almost as much fun—flipping on the TV, or asking one of the writers, "What's their score? What? They lost again?" We're all cracking up—"Can you believe it?" We're holding up our end. We can't believe they're not winning.

REX HUDLER
Former Angels Infielder (via the *Seattle Times*)

It was devastating. We knew they were there, but we definitely tanked that. That was on us. We couldn't stop the bleeding. The hitting carried the pitching all year long. We had a great lineup—[Tim] Salmon, Chili [Davis], Tony Phillips. We had some players. And then when the offense shut down, our pitching couldn't hold it. It was a desperate feeling I'll never forget. What happened was, Lach [manager Marcel Lachemann] was not skilled on the motivational side of things. He didn't have a way of rallying us verbally. He was a hard worker, a very prepared manager—I loved Lach—but he didn't have the motivational skills, and looking back all these years later, that's what we missed, someone to say, "Don't worry, guys. We'll be okay."

We couldn't get out of it. It was the nastiest funk I've ever seen in baseball. Just my opinion, but we needed our manager to step up, and Lach couldn't do it. He went into his shell, went into withdrawal. He let us figure it out ourselves. They had Lou, who had been through this before, and he had the intangibles. He knew how to handle his boys. We had a manager who had never been there before.

What I do remember on the positive side is the last week of the season—we swept the whole week and the Mariners lost three games. We forced that one-game playoff.

MARK LANGSTON
Former Angels Pitcher

I look at it from the standpoint, that was the first year of the wild-card. I truly believe had there been no wild-card, I don't think the Mariners do what they do. They were right there in the wild-card. We had a huge lead. Usually when you have a big lead like that it always seems impossible because now you're going against the clock trying to climb back into it. But for the Mariners, they were right there in the wild-card, one game out, two games out, so every game was meaningful. And so when we started our tailspin, we weren't able to really get back on track. And that's the difference, where they kept climbing. All of a sudden, where we seemed an impossible hurdle to get to became possible for them. All of a sudden they started saying, forget this wild-card, we can take this division, and that became a different focus for them.

This game is about momentum, about carrying that energy on a daily basis. We could not get this thing back on track until the very end of the season, when we were three games out with five to play. People forget that, that Seattle actually coughed it up to force the one-game playoff. The clock was completely against us on that side of it where we looked at the games and go, "Man, we have to win out and they have to lose two out of three to Texas." And that all materialized.

From my standpoint, I look at it as disappointment, having the big lead we had, allowing those things to come into shape. I do believe if there's no wild-card, I don't think Seattle catches us. I don't. They don't make all those different moves they made—Andy Benes, Vince Coleman. Because they were fighting for the wild-card, the whole entire time. That was the first year, and it became really big.

We were up two games with six to play, with the Angels coming to town for two games. We split those, but won our next two over the Rangers. All we needed was to win one of our last two scheduled games to win the division. But wouldn't you know it—we lost them both in Texas, and the Angels won their final five games in a row. We finished in a dead heat at 78–66. It was going to take a one-game playoff the next day against the Angels to decide the division champion. The Yankees had surged to 79–65, so the wild-card was out of play. Whoever lost this game, their season was over.

Here's where we got a couple of huge breaks. One, we had won a coin toss a couple of weeks earlier, so the game was going to be in Seattle and not Anaheim. The Seahawks had played at the Kingdome the final Sunday of the season, and our fans waited in line until that game ended to scoop up all 52,356 tickets for the game. It took a while, but the fans in Seattle had fully bought into our season and were rallying around us, not just filling the Kingdome on our final homestand but raising a ruckus. It's no coincidence we went 7–1 on that homestand.

Having those fans on our side for the one-game playoff, creating a wild atmosphere like we knew they would, was going to be a huge boost. But not as big as having Randy Johnson on the mound, the other massive advantage we had. Lou had wisely lined the Big Unit up to pitch this game, and we knew his intensity was going to be off the charts. We just felt very good about this game with Randy on the mound, and the guys we had, like Junior, Jay, Tino—another great leader. We knew how loud it was going to be, too.

REX HUDLER
Former Angels Infielder

I remember getting on that plane after that one day in Anaheim, and now we're heading up to Seattle, and we were thinking, "Who's going to pitch— Tim Belcher or the Big Unit? If Belcher pitches, we win. We beat Belcher." There's no doubt he couldn't have beat us. But Randy Johnson... uhhhh. I know he was on short rest, too, but the Unit stepped up. He stepped up and the rest is history. But I have great memories. Nothing is woe is me, poor me—no, great for Seattle. I have complete joy that the Mariners are still here in Seattle, playing in Safeco Field, largely because of that game. It was a historic game, and I was happy to be a part of it.

The one-game playoff was a classic. The Angels started Mark Langston, who had been my teammate during my first couple of years with the Mariners before he was traded to the Expos for... Randy Johnson. How perfect was that to have those two facing each other? Mark was a great pitcher himself, with a sharp breaking ball and a good fastball he moved around. He was a competitor, too. Sure enough, the game was as tight as you'd expect, scoreless for the first four innings before we took a 1–0 lead in the fifth inning on an RBI single by Vince Coleman, one of the guys we had picked up mid-season in a trade.

That score stood until the seventh, with the game still hanging in the balance. Randy was fantastic, as we knew he would be. He had given up just one baserunner, a sixth-inning single by Rex Hudler. It was looking like one run might be enough, but we made that a moot point in the seventh inning with one of the freakiest plays you'll ever see.

With two outs and the bases loaded against Langston, our shortstop, Luis Sojo, hit a little broken-bat squibber toward first base. It looked like it was going to be the third out of the inning, especially with J.T. Snow, a Gold Glove fielder, at first base. It was one of those plays where you went, "Oh, no—oh, yes!" The ball went under the glove of Snow and down the right-field line. Two runs scored, and when the throw home was wild, Joey Cora came home, with Sojo right behind him. As our announcer Rick Rizzs said in his famous broadcast, "Everybody scores!"

The Kingdome went absolutely nuts. You couldn't hear yourself think. We knew that was the ballgame. We had momentum, we had a five-run lead, and we had Randy. He was electric that afternoon, just what you'd expect from the best pitcher in the game. His focus and determination was off the charts. He went the distance, pitching a three-hitter with 12 strikeouts, and we won 9–1.

MARK LANGSTON
Former Angels Pitcher
A lot of people don't realize, it came down to a coin flip on who got to have home-field advantage. The Angels lost the coin flip. I'm not saying it would have been a different result down in Anaheim, where you have your

own fans. But the Kingdome was as loud as I've ever heard it in my entire life. It was crazy loud. So I went into it, you knew what Randy was going to do and what he was very capable of doing is what he did. He's basically going to shut a team down. Your responsibility is try to keep this game as manageable, as close, as you possibly can, to hope if it's that close, one swing of the bat can be the difference in a game.

We were unable to do it. It was just a freaky little deal with Sojo that still to this day—I finally saw a recording of it, because I can play it in my head. I remember the pitch being outside, I remember him breaking his bat, I remember flinching, and J.T. Snow—who I think was the best first baseman in the game at that time—I talked to J.T. a million times, he still does not know how that ball got underneath his glove. But it did.

Once it got rattled around in the corner—you give Randy that kind of lead, there's no way you're going to come back. Up until the seventh inning, it was one of those games you were hoping to just keep it close. Once Seattle got that 1–0 lead, if you could just somehow keep it at that point… then you hope you get a guy on and one swing of the bat could be the difference. But once he got the big lead, he was not going to relinquish it.

We had done it. We had come all the way back from a 13-game deficit to make the playoffs for the first time in Mariners history. I'll never forget the celebration in the clubhouse. We let it all loose. At one point, team president Chuck Armstrong hugged me, and we both had tears in our eyes. "After all these years, Edgar. All these years," he said.

Late in the game, with a big lead and Randy dominating on the mound, I had let my mind wander to the ups and downs of my time with the Mariners. "I tried to stay calm, and it was easy when the game was close," I told reporters afterward. "But when we went way ahead

I started to think back over the years and the players who have been here and gone without this. And when we won, I was glad for myself and maybe for all of them, too."

Eventually, though, we had to end the party, because we had a plane to catch to New York. We were going to open the best-of-five AL Division Series the next night against the Yankees at Yankee Stadium. We had a police escort to the airport.

We'd run at such high intensity throughout September, I don't know if we unconsciously crashed a little bit. But we lost the first two games in New York, 9–6 and 7–5. The second game went 15 innings and more than five hours, an intense, back-and-forth affair that didn't end until past midnight on a game-winning home run by Jim Leyritz. As a result, we didn't get back to Seattle until the early morning. Once again, we were one loss away from the season coming to an end. We had to beat the Yankees three games in a row to stay alive—but at least we were heading back to Seattle for those three games.

Lou told us that we were going home, and we were going to win. He felt very confident, and that filtered down to us. Lou always knew what buttons to push. Before the first game at Yankee Stadium, with the tension building as we were about to take the field, Lou showed up in the dugout eating a piece of pizza. "We just started laughing," Vince Coleman would say later. "I could see how tight the guys were. And here comes Lou, acting like it was a day in spring training. You could see the nerves loosen after that."

Heading back to the Kingdome, we knew how much the home crowd had helped us down the stretch and in the one-game playoff against the Angels, and that they were going to turn the energy up another notch. I remember Lou walking around the plane on the flight from New York, talking to his players, pumping us up. We may have been down two games to none, but we felt very good coming home.

Having played the bulk of his career for the Yankees, and then managing them (and even serving a stint as their general manager) after he retired, Lou had a special passion whenever we played the Yankees. It was even higher than his normal passion. He loved to beat New York. Or maybe it was more that he hated to lose to them. All I know is that he would get really mad if we lost to the Yankees. You could tell there was a little higher motivation. As for me, for some reason I always hit really well against them. For my career, I hit .317 against the Yankees. That season, I hit .391 in 13 games against them, with seven home runs. It didn't matter whether it was at Yankee Stadium or the Kingdome, I just raked against New York. Even in those two playoff losses, I had three hits in each game.

I don't know if I got more intense playing against them, or if it was the matchups, but the way they pitched to me, it was something that fit me. I almost felt like I knew how they were going to pitch to me. And I knew what I had to do to handle it. Everything was falling into place in this series. I felt at the plate like I didn't have to do too much, just try to make solid contact with my same approach. It was very consistent.

Much has been made about my success against Mariano Rivera, who is unquestionably the greatest closer of all time (although he hadn't yet become the Yankees' closer in 1995; as a rookie that year, he had started 10 games and was being used in long relief in our Division Series). In 19 career at-bats against Mariano, I had 11 hits for a .579 batting average. That included three doubles and two homers for a 1.053 slugging percentage. He also walked me three times and hit me once, so my on-base percentage against him was .652.

First of all, just because I had success, it doesn't mean I didn't recognize what a great pitcher he was. And he got me one time—with the tying run on base in the ninth inning, I grounded out to shortstop for the final out in the clinching Game 6 of our ALCS against the Yankees in 2000. I was looking for the cutter all the way, like he always threw. And instead, he threw the first sinker I saw from him his whole career. Game over, we go home. I would change all those hits just for that one at-bat.

I think what helped me against Mariano is that he was very consistent in how he pitched. He changed his repertoire when he became the closer. As a starter, he had the fastball and breaking ball—not yet the cutter, his signature pitch. His fastball had good velocity—hard but straight. As a reliever, though, he would throw only that cutter. He stayed with his strength—the cutter, middle away.

My approach was pretty much middle away. The only difference is, I said, "Okay, because he throws hard and the ball moves that way, don't try to do too much." So I didn't try to do too much. I just tried to make sure when I got a good cutter to hit, I would make solid contact in that direction. I think that helped me, because every time I'd get a good pitch to hit, I'd make sure I controlled my swing and just tried to make contact. That's how I found a lot of hits. It wasn't like I hit a ton of home runs against Mariano. He struck me out four times, too. I just managed to get a lot of hits from not trying to overswing—just make contact.

DAN WILSON
Former Mariners Catcher

As a player, you always wonder, Edgar's your clutch hitter, no question, but can he really do it every time? It seemed like against the Yankees, he did it every time. Every time we needed that big hit, he delivered. I think there's a strong competitive nature to him…you can't get this far in the game without it being there. But his ability to control it, his ability to control his emotion, his ability to think in those circumstances, where most of us are fight or flight—I don't know how he does that. I think that's the key. Yeah, he's got a great swing. He's got great mechanics, and he worked a ton on his mechanics. But I think the separator is what's between his ears and his ability to control his emotions and deliver in those situations.

We had Randy on the mound for Game 3, so we felt good about our chances. Sure enough, the Big Unit pitched seven strong innings and we won 7–4. I didn't have any hits, but I walked three times and scored two runs. Tino had a big home run off the Yankee starter, Jack McDowell, a guy we would famously see again. We felt that if we could just somehow win the next game, there was no way we'd lose Game 5 in front of our fans at the Kingdome.

Game 4 turned out to be a big one for me. I drove in seven runs, which set a major-league record for a postseason game. After we fell behind 5–0 early, I hit a three-run homer in the third inning on a two-seam fastball, up-and-in, off Scott Kamieniecki.

After I hit that home run, I said in my mind, "Okay, they're not going to pitch me inside any more. They're going to pitch me middle away." That's what happened when I came up in the eighth inning. I got a middle-away pitch, and I was focusing on the middle of the field, and just got the right swing. It was a grand slam to center field in the eighth inning off John Wetteland that broke a 6–6 tie.

Dave Niehaus, in his radio call, said: "Baby, he pickled it! He deep-sixed it!" Steve Kelley wrote in the *Seattle Times*, "Edgar Martínez took a swing for eternity. A line drive that cut through 18 years of ennui. A line drive into the blue curtain in center field that rocked the building and the city and the game to its foundations."

Years later, I was in a card show with Wetteland. He shook his head when he saw me and said, "My nemesis." I rarely showed much emotion on the field, but I pumped my fist on that one as I ran around the bases.

MIKE BLOWERS
Former Mariners Third Baseman

I think the thing for me with Edgar is how even-keeled and level his personality is, which goes right into his game. You could see it the way he played, the way he hit. One of the things I'll never forget is the fist pump coming around first when he hit the home run to dead center in the postseason. The grand slam, which is something incredible. At the time, I didn't see it, but when I saw the replay, I thought, "Wow! There's some emotion out of this guy." Which was great, because you never saw it. He had so many huge hits in big moments and he was so important to our club.

We won that game 11–8, and when we were driving home afterward, Holli exclaimed, "Honey, what a great game! Are you excited?"

My answer, as recounted in *Sports Illustrated* a few months later: "I'm thinking about the next game."

It all came down to Game 5 the next day at the Kingdome. That's all we could have hoped for, and we were ready. It was the best game I've ever been involved with—do-or-die the whole time. Every pitch counted. Incredible tension. Incredible electricity at the Kingdome. The focus was at such a high level for both teams. Incredible strategy and counterstrategy by both managers. We felt like there was no margin for error. It was tied 2–2 after four, but they scored two in the sixth to take a 4–2 lead. We didn't score in the sixth or seventh. They were six outs from ending our season.

In the eighth inning, however, we tied it. Griffey hit a home run, his fifth of the series, and Doug Strange, who had come up big so many times, had one more bout of heroics inside of him. Pinch-hitting, Doug drew a bases-loaded walk off David Cone, one of the best pitchers in baseball, to force in the tying run. The guts it took to take that pitch on a 3-2 count was off the charts.

At that point, the Yankees pulled Cone, who had thrown 147 pitches, and brought in Rivera. Mariano was a 25-year-old rookie who had started more games than he relieved that year. No one knew he was going to become the best closer in baseball history. But I've always been glad they didn't bring Rivera in at the start of the inning, because even then, his stuff was great.

The drama was only getting started. Randy, remember, had pitched seven innings (and 117 pitches) just two days earlier. But he'd told Lou he was available to pitch if they needed him. That's the kind of competitor Randy was. So in the eighth inning, Lou told Randy to go to the bullpen. Part of it, I think, was to fire up the crowd, which is exactly what happened. The fans went absolutely nuts when they saw Randy trot out of the dugout. Part of Lou's motive was to put the thought in the head of the Yankees that the Unit might come in. I don't care how tired he was, that's not a comforting thought for a hitter.

But the biggest part of it was, we needed him. And sure enough, when Norm got in trouble in the ninth, Randy Johnson came in from the bullpen, receiving the loudest ovation I've ever heard. It was bedlam. That reaction fueled us even more. It made everything that much more intense, if that was even possible.

Randy got out of the jam with three straight outs. If we could push across a run in the bottom of the ninth, we'd win. Vince Coleman led off with a single off Mariano and moved to second on a sacrifice. When they walked Griffey intentionally, the Yankees created a little drama of their own. They brought in Jack McDowell, who had been Randy's opponent in Game 3, working 5⅓ innings and throwing 85 pitches. He, too, was on one day's rest, like Randy, trying to gut it out.

The first man McDowell would face was me. With the speedy Coleman on second, I knew I could win the game with a single. But McDowell—who had won the Cy Young Award two years earlier—struck me out on a split-fingered fastball, up in the zone. I swung right through it. It was a pitch I should have hit, and I was very upset when I got back to the dugout. Norm came up to me and said, "Stay ready, Gar. You're going to win the game for us."

Alex Rodriguez, who had entered the game as a pinch-runner, grounded into a force out to end the threat. We were headed to extra innings. It couldn't have been any other way, right? Randy struck out the side in the 10th, but we didn't score off McDowell. So Johnson went back out for another inning. It was an amazing display of guts, but he was on fumes now. Randy gave up a walk, and then after a sacrifice moved the runner to second, Randy Velarde got a base hit to score the go-ahead run. So we headed to the bottom of the 11th trailing 5–4. Everything we had worked so hard for was in danger of going up in smoke. We had one last chance to get something done.

Joey Cora, one of my best friends on the team, led off with a bunt single, just barely eluding the tag by Yankees first baseman Don Mattingly. Donnie Ballgame, as he was known, had announced his retirement and would be playing the final game of his great career if the Yankees lost. In his 14 seasons, Mattingly had never been in the postseason before, so there was a lot of sentimental support for him to go out with a World Series appearance. Mattingly still claims Joey went out of the base line and should have been called out, but the umpire didn't see it that way, and that's all that mattered. I'm kind of glad they didn't have replay review yet, though. Griffey came up next and drilled a base hit to center off McDowell, with Joey motoring to third. In his first appearance on the national stage, Junior really came through, hitting .391 with five homers in the series.

It was on me now. I walked to the plate, with Norm's words ringing in my ears: "You're going to win the game for us, Gar." I tried to stay calm, even as the rest of the stadium was going berserk. I wasn't about to let another opportunity slip away, as I had done in the ninth. Even though I had struck out last time, my confidence was still sky-high, because I had been swinging the bat so well that entire series. I wanted another chance. I felt I could get to him. Alex Rodriguez was waiting on deck.

NORM CHARLTON
Former Mariners Pitcher
Who would you rather have up there? You could pick a handful of guys you'd like to have at the plate at that moment in time. Think of all the clutch hitters, Jeter, Junior. I'm not sure anyone who played with Edgar on a daily basis would pick anyone else to have at plate at that time.

DAN WILSON
Former Mariners Catcher
You knew something good was going to happen because Edgar had delivered every single time. Obviously, no pitcher scared him. No pitcher intimidated him. He had a lot of experience with Jack McDowell. He was

just so prepared, and just so comfortable in those situations that you knew it was going to be a good result. The question was, was he going to get one runner in, or was he going to get both in?

The first pitch was a fastball down the middle, which I took for strike one. I was looking for the split-fingered fastball, the pitch he had struck me out on. I said to myself, "Here it comes. He's got to come with the split." Sometimes, as a hitter, you just know. Sure enough, that's what I got, same location, a little up.

I didn't try to do too much with that one. I tried to make sure I just made solid contact. That's all I needed to do with a man on third. I didn't try to lift it in the air to ensure a sacrifice fly that would score the run. I didn't try to hit it out of the park. Just the same swing, not trying to do too much. I was very focused and very sure of what I wanted to do.

JAY BUHNER
Former Mariners Outfielder

Right person, right time. No one set up pitchers better. He knew in his heart of hearts, if a guy made him look silly on a pitch, he'd go up and sit on it, because he knew the guy would come back to it. He knew McDowell would throw that split. He had a hard time picking it up. It was his bastard pitch. But he hung in there that at-bat. Watch it in slow-motion. Watch how his hands stay inside, until he gets to the point of impact. He stays through the ball, and then extends way out, just to keep it fair. No one did that better than him, staying inside until the last minute and then frickin' squaring it up.

LOU PINIELLA
Former Mariners Manager

I was confident he was going to hit the ball hard, so I felt good we'd at least tie the score. But that's a perfect situation for a professional hitter. He's not going to panic He's going to give you a good professional at-bat and hit the ball hard somewhere. By that time in his career, he was already hitting for a lot of power. What happened next, I still remember like it was yesterday. It was as big a hit as we've ever had in that organization.

I lashed the ball into the left-field corner. It was one of those where you barely feel the ball hit the bat, it was so clean. At that point, it became almost dream-like. It's a great feeling, don't get me wrong, but you don't feel much as it's happening, in the moment. I knew Joey was going to score the tying run. But I wasn't sure if Junior could score from first. After I went around first base, I started looking back over my shoulder for Junior, and he was nearly home. I was amazed. If you've seen the clip, you know that he ran around the bases faster than he's ever run before, taking a virtually perfect route with the way he approached each base and cut the corners.

Textbook. It was as if all Junior's baseball instincts—developed from being around his father, Ken Griffey Sr., a major-league star with the Reds, and which he had been blessed with from birth—crystallized in that sprint home. It's almost like he anticipated a ball in the gap and said, "I'm going to score. No one is going to stop me."

Our third-base coach, Sam Perlozzo, waved him home, and Kenny easily beat the relay from Yankees shortstop Tony Fernandez. I'm willing to bet he had never run that fast, and never would again. But Junior was not going to be denied. If you look at photos from that game, you can see our dugout just erupting as he rounded third, most of them spilling onto the field as if to will Junior home. Bob Wolcott, a rookie pitcher, must have jumped five feet in the air. Alex Rodriguez, the on-deck hitter, was the first to get to Junior as he crossed the plate, but the whole team swarmed him.

DAN WILSON
Former Mariners Catcher
I remember being split. You're running out of the dugout, and you're not sure whether to go to second base, or to Junior. I remember doing that and then thinking, "Well, Edgar got the hit," so then I veered out and went out to second base. I think it was just disbelief, almost like that childhood joy. You felt like a kid, and that was such a good feeling.

It was just starting to hit me. We had won the game. We had come back from down two games to none when everyone was writing our obituary, just as they had when we fell 13 games behind the Angels in August. My teammates poured onto the field to mob Griffey, who lit up the Kingdome with his smile from the bottom of the pile. And then they came after me. I remember Joey running out to greet me at second base. After a while, there were two dogpiles, one at second, one at home. That was tremendous.

MIKE BLOWERS
Former Mariners Third Baseman
I think we all knew the moment was never going to be too big for Edgar, because of his personality, the way he prepared, the way he handled

himself. To me, hitting the double, I'm sure it wasn't the case, and I've never talked to him about it, but it just seemed like he looked exactly the same as always. The way he would take a pitch, the way he walked to home plate, it was just another at-bat. I know that it wasn't, but that's the way it looked to me.

It wasn't until later that it all sunk in, what we had accomplished and my role in it. It took a little time for me to savor the aftermath. When you see the reaction of the players and the fans, and even more, when you go out of the stadium and see the utter joy in the community, that's when things started hitting you. But when you are in that moment, it's weird—it's like another game, another at-bat. I was happy I hit a double and the team won, but it really starts hitting you when you see the effect it causes in other people and in the city. When people talk about my career, the double usually comes up first. They talk about that year, that series, and the double. I don't have any problem with that.

It was another great celebration. I remember Alex, my son, was very young, and I brought him to the clubhouse. It got pretty wild in there. David Cone came by to congratulate us, which was classy. I'm pretty sure the mayor of New York City, Rudy Giuliani, came in, too. I remember ending up in the Jacuzzi with Jay, Junior, Norm, Randy, Mike Blowers, and our trainer, Rick Griffin, all of us smoking a cigar. You might have seen that picture—it shows the pure bliss on our faces. I think Norm was the first one to go in, and we all jumped in, too. I remember thinking, "Oh, so this is what it feels like to win."

NORM CHARLTON
Former Mariners Pitcher

Someone ended up in the Jacuzzi, and we all piled in. I still had my spikes on, three or four of us had cigars, a few had Coors. A couple of times that happened when it was around the dinner table, the same group of guys, with cigars and beer. We did a lot of stuff together. We were so close knit. That's why we won.

RICK GRIFFIN
Mariners Athletic Trainer, 1983–2017

Somebody was handing out cigars and we all had a bottle of champagne, and we were all in the training room. Everybody was excited because we won that series, and that was a really big deal. I probably have 200 pictures at my house—little teeny ones, big ones that people took that I got. We were in the training room and everyone was smoking cigars. Next thing, Norm runs in there and he jumps in the hot tub. He's holding up his bottle and he goes, "You guys get your ass in here. Let's go." Then we went in there and they took that picture. I think more guys would have got in there, but it wasn't a very big hot tub.

At one point, I excused myself and went into the weight room to work out, as I had done after we beat the Angels to clinch the division. It was part of my routine and I wasn't going to miss it, even if we were celebrating the first playoff series win in Mariners franchise history. While everyone else partied and continued to spray champagne, I rode the exercise bike for 20 minutes. Once again, if you asked me what I was thinking about, I would have said, "The next game."

I knew we had another series coming up, the American League Championship Series against the Cleveland Indians. That was one thing running through my mind: Don't get too high. Stay with the goal in mind, stay focused. You didn't want to get to such a high you lost sight of what was the bigger picture. We wanted to get to the World Series. In fact, we thought we were destined to not only get to the World Series, but to win it. You start to feel that way after you've staved off elimination four times in seven days.

But that was a great Cleveland team, filled with All-Stars at every position. They had veteran players that really knew what to do. They had the talent, and they also had a catcher, Sandy Alomar, who had been good for a number of years. Not only defensively, but how he called the game. He was smart. They had pitchers like Dennis Martínez, who knew how to pitch. They had a strategy for us, they had a plan, you could tell. I never saw one at-bat where they pitched me the same. They were always changing. No patterns. They kept switching back and forth, making great pitches with two strikes.

I think I started pressing a little and swinging at pitches out of the zone. Our hitting coach, Lee Elia, observed after the series: "They worked hard to get him out, get him off stride. Eventually, they succeeded. They gave him nothing to hit. You got to a point you wanted to scream, 'Pitch to him!' But credit to them, they had a game plan and made it work."

I hit .571 against the Yankees. I hit just .087 against the Indians, with two hits in 23 at-bats. They had a good strategy to neutralize me. In Game 5, with the series tied at two games apiece, I nearly tied the score in the ninth inning, but Kenny Lofton caught my blast at the wall in dead center. Lou said I hit it so well on a line drive that it never had a chance to get caught up in the wind that was blowing out. Earlier in the at-bat, I hit one into the seats, but barely foul. As I said after the game, "That's baseball."

NORM CHARLTON
Former Mariners Pitcher

I don't know if we could have had any more confidence than we did going into the postseason, because of the way we won games down the stretch and the deficit we came back from. But everyone in the back of his mind thought reality would hit us eventually. We laid everything on the line every night; we'd run out of gas sooner or later.

We did, when we hit Cleveland. First, Cleveland was probably the better team, and they were fresh and we were flat out of gas. We had to use Randy in the one-game playoff, then used him as a starter and reliever against the Yankees. By the time we faced Cleveland, we were pretty burned up.

MIKE HARGROVE
Former Indians Manager (via sportswriter Jim Street)

Sitting in the opposite dugout before I really got to know Edgar, it struck me how calm and focused he always was, but still approachable. He wasn't arrogant, condescending, or any of those things. He was a ballplayer's ballplayer. He played the game the way it was supposed to be played. He showed a lot of respect for the players he played with and against and you just couldn't throw a fastball by him.

For me, he was a more dangerous hitter day in and day out than Griffey. As strange as it sounds, because I wouldn't want to face either one of them, but on a day-to-day basis, big RBI situations, I would rather have Griffey at the plate than Edgar. He was just a professional hitter that would put the ball in play and put the ball in play hard to any part of the field. He wasn't a big swinger.

Thinking back, I don't ever remember a time when I saw him over-swing. He had a short, compact swing and the ball jumped off his bat. For me, again, not taking anything away from Jay Buhner, Griffey Jr., or any of those guys, Edgar for me was the most feared bat Seattle had in their lineup.

We never figured out how to pitch him. To this day I remember in 1995, watching him play the Yankees in the playoffs. I was watching the game on TV and Edgar came up and hit a rocket, I believe for a home run, to right-center field, but more center field than right. It either tied the game or put the Mariners ahead. Later, when we played them in the ALCS, we had the same situation in Seattle, in Game 5. That scene I saw on TV kept replaying in my mind and I will be damned if he didn't hit that same ball in the same location, a bullet that we just happened to have [center fielder] Kenny Lofton in the right position and he made the play on the ball. Every time he came up in a big situation, my stomach never seemed to settle down."

We lost the series in six games, but none of us will ever forget what happened after the last game, when the Indians clinched the American League pennant with a 4–0 win at the Kingdome. We had been shut out just twice during the regular season in 144 games, but we were blanked twice in the final three games of the ALCS by Cleveland. We were in the clubhouse, feeling down, of course, when someone came in and told us, "Man, you've got to go back onto the field."

None of the fans had left. They were on their feet, cheering in appreciation for what we had done that season. It was such a moving moment. It made us feel like, "Hey, we've got to do this next year." We left for the winter with that in mind.

Oh, yeah—we got our stadium. The legislature voted in favor of a funding package that was approved on October 23—six days after our final game. That was just one week before our owners' deadline to put the team up for sale if no agreement was reached. Would that agreement have happened without the excitement caused by our run to the ALCS? I don't think so. We truly did save baseball in Seattle.

I had such mixed feelings, though, after the final game. Losing to the Indians was a disappointment, I can't sugarcoat that. We felt we were going to beat Cleveland. We truly felt like a team of destiny, but we didn't quite reach our destination.

A lot of Mariners' fans remember Joey Cora sitting on the bench, crying, after we were knocked out. Alex had his arms around Joey, comforting him. When you feel you should beat this team, and you don't, it's a bitter disappointment. If you feel you're completely outmatched, then it's different. But we felt we could beat the Indians, and should have beat them. So that was a disappointment. They just executed better.

Part of the sadness, though, was the fact that it had been so much fun, and we had grown so close, that we weren't ready to go our separate ways. Joey said he couldn't remember the last time he cried like that, especially over baseball, something he had fun doing.

"But this has been so special for so long a time, it hurts to end," he said.

We all felt that way. I admitted afterward that I felt some guilt about not hitting better. "I feel a responsibility for not doing more," I said. "I feel if I had produced some more runs, our chances to win would have been so much greater. I came up with men on base so many times. If I only had gotten a hit here or there, a double, a simple hit, the series would have been different for Seattle."

On the other hand, the run to the playoffs, the comeback to catch the Angels, the incredible tie-breaking game, Game 5 against the Yankees, the thrill of the postseason, the way the baseball fans in Seattle came alive—those were once-in-a-lifetime thrills. The energy in the stadium for the final month, it was the best I saw in any year I played. Beating the Yankees the way we did, that remains in my heart to this very day. We proved that Seattle could be a baseball town, and that baseball would stay here for the long-term. Some say we helped save baseball after the strike.

I just wish we could have kept going.

Chapter 9

Back to the Playoffs

IT WAS BACK TO REALITY for us in 1996.

On the plus side, we had the new ballpark on the way, and we had awakened a fervor for baseball in the Pacific Northwest. Our attendance at the Kingdome shot up by more than a million fans, from 1.6 million in 1995 to 2.7 million in 1996—more than double our total from 1987, the year I broke into the majors. Not only was local interest in the team at a sky-high level, but we had become one of the glamour teams in baseball. Jay was on the cover of *Sports Illustrated* in March, and Junior was on the cover of *GQ* with the headline, "Ken Griffey Jr. saves baseball." Some people even dubbed us "America's team."

But that didn't mean that the Mariners' financial problems had been completely solved. To meet their payroll budget, they shipped two of our key players—Tino Martínez and reliever Jeff Nelson—to the Yankees for pitcher Sterling Hitchcock and third baseman Russ Davis. In another deal, Mike Blowers went to the Dodgers for two minor leaguers. Tino and Mike had combined for 54 homers and 207 RBIs in '95, but it was more than numbers with those guys—it was the intangibles. They both were a big part of the clubhouse chemistry. Tino was a gamer with a knack for coming up with the clutch hit. He would give you that extra every time. Mike was always such a positive player and he lifted everyone up with his attitude. They were a great complement to the core of Junior, Randy, and Jay, and their departure definitely left a hole.

We did make two nice free-agent signings by adding Paul Sorrento to play first base and Mike Jackson for the bullpen, and we brought in John Marzano, a great guy, as a backup catcher. And Lou got a well-deserved contract extension through the 2001 season. Believe it or not, there were more trade rumors over the winter involving me—even after a season in which I led the American League in batting average, on-base percentage, OPS, doubles, and runs, and became the first American League right-hander to win two batting titles since Luke Appling in 1936 and 1943.

Fortunately, the trade didn't happen. Holli and I were planning on raising our family in Seattle, and we didn't want to go anywhere. In fact, I was hoping for a long-term contract extension, maybe four years. My agent, Willie Sanchez, couldn't reach an agreement with the Mariners in the off-season, but in October, they picked up the one-year option on my 1996 contract, so I wasn't going anywhere. That was cemented in late March, when we finally reached agreement on an extension—two years through 1998, with a club option for 1999.

"I wanted to stay in Seattle," I said that day. "It's the only team I've played for. My wife is from Seattle, the fans, my teammates, the way we played last season. There are many reasons. There is a big difference from last year to the first year I came up in 1987."

I was hoping for another year like 1995, when I stayed healthy, played in every game for the first time in my career and (not coincidentally, I don't think) put up the best numbers of my career.

One nice honor was finishing third in the voting for the American League's Most Valuable Player Award, behind Mo Vaughn, who narrowly edged Albert Belle. I even received four first-place votes. Jay finished fifth and Randy was sixth, which reflects what sort of team effort we had in '95—and needed to have again. In talking to reporters the day of the vote, I mentioned that I only felt one time all year in 1995 that I needed to try to carry the Mariners. That was the night Griffey broke his wrist on May 26.

"I thought about it. I don't deny that. Tino and I talked about it after the game. We thought we really have to have great years now for us to make it. We've got to do it. But that was it. I did not think about it again."

By the time we reported for spring training in 1996, I was settled into my role as a full-time designated hitter, but that had taken some adjustment, mental and physical, on my part. These days, I'm thought of as a DH; it's part of my identity, which probably was a big reason I needed all 10 years of eligibility before I made the Hall of Fame. When Lou, before the 1995 season, proposed that I moved to the DH position, I was initially skeptical. At that time, I still very much thought of myself as a two-way player and took a lot of pride in my defense.

Lou told me, "I need you in the lineup. You need to stay in the lineup." I couldn't fight that. It was true. Since Lou took over as manager, I had missed most of '93 with the hamstring injury, and then much of '94 with a wrist injury. I also had a history of knee problems and a shoulder issue as well. It wasn't a long conversation that I can remember. I wasn't the type of person to get into arguments and say, "No, I'm not going to do this." But I was frustrated about it, because at that stage of my career—I was just 32—I never saw myself as a DH. One concern that came to my mind was, what if I got hurt? Now I'm just a DH, and someone comes in and has a good year—what would my options be? I was kind of concerned about the future of my career.

I had to fight those thoughts in my mind. I told myself, "You can't go there. You have to look at the positive. The team is better if I'm healthy and playing DH, and Mike is at third." And eventually I realized that if I stayed healthy, I would have a longer career. I trusted Lou with what he wanted to do, and I understood that his motivation was to do what was best for the team, but also what was best for me. So that's where I started wrapping my mind around it. My attitude become, "Okay, let's go and just be a DH. Give it a try."

MIKE BLOWERS
Former Mariners Third Baseman

Edgar did not want to be a DH, I can tell you that. He fought Lou on that a little bit. Oh, yeah. He did not want to do it. He finally understood with the injuries he had, it was important to keep him in the lineup, which was great for me, obviously, because I got to play because of that. But that was something that was interesting. He was actually a pretty good defensive third baseman, too.

We talked about it. I remember Lou talking about it, and I think the whole thing with Edgar, he just wasn't sure. Now he had to learn how to be prepare, how to be a DH, all these different things. It was something that was foreign to him. It's one thing to DH in a game every now and then. But now it's going to be your job every day. The total of what you're bringing to the club is your ability to swing the bat. We all have bad days, but you can make up for it by making a play in the field, right? There's something to that. It takes some of the pressure off. Now all of a sudden that was not going to be there for him. How do you prepare and do all these different things?

I think at that point in his career he had already won a batting title. He was already emerging as a star in this game. I think all those things—trying to figure out, how am I going to do this all over again and how do I reinvent myself as just a hitter—would have been difficult for just about anybody. At that point, there were some pretty good DHs, but it wasn't like there were a lot of them. There were a few that were really good. He became the best.

The one thing I'll say: once that decision was made and he was on board with it, Edgar was all in. He figured it out, the way it worked best for him. It was interesting because for Edgar, he'd probably tell you it took some time, but for me it seemed like it was almost overnight. It didn't stop him from hitting at all.

RICK GRIFFIN
Mariners Athletic Trainer, 1983–2017

Edgar was mad because he still wanted to play in the field. The way Lou approached it with him, he said, "I need you on the field every single day. The way to keep you on the field and keep you healthy is to be a DH." And he said, "Plus, we have Blowers, and he's a really good player, and we need to get him in the lineup."

I know Edgar and Lou had several conversations. Some of them were in Spanish and probably a little bit heated. Edgar wanted to continue to play. He was still fairly young. He wanted to play in the field. But Lou was right. By Edgar doing that, it allowed him to stay healthy, and gave him a better opportunity to play on an everyday basis. That's one of Edgar's qualities—whatever needed to be done to help the team, he did it.

LOU PINIELLA
Former Mariners Manager

Edgar resisted it. No question about it. He wasn't happy. Edgar considered himself a two-way player. He was actually a good third baseman. When I went there to Seattle, Edgar was hitting second in the lineup, stealing some bases. He could run. It was just the fact his legs were a little thick, and he was getting leg pulls. After a few years of playing in the Kingdome with that hard turf, he started having leg problems. Lee Elia and I talked about how we could maximize him. We decided the best thing was if we could somehow get a third baseman to play in the field and let Edgar DH and become a hitter. That's exactly what we did. Woody got us Mike Blowers, a really good defensive third baseman with an excellent arm. That allowed us to move Edgar full-time to DH.

He fought it; he fought it hard. We told him, "Look, it's not a demotion. DH is an integral part of a major-league lineup. And we need you in the lineup, not nursing leg pulls." He finally accepted it, and the professional he was, basically became the best DH in the league.

Throughout my career, I worked hard at being a good fielding third baseman, and I actually enjoyed being on the field. It just felt like you were a part of the team when you were out there with a glove every inning. A DH is, in some ways, kind of a lonely place.

Right away, I set about learning the best way to do it. Routine is very important to me. I have to have a routine. Focus is important, too. I realized I had to be into the game like I was playing in the field, and be prepared. Anticipation. Those things were part of my everyday routine, and that helped quite a bit. I saw what happened when I wasn't fully focused, or I wasn't anticipating the situation.

Eventually, I developed a constant awareness of being prepared, and staying consistent, as a DH.

I didn't really talk to any of the primary DHs of that era, like Harold Baines—who will be going into the Hall of Fame in 2019 in the same class as me. Harold and I used to say hi to each other, but we never had any communication about DHing. Mainly, it was just trial and error, going game by game and learning about what I needed to do to stay consistent. The more I DH'd, the more comfortable I became. By the second month of the '95 season, I felt like it was working. Our team looked good, I was hitting well. I felt like, "Okay, this might actually work out."

Eventually, I came to enjoy being a DH. It happened that year, in fact, and I felt that way throughout the remainder of my career. For a few more years, I would occasionally play the field, especially when we went to National League parks for interleague games, where there was no designated hitter. If the manager wanted to keep my bat in the lineup, I had to play either third base or first base. But the more infrequently I played, the less comfortable I felt in the field. Eventually, it became hard for me to make the throw from third base, and at the end of my career, when my eyes worsened, it was hard for me to see the throws when I played first base. It came to the point where my comfort zone was as a DH. When I had a glove on, I just felt like I was out of place at times. It switched around completely.

At the same time, I bulked up a little more once I became a DH, because I didn't have to worry so much about quick movements in the field. I made sure I didn't get too big, but now my concentration was on hitting, and only what I needed to do to be more productive as a hitter. Plus, when you're not in the field, you gain more weight because you're not as active. My training became more weights than cardio. When I was still playing in the field, it was more cardio than weights, because you needed to be agile.

I adhered to my routine very strictly. That was part of my personality, I guess. Once I figured out what worked for me—and that evolved over the early years—I felt it was very important to stick to that. I would wake up at seven o'clock in the morning, have breakfast, and then go back to sleep for another couple of hours. I wanted to make sure I slept eight hours. Once I had my eight hours, usually about 10:00 AM, I would get up, have a snack and do whatever personal errands I needed to do. At noon, I would have my lunch, and then do my eye exercises at 1:00. As I mentioned earlier, that could take up to an hour, though later in my career, when I had become familiar with the exercises, I cut it down to 20 minutes.

At around 2:00, I would head out to the stadium. When I got there, I would have a snack, then do whatever treatment I needed to do in the training room, and especially do what I needed to do to take care of my legs. As a DH, you're sitting, sitting, and all of a sudden you go and hit, and you have to run hard. Your legs had to be loose and ready. And my legs, throughout my career, had a tendency to give me trouble. Rick Griffin, our trainer for my entire career, did a magnificent job keeping me healthy. I owe him a lot.

RICK GRIFFIN
Former Mariners Athletic Trainer

When you're an infielder, you do 150 to 200 squats, every single game. So your quads get overdeveloped and you don't do enough hamstring work because your quads are usually two or three times stronger, and it's supposed to be an even balance. So that was part of it. Edgar had really big legs, very strong legs, and a lot of quad work, and his hammies were not as strong. And when he ran, he didn't have the most efficient running style. He put a lot of pressure on his hamstrings. He fought those.

If I gave Edgar a hundred massages, I gave him a thousand. Every single day, I'd work on his legs, work on his hammies, do different things. He spent a lot of time in the training room, a lot of working. He did everything he could to stay on the field. There's some guys you can tell, "You can only run 60 percent. If you run 70, you're going to pull your hamstring." Edgar knew what his limits were, and most of the time he'd stay within his limits. Lou was really good, too. He knew certain situations when he'd get Edgar out of there. If it was a winning-run situation, Edgar's going to run, and he'll pull his hammy, he doesn't care. Lou made sure he got him out of the game. Lou was really good about managing those situations with him.

It started in Vancouver, and then he pulled it in Anaheim one time real bad. He popped the tendon off the bone, and he ended up having surgery. He pulled it in Boston once really bad. It was usually his left hamstring. His right one never really bothered him. When he pulled it off the bone, it was a little bit of a disadvantage because then he really had only one of the three hamstring tendons attached. Then he had a little bit of a mechanical disadvantage, and that affected him running.

After treatment, I would go to the batting tee, take my swings, and then do some work in the cage, followed by batting practice. When BP ended, I'd come in, have something to eat, and do another 15 to 20 minutes of eye exercises. Then came the game. After it was over, at 10:30 or 11:00, I would have a protein shake and then work out for about 20 minutes in the gym at the stadium. I'd head home, go to bed, and at 7:00 in the morning, wake up and do it all over again. That was my routine pretty much every day of my career.

Once I became a DH, it became important to figure out what to do in between at-bats. I would stretch, I'd ride the bike a little bit to stay loose, I'd take some swings off the tee. But all the while I would watch the game and follow what was happening on the field. If I was doing the bike, I would be watching on television. I would start thinking about the pitcher, and how he would try to get me out. "Are we ahead or behind? Who's warming up, and what kind of stuff does he have?" When it came closer to my at-bat, I'd make sure I was in the dugout, so I could adjust to the light.

I liked to keep moving. I didn't like to sit. That's how you get hurt, by sitting and then all of a sudden going up to hit while you're cold. I was moving, doing the bike, stretching constantly, but always in tune with the game, what was happening. It was just as important as the physical activity to be focusing on what was going on.

The more I watched, whether it was on TV or actually being in the dugout watching the game live, the more I would pick up little things that could help me. Maybe I'd see that the second baseman, when they threw breaking balls, would move one step to the right side, and when it's a fastball, he moves the other way. If he does it early enough, I could pick that up. Or I'd see that the pitcher does something with his glove when he throws a breaking ball, or he goes to his chin. You never know what you're doing to pick up. I would share what I learned with other players on the team. It's amazing what you can pick up when you're in tune with what's going on.

I was consumed with baseball during the season. At the end of each year, it was like you unplugged me. During the season, I went to bed thinking about the game, and I woke up thinking about the game—to the point it was kind of frustrating to Holli at times. But that's the life of the ballplayer. The game is every day. It doesn't give you time to relax. Every day you have events that stick in your head and work on your mind the whole night.

One aspect to my training that intrigued a lot of people—even my teammates—was the way I would take batting practice. For a certain amount of time, I would swing with the weighted donut still on my bat. But what amazed a lot of other players was when I would hit with the donut on my bat against live pitching, and not just off the tee. In general, I felt the donut was good for the strength of my arms, and the grip. I would always have the donut on the bat, just working the hands. I felt that the heavier I made the bat, the quicker my hands would be when I took it off. That was the thought behind it—swing with something heavy so when you take it off, the bat becomes so light you can wait on the ball as long as you can.

As far as taking BP with the donut still on the bat, I thought it was good for hand-eye coordination. My swing was more inside out. Players who tried doing what I did who had an outside-in swing, they would end up hitting the donut with the ball quite a bit. The concentration it took to actually square the ball right on the barrel, with the donut on, that helped me. That focus, as well as the strength I felt I developed and the sensation of making the bat lighter, all of that made it worthwhile for me to hit with the donut. Honestly, I can't remember if I once saw another player doing that and picked up on it. I feel like I must have. I wonder if it was José Cruz, since I picked up so much from him.

MIKE BLOWERS
Former Mariners Third Baseman

I remember one time watching Edgar, and he was hitting off the tee, and he had one of those old red donuts on his bat. I thought, "That's kind of odd," so I asked him about it. He said it was for bat control. If you're out of balance, or you're out of position, that thing is going to drop. I said, "That makes sense." He was hitting off the tee with the donut on his bat. Then one day I showed up and walked out on the tunnel for early batting practice. He was in the cage on the field with a donut on his bat.

Now, think about that. My first thought is, "If I try it, that ball is going to hit off the donut and hit me in the face. You're talking about just a real small area to hit the ball. And he's just, line drive, line drive, line drive. Then he would kick it off and take his regular batting practice. I had never seen anyone do it before. I've done it just to try it. It was a little scary for me, so I kind of stayed away from it. But I always thought that was just amazing. He had an M356 model Louisville Slugger, and it was a bigger barrel, so the donut wouldn't go all the way down, it sat a little higher, like where the label is, but still it was amazing.

NORM CHARLTON
Former Mariners Pitcher

One thing that stands out about Edgar's hitting—he'd be taking extra BP on the road, and I'm watching him hit balls out of the park with the donut on his bat. Granted, he's not facing major-league pitching; he's facing coaches. I can't hit them out of the park without a donut when I'm facing coaches. To watch him move the ball around the park at will, and watch him do stuff like that, hitting the ball out of the park with a donut, I still shake my head.

The 1996 season turned out to be a very frustrating one for the Mariners, especially coming off our success in 1995. Randy Johnson, fresh from a Cy Young season in which he went 18–2, made just eight starts in 1996, missing all of June and July. He suffered from a back injury—two bulging disks—that eventually required season-ending surgery. They shut him down for good in late August. Obviously, that was a huge blow, because Randy meant so much to our team. We had other issues as well—a hand injury (broken hamate bone) that kept Griffey out for nearly a month (but that didn't stop him from hitting 49 homers and driving in 140 runs), and an arm injury that limited Chris Bosio to just nine starts. Third baseman Russ Davis broke his leg, and Alex went on the DL early in the season with a hamstring strain.

Put it all together, and it added up to an 85–76 season in which we barely missed the playoffs. Considering our high expectations after '95, it was a huge disappointment, though a couple of good things did happen. One, Alex Rodriguez had a massive breakout season. He succeeded me as American League batting champion with a .358 average, hit 36 homers, drove in 123 runs, and led the league with 54 doubles and 141 runs scored—all at age 20, in his first full big-league season!

He finished second to Juan González in the MVP balloting, with Junior finishing fourth. When Alex came up, you could see all the raw talent, but it was just that, raw. He would chase a lot of pitches. But when he connected, you could see the power he had. Alex was also very smart and wanted to learn everything he could about the game. He asked me a ton of questions. Like I said, I heard that after the '95 season he took home a hitting tape of me. And I believe it, too, because in '96 he came to spring training and he had my stance, my high leg kick. And then he went out and hit .358.

Of all the guys I played with, him and Junior were similar—five-tool players who could do pretty much anything on the field. They had the makeup, preparation, work ethic, and the mental strength to play the game.

The other positive development of 1996 (with a ripple effect that went far beyond) was an unheralded trade we made on July 30. We sent outfielder Darren Bragg to Boston for a journeyman left-hander named Jamie Moyer. Jamie was already 33 and had been with six organizations, released several times. But we got him just when he was figuring out how to pitch, and reaped the rewards for the next nine-plus seasons. Jamie was a marvel. He pitched in the majors until he was 49, and won 269 games, which is a tribute to his dedication, work ethic, and how smart he was. Everything he did had a purpose. More than almost anyone I played with, he got every bit out of his ability. Jamie realized, "I don't throw hard, but I can be creative." You really have to know yourself, and what it's going to take to be successful, to make that work. He not only made it work, he was one of the best pitchers in the league for an extended period and a key part of three playoff teams for us.

Jamie was such a master of the changeup. You could sit on it, but that didn't really help, because he threw different changeups. He knew when to pitch in. He would get feedback from every pitch, every nuance—"Okay, this guy is leaning over the plate, this guy is pulling out." He was very aware of all that. That's what it takes for a pitcher who doesn't throw hard: to have a really good feel for what the hitter is looking for, or his weakness. Jamie would exploit those weaknesses like no other pitcher. Mechanically, he was able to locate, and mentally he knew how to stay away from a hitter's strength and attack his weaknesses.

Given the choice between facing a power pitcher, or one who thrives on deception like Jamie, give me the flamethrower any day. At least with a guy who throws hard, you pretty much know when he's going to throw the fastball. Finesse guys like Jamie, you don't know what he's going throw, or where. Those kind of guys could be a little more of a problem for hitters. But I'll tell you who I least liked to face: knuckleball pitchers. They drove me crazy, especially Tim Wakefield of the Red Sox. Everyone talks about my numbers against Mariano. I hope they don't look at what I did against Wakefield: 1-for-19 (a single) with seven strikeouts. I did walk 12 times, probably because I figured out my best strategy against him was to wait for him to throw a ball, since I couldn't hit his strikes.

Some people have asked me how I think I'd do against modern pitchers, who have such a greater velocity than they did when I played. That's not to say we didn't face hard throwers. Guys like Troy Percival and Billy Koch in my day threw 100 mph, and there were others, too. But nowadays, every team seems to have a whole staff of guys at 98 or above, especially coming out of the bullpen. One thing I've noticed, though: hitters, over time, get used to higher speed. At the beginning, it's almost like it doesn't register in the brain. But if you constantly face guys throwing 100 mph, you adjust, just like a Single-A player adjusts to Double A, and then Triple-A, and then the big leagues. I feel like I would have adjusted.

Personally, I had a mixed season in 1996. I had ended the year before feeling bad about my performance in the ALCS against Cleveland. Even with all my success in 1995, including the Division Series, it took a while to get the disappointment of the ALCS out of my head. I told a reporter in spring training, "For some time, it took away some of the joy in other things we had done as a team." But I tried to use it as a learning experience about how to handle slumps, because I realized I had begun to press when I got off to a slow start against the Indians.

One person who helped me immensely throughout my career whenever I got into a funk—or really at all times—was our hitting coach, Lee Elia, whom everyone called "Uncle Lee." Working with

Uncle Lee was so much fun. He was a guy that always knew what to say, and when to say it. And he never said anything negative. In this game, you fail so often, you don't want to hear negative things on top of that. When you were down, Lee tried to switch it to a positive and make it light, make it fun, help you relax and not worry too much. That helps the player to actually use their skills instead of being worried about what a coach might think or say.

Yet he was also a great technician of hitting. We worked together to come up with three checkpoints in my swing. When one of them was off, Lee would spot it, and we'd head to the film room to check it out. Having him as a watchdog helped keep me from prolonged slumps. When I became the Mariners' hitting coach in 2015, I tried to model my approach on Uncle Lee.

I hit .327 in 1996, with 26 homers and 103 RBIs, while putting up a .464 on-base percentage and .595 slugging percentage. I made the All-Star team, along with Junior (of course), Jay, Alex, and Dan Wilson—the first time for those three.

But I was headed for an even bigger year until I suffered a freak injury in July. In fact, I was having the best season of my career, even better than 1995. Until I got hurt, I was way ahead of the pace to break the American League record for doubles, which was set by Earl Webb with 67 in 1931. I had hit .491 in spring training, a new Mariners' record, and used that as a springboard to a torrid start (despite wrenching my shoulder trying to break up a fight in one of the final exhibition games of the year).

In mid-May, I was hitting .354 and had more doubles (29) than singles (24)—a pace to hit 96 doubles. On July 4, I had 41 doubles, still on pace for 82, and Lou said, "You can put an asterisk by Webb's record. It's just on hold now."

I was hitting so many doubles I actually told a reporter, "I want to get a single, a simple single." I said I felt that too many long hits meant my swing might be getting too long. "Singles tell me my swing is right," I said. "The longer the swing, the bigger the holes in it." A couple of days later, I hit three homers in a game for the first time in my career, so I guess the holes weren't too big.

That's not to say I didn't love doubles, mind you. I was a gap-to-gap hitter, so when I was in a groove, I would rack up two-base hits. My most well-known hit was a double, of course, and one of my nicknames was "Señor Doble."

"Doubles are the best hit of all," I once said. "I call them the rally hit. If there is anyone on base, a double gets them home, maybe even from first. It automatically puts a runner in scoring position. It's a hit that keeps pressure on the other team."

But my doubles parade halted on July 20 in Anaheim—the first game all season I started at third. In fact, it would be the final start of my career at third base. In the second inning, Pat Borders of the Angels hit a popup between home plate and third base. Our catcher, John Marzano, chased after it, and so did I. We looked at each other—and kept going hard until we collided. Each of us thought the other was going to pull off.

At the last minute John saw me and went into a slide, and when he did, he upended me, so I did a flip. My elbow smashed into John's left eye, and he needed 30 stitches for a gash along his left eyebrow. I ended up with four fractured ribs and a sore back that landed me on the disabled list until mid-August. A few years later, when I played first base against the Giants in San Francisco, Lou joked, "We instructed Edgar that on popups between home and first base to let the catcher catch them... or let them fall."

I was out 21 games, the first games I had missed since June 11, 1994. But even when I came back, I just wasn't the same. I couldn't turn on the ball like I did before, and I didn't feel like I had the same bat speed. It was almost like I was dragging the bat through the zone. At the time of the injury, I was hitting .334 with 22 homers, 44 doubles, and a .663 slugging percentage in 95 games. After I came off the DL, I hit .309 with just four homers, eight doubles, and a .441 slugging percentage in 44 games. I finished with 52 doubles—two behind A-Rod, who led the league. Some people have wondered if a major record like most doubles in a season might have put me in the Hall of Fame sooner. We'll never know, I guess.

Marzano said later he thought that when we locked eyes, I was indicating that he should take it. John was a funny guy—and a tough guy. Everyone remembers the fight he got in with the Yankees' Paul O'Neill in August of that year after our pitcher, Tim Davis, knocked down O'Neill. They were firing punches at each other at home plate.

John tragically died in 2008 at age 45 when he fell down the stairs at his home. In 2005, reminiscing with Bob Finnigan of the *Seattle Times* about our collision, he couldn't help but laugh. "I was lying there bleeding, I needed 40 stitches, and everyone ran to Edgar. Only one guy came to me. Junior. He leaned over me as I lay on the ground, my eyelid hanging off, and told me, 'Edgar's hurt. You're screwed.'"

You want to know the worst part? The umpire had called the infield fly rule, so we didn't even have to catch the ball. The batter was already out.

I was the first player in 59 years to have 50 or more doubles in back-to-back seasons. A-Rod and I had the most combined doubles by teammates since Hall of Famers Hank Greenberg and Charlie Gehringer had 113 for the Detroit Tigers in 1934. But I couldn't help but think about how much more I could have produced if I hadn't gotten hurt, and wonder if I could have helped us make up the games we needed for the playoffs. We made a late charge by winning 10 straight games in September to pull within one game of Texas in the division. But we finished the season with six losses in our final eight games, and wound up 4½ behind the Rangers and 2½ behind the Orioles for the wild-card.

The most frustrating part was we had one of the best offenses in baseball history in that period, but didn't quite have the pitching to match. We scored 993 runs in 1996, barely missing becoming just the seventh team in major-league history to score 1,000 runs. And in 1997 we blasted 264 home runs to set a major-league record for homers in a season that stood until the Yankees slammed 267 in 2018. That 1997 season was the only year we had Randy, Junior, Alex, and myself all healthy for a full year, with great performances as well from Jay, Dan, Joey, and Paul Sorrento.

Randy came back from his back surgery to go 20–4 in 1997 and finish as the Cy Young runnerup, with a 19-strikeout game in August to reinforce he was as dominant as ever. Junior hit 56 homers, drove in 147, and was the American League MVP. Alex hit .300 with 23 homers. Jay hit 40 homers, Sorrento had 31, and Russ Davis had 20. I had a rare injury-free year. (Excluding the time Russ Davis's bat slipped out of his hands and flew into the dugout, hitting my head and opening a wound that required five stitches; and later the same week, I got another gash in my head when I slammed into the catcher's mask during a play at home plate, requiring eight more stitches. That's 13 stitches in five days, but I didn't miss any time.) I played in 155 games, a career high, and hit .330 (second in the AL to Frank Thomas's .347), with 28 homers and 108 RBIs.

If that sounds like a playoff-caliber squad, you're right. We won 90 games in 1997, the most in franchise history at that point, and took the AL West by six games over Anaheim. But it wasn't quite as easy as that makes it sound. All season long, our bullpen was an issue. We had trouble settling on a closer who didn't struggle, and when the trade deadline came around, Lou was desperate to get some reinforcements. On July 30, the day before the deadline, we squandered a 7–2 lead and lost 8–7 to the Red Sox—our 15th blown save, tops in the majors. That just added to the urgency to shore up our relief corps.

We swung two big trades on July 31. The first one sent outfielder José Cruz Jr., who had been our first-round pick in 1995 and an impressive young talent, to the Blue Jays for relievers Mike Timlin and Paul Spoljaric. Of course, I was sad to see José go. I took a special interest in him because of my affection and respect for his father. When I watched José in the outfield, I could see his father's mannerisms, and even the way he ran reminded me of his dad. I tried to take him under my wing, but having grown up the son of a major-leaguer, José was like Griffey—he already knew what to do in the major leagues. It was tough to see him go. José was shook up, because he enjoyed playing for the Mariners. José actually started the game that night against the Brewers, but Lou pulled him in the fifth inning when the trade came down. Several of us—Joey, Russ Davis, and Dan Wilson, in addition to myself—came into the clubhouse to talk to José and wish him well before he left.

The other trade that day was one that came back to haunt the Mariners—catcher Jason Varitek, our first-round pick in 1994, and promising young pitcher Derek Lowe going to the Red Sox for reliever Heathcliff Slocumb. Varitek and Lowe, of course, were instrumental in bringing Boston its first World Series title in 86 years in 2004, and Varitek added a second ring in 2007. Our immediate reaction in the clubhouse was, "It's great to get some help for the bullpen." At the same time, we were thinking, "What about the price we're paying to get those guys?"

José Cruz was a great talent and looked like a very promising player for the future. Varitek and Lowe also. So we gave up a lot to get that pitching we needed. Sometimes, you have to pay a high price. You just hope it works. But we still struggled with the pen after that, and finished the year with a whopping 27 blown saves. We lost seven games that season in which we scored eight or more runs.

To be fair, Slocumb and Timlin did help stabilize our bullpen enough to get us through that crisis period and into the playoffs. Unlike 1995, when we stormed from behind, in 1997 we took the division lead early and had to hang on for dear life, which brings its own kind of pressure. And satisfaction. A turning point came on August 31, when we were struggling to hold off the Angels. After an 11–2 loss at Dodger Stadium, Lou called a bunch of the veterans— Griffey, Buhner, Rodriguez, Johnson, Cora, Sorrento, Wilson, and myself—into his office. As A-Rod recalled in the *Seattle Times*, "I've never been in a meeting so intense. I'm not going to say just what Lou told us, but he motivated the hell out of us. This team has so much heart."

We won 15 of our next 22 games to take the division by six games over the Angels. I missed the last week of the season with my only injury of the year—a pulled muscle in my left side. That was bad timing. I could still feel it at times, but I was determined to play in the postseason.

Heading into the Division Series against Baltimore, we felt good about our starting pitching. Not only had Randy gone 20–4, but Jamie Moyer was 17–5 and Jeff Fassero was 16–9. No trio in the league won more games. Our staff ERA dropped from 5.17 on the day of the trades to 3.88 afterward, and we went from six blown leads in the ninth to just two, so you could say the deals had their desired effect. During our clubhouse celebration when we clinched the division with a win over the Angels at the Kingdome, I told reporters that our goal was to take the step we had missed in 1995 and make it to the World Series.

Instead, we didn't get out of the best-of-five divisional round, which was a bitter disappointment considering our talent and expectations. The Orioles swept the first two games in Seattle, and after we took Game 3 in Baltimore behind a strong game from Fassero, they finished us off the next day. Randy, who was pitching with a bruised middle finger that definitely cost him a little bit of his power, lost twice to the Orioles' ace, Mike Mussina. Jamie was pitching brilliantly in Game 2 but had to leave in the fifth inning with an elbow injury, and our bullpen couldn't hold the lead.

We hit just .218 as a team with six homers, all solos. Junior and I were combined 5-for-31 (.161), although I did have two home runs in the four-game series. Jay summed up our mood after the final game: "We didn't get to the level we wanted. It's bittersweet. It's almost like we didn't achieve anything, to be honest with you."

DAN WILSON
Former Mariners Catcher

In 1997, for the first time, we played a season with expectations. In '95, we were not expected to do anything. In '97, we were expected to win the division. I remember winning the division and feeling very satisfied we had met expectations. But in the playoffs, Baltimore beat Randy twice. Mussina was on fire. They were the one team that had given him trouble during the year. Jeff Reboulet, oddly, and Mike Bordick, he just couldn't figure them out.

JAY BUHNER
Former Mariners Outfielder

Man, '97 was it. That one hurt. We had the chemistry, we had the right guys. We might have been a little short here and there. I'm not going to throw anyone under the bus, but I wish we got that one more guy. I would hear Lou say that over and over. Look at that lineup—it's like a who's who. It's a shame. But a lot of things come into play. It's hard for Seattle to grind it out for 162 games in 185 days with all that travel from the Pacific Northwest. That's not an excuse, but going cross-country all the time, it takes a toll.

And Cleveland was loaded, the Yankees—everyone else was loaded. We were the meek Seattle Mariners no one expected—who the hell are these guys? But they knew we'd go toe to toe with you. We'd scrap in the trenches or wherever. That was the personality of our team, trickling down from Lou. You knew you were in for a friggin' battle. We were not intimidated in beanball wars. It was fun, man. But '97—I still shake my head.

It was an empty feeling, and I had more than just the pain of early elimination on my mind.

One backdrop to the 1997 season that caused me a lot of distress and concern was the serious discussion going on within baseball of undergoing radical realignment after the season. There were stories and speculation about that all year. And the plan that gained the most traction involved the Mariners switching to the National League in 1998. Of course, that would have major ramifications for me, as a designated hitter. In the National League, which doesn't use the DH, I'd be out of a job.

247

For the first time in my career, I had sincere questions about whether I would still be with the Mariners beyond the year. The Mariners could conceivably keep me as a first baseman, but the longer I was removed from playing in the field, the harder it became. The ballclub would likely be forced to trade me to an American League team so I could remain a DH. I wasn't sure that I wanted to go somewhere else at that stage of my career. I even began to discuss seriously with Holli the possibility of retiring, although at 34, I felt I had a lot of good years still in me. I told Bob Finnigan of the *Seattle Times* that I had briefly considered retirement after my hamstring injury in 1993, but this time it was more tangible.

"If Seattle goes to the National League, it will create big changes for a lot of our players, especially me," I told him. "What is my role? I don't know if I would be happy in what the team would want me to do. Holli and I want to stay in Seattle. We want a bigger family, brothers and sisters for [my 4-year-old son] Alex, and we want to raise them in Seattle. I don't say anything about retiring easily because I do love to play the game. But I have to be happy to help my family be happy."

When we were knocked out by Baltimore, I went home not knowing if I had played my last game for the Mariners—or if I had played my last game, period. At that point, I thought it was likely the team was headed for the National League in 1998. That's what all the buzz was at the time. So I had that playing on my mind on top of the disappointment of having our season abruptly ended.

"If they go to the National League, right now I have no clue if they want to keep me or if they want to trade me," I said in the clubhouse at Camden Yards after we were eliminated. "I'd rather stay, but it's not up to me."

Later in October, however, MLB abandoned its more radical realignment plan, which would have resulted in Anaheim, Oakland, and Seattle all moving to the National League. They settled for the smaller move of just Milwaukee into the NL. The Mariners stayed right where we were in the American League—with the DH spot in the lineup still intact.

That was a huge relief to me, to know that I wasn't going to have to leave Seattle or even retire. But huge changes would soon be coming to the Mariners involving three of our core players—followed by the winningest season in American League history.

Chapter 10

Soaring to New Heights

WITH THE MARINERS STAYING PUT in the American League, one more mystery hung over us when the 1997 season ended: What would happen to Randy Johnson, who was entering the last year of his contract?

That would be a common theme in the next couple of years as the Mariners grappled with the challenge of retaining our three superstars—Randy, Ken Griffey Jr., and Alex Rodriguez. It turned out, they couldn't do it.

Randy was traded to the Houston Astros on July 31, 1998, bringing back three minor leaguers—pitchers Freddy Garcia and John Halama, and infielder Carlos Guillen. Junior was traded to the Cincinnati Reds after the 1999 season in a deal that netted us outfielder Mike Cameron, pitchers Brett Tomko and Jake Meyer, and infielder Antonio Pérez. And after the 2000 season, Alex signed a free-agent contract with the Texas Rangers for what at the time was the most money in professional sports history, $252 million over 10 years.

If you had asked me what the net result of losing the Big Unit, Junior, and A-Rod would be, I'll admit I would have told you that I thought we'd be headed for trouble. Big trouble. And I wouldn't have been alone in our clubhouse with that line of thinking. Those three were the biggest part of the core of our team, the best pitcher and two best position players in baseball. It was frustrating for everyone to see them leave Seattle. But something amazing happened in their wake: in 2000, with Randy and Junior both gone, we made it back to the playoffs as the wild-card team in the American League. And in 2001, with all three of our superstars playing elsewhere, the Mariners roared to a 116-win season, the most victories in American League history and tied with the 1906 Cubs for the most in major-league history.

We still didn't make it to the World Series, which remains a major regret to this day. I feel like we should have been able to get it done. Each time we made the postseason, it was a precious gift, as Mariners' fans have painfully learned. As of this writing, we have not been back to the playoffs since 2001. And each time we got there, we truly felt we were going to win the pennant and bring the World Series to our great fans in Seattle.

In 1995, it was maybe easier to put behind us because it was the first time. There was great satisfaction in our miracle comeback and saving baseball in Seattle. With our loaded roster in 1997, Joey Cora said at the outset of the playoffs, "We're at the point where experience and opportunity cross. We're right there. We have it all." But we let that one get away. And in 2000 and 2001, we came agonizingly close each year, making it to the American League Championship Series, but couldn't get to the finish line. The Yankees stopped us both times.

As I reflect, it feels like we were always missing one piece, even with the massive talent we had. Maybe it was a leadoff hitter or a left fielder or a starting pitcher or a reliever. One more bat, or one more arm. That was frustrating. Sometimes, the piece we got didn't turn out to be the right piece. Sometimes, the deal wasn't there to be made, for whatever reason. It's just what happens. And in 2000 and 2001, we ran into those great Yankee teams that won five pennants and four World Series titles in six years. They found a way to execute against our offense and get a big hit at the right time.

That's the big-picture view. It doesn't take away from my feeling that with that lineup, we should have at least made it to the World Series. And I guarantee you everyone who played on those teams feels the same way.

The 1998 season was a major disappointment for our ballclub. We finished 76–85—our first losing record since the strike-shortened year of 1994. The Mariners had picked up Randy's option for 1998 in September of '97, but they broke off talks on an extension and started actively looking to trade him. Rumors were flying all winter and into the season—including one rumor that the Mariners turned down an offer of Mariano Rivera for Johnson. That would have changed the course of history. The uncertainty over Randy's status hung over us all year until he was finally dealt to Houston at the trade deadline. It was an uncomfortable situation for everyone, particularly Randy, who was an uncharacteristic 9–10 with a 4.33 ERA in 23 starts for us.

It's funny—the trade with Houston was extremely unpopular in our clubhouse when it came down. Everyone was disappointed that we hadn't gotten back players that could help us right away, and some guys were angry. Our GM, Woody Woodward, even had to meet with a group of the veterans to explain the deal and try to ease our concerns. David Segui called it a "lousy" trade and Griffey said to a reporter that if Randy was worth three kids with no reputations then, "They would get a bag of balls if they traded me."

But in retrospect, it wound up being a very good deal by Woody, considering that Randy was going to be a free agent at the end of the year. Freddy Garcia quickly became our ace, winning 17 games in 1999 and going 76–50 in six seasons in Seattle while making two All-Star teams. Carlos Guillen was our starting shortstop when we won 116 games in 2001 (and went on to make three All-Star teams when Seattle traded him to the Tigers). John Halama was a solid pitcher who won in double figures three times for the Mariners.

But that didn't help us in 1998. We felt a lot of pressure to win that year, because we knew our window with this group was starting to close. My contract was up at the end of the year, too, and everyone was getting a little older. Lou told us in our first meeting in spring training that we had unfinished business. That is how we all felt after getting knocked out in the first round of the playoffs by Baltimore the previous year. But it would remain unfinished. Jay missed two months following knee surgery, and as I said when he came back in June, "Jay means so many things to us. He means so much in our lineup, yet sometimes that's just small stuff compared to what he means in our clubhouse. He is our leader." Unfortunately, Jay ended up undergoing Tommy John elbow surgery in September. He played only 72 games that year, another big factor in our struggles.

On Opening Day at the Kingdome, we blew a 9–6 lead in the eighth inning and lost 10–9 to Cleveland. That set the tone for the season. We got off to a 3–10 start—including a seven-game losing streak—and never could dig out of that hole. By the end of May, we were already 10½ games behind the Rangers in our division, and by the end of June the deficit had grown to 16 games.

Randy was up and down all year. He was as brilliant as ever in some games, but knocked around in others. After he dominated Tampa Bay in a 15-strikeout game in May, Joey Cora said, "No one can lift this team like Randy can when he's hot."

But two starts later, he got touched for six runs against the Angels. I felt for Randy, because he had to deal all year with the uncertainty over his future. We all were wondering what was going to happen, too. In June, according to many reports, Randy was on the verge of being traded to the Dodgers, reportedly for pitcher Ismael Valdez and others, but one of our owners reportedly vetoed the trade. We lost 12 out of 15 games following the trade veto. I said to reporters, "We haven't been hitting or fielding or making plays or pitches. We stink."

When that quote was relayed to Griffey, he said, "We don't stink. We suck."

It had been a long time since we had gone through such a struggling season. That had been a common occurrence for the Mariners early in my career. When the losses mount, "you are unable to concentrate as well," I told a reporter. "It's almost like we're thinking too many things instead of just thinking what you are doing." We had some great individual performances that year. Junior hit 56 homers for the second year in a row and drove in 146 runs, while Alex became the third player in history to join the 40/40 club, with 42 homers and 46 steals. But our bullpen struggled all year and our fielding was an issue.

The trade of Randy on July 31 drew all the attention, but in August we traded Joey Cora to the Indians for David Bell. David—who is now the manager of the Reds—would become a big contributor for us on two playoff teams, playing second and third base. But I hated to see Joey go. Besides being one of my closest friends, he brought intensity to our team. He had a lot of great years in Seattle, and always played hard, doing the little things at the plate, and in the field, that helped us win. It was always fun to have Joey around and his trade hit me hard.

Here's what I said at the time: "He was my closest teammate and a good man. I will miss him, we all will miss him. We talked in the early hours of the morning after he heard about the trade. This is sad. We all know baseball is a business, but sometimes it is a cruel business."

Personally, I had a pretty good year at age 35 in 1998, staying healthy for the most part once again (154 games played) and hitting .322 with 29 homers and 102 RBIs. I actually got off to a slow start and was still hitting under .300 at the start of June. But over the final 100 games I hit .342 with 20 homers.

When I was struggling, the speculation began that I might be traded by the deadline. I could be a free agent after the season if the Mariners decided not to pick up my option. I told the *Seattle Times*, "I know this game is a lot of business, and they are going to do what's best for the team. Whatever they do, there is nothing I can do. I would be disappointed [if traded or the option is not picked up]. This is the only team I have played for. But life goes on, and I would have to move on."

But happily, once again nothing happened that drove me out of Seattle. In fact, Mariners' management called me in for a meeting to assure me I wasn't being traded, despite the rumors. At this stage of my career, I had been in trade rumors so often I was able to tune them out, for the most part.

The strong finish was gratifying because I heard a lot of comments that I was getting old, I was finished, my bat speed was slowing. But I was just struggling. That doesn't mean you are finished. That was the year, remember, I was really having trouble with my eyes. When that problem was solved, my hitting took off.

On the next-to-last day of the season, I went 4-for-4 to raise my average from .316 to .321. After going 3-for-3 in the game, including my 29th home run, to move to .320073, Lou asked me if I wanted to sit on .320 or go for my 30ᵗʰ homer. I said I'd go for 30. In my last at-bat, I hit a double. Lou then gave me the option to sit out the season finale to protect my average. After all, .320 sounds a lot better than .319. But I chose to play and went 1-for-2 with three walks to finish at .322.

It was the fourth of six straight years of hitting .320 or higher, with an on-base percentage over .420 and a slugging percentage over .550. I feel like these years were the heart of my career, where everything was working. My confidence was high. I felt great at the plate mechanically. I stayed more or less healthy. And I was very, very motivated. I loved coming to the stadium, I loved competing, I loved the guys we had on the team, I loved playing for Lou. There were obviously frustrations along the way—such as the Mariners' potential move to the National League that festered in 1997, and an (unsuccessful) effort by MLB in 1998 to eliminate the DH altogether. But for the most part those were great times.

HAROLD REYNOLDS
Former Mariners Second Baseman

I remember talking to Ken [Griffey Jr.] when he was hitting his 40, 50 homers a year, and he's saying, Edgar's the best hitter on the team. Repeatedly. He'll say that today. Edgar was the best hitter. When you're around great players, it makes you better. It brings that greatness out of you.

Edgar's understanding of what that guy on the mound was going to do to him was amazing. He'd say, "I'm going to sit on a changeup this whole night. He's going to throw it to me. You'll see. My third pitch will probably be a changeup." I'd be sitting there—dang, he got that changeup on the third pitch.

We hit in the same group [in batting practice] for a year or so. I actually started acting like I was Edgar when I hit right-handed. "I'm doing my Edgar Martínez tonight!" He would explain why he held his hands where they were, that he felt like from that position he could go inside-out a ball, before it was vogue to say, "I'm going to inside-out a baseball." Be able to manipulate the field by having his hands here. He had that little rock at the plate, so I'd start doing my Edgar Martínez against a lot of left-handers that would sink the ball away. It allowed me to do that.

JOHN McLAREN
Mariners Coach, 1993–2002, and Manager, 2007–08
One thing I really observed during my time was opposing teams watching Edgar take batting practice. They wanted to watch his routine, how he went through BP. They tried to study his stroke.

NORM CHARLTON
Former Mariners Pitcher
Edgar was like EF Hutton on those Mariners' teams. He really doesn't talk a lot, but when he does speak, young or old, you probably need to listen. When something needs to be said, when someone needed to take a stand with the front office, he was definitely willing to do that.

In 2001, when we were in the playoffs and they were talking about not letting the wives go on the charter and were going to make them fly commercial after everything that had gone on, we were saying, "That's probably not a good idea."

They said, "Well, our policy is, wives are never allowed on the plane." First of all, we haven't made the playoffs that often. Second of all, the policy probably changed after 2001, when we lost two buildings in New York.

Edgar was one of the guys who went into the office and said, "Things are different right now." He didn't have to go. A couple of us could have handled it fine, but it's always nice to have a guy like Edgar on our side.

At the end of the year, the Mariners picked up the option on my 1999 contract, so that worry was lifted. At one point, I thought there was a chance they might trade me or pay the $150,000 buyout that would have made me a free agent. They had a few guys, like Jay or Russ Davis, who could have been moved to DH. It was a relief to stay put. Right after the year, though, I had another surgery to clean out my left knee. I was 35, and I knew that I was much closer to the end of my career than the beginning. I figured that the 1999 season might be my last, or maybe one more after that. It turned out, of course, that I played until 2004, but I pretty much went on a year-to-year basis from that point on. What I really wanted to do was win again and get us to a World Series. That's what kept me coming back.

We finished under .500 again in 1999 at 79–83, but it was an important transition year for the organization that set the stage for some great times to come. One significant change for the Mariners came on July 15, 1999, right after the All-Star break, when we moved into Safeco Field, our beautiful new stadium. And the other move that had far-reaching implications—positive ones—occurred shortly after the season on October 25, when Pat Gillick was hired as general manager. Woody Woodward had retired in September.

Initially, I had mixed feelings about Safeco Field, and I wasn't alone. We all loved the facility. It was beautiful, the clubhouse and training areas were great, all that was wonderful. But a hitter is a hitter. He wants to hit under the best conditions. He doesn't care how it looks. We were thinking, "Oh, man, it's going to be hard to hit here. This is not going to be the Kingdome." For all the other structural problems with the Kingdome that made it necessary for the Mariners to move, it was a fantastic place to hit. It was always 70 degrees, the ball carried, and the dimensions weren't imposing. The hitter's mentality was, "Aw, man, I wish we had the Kingdome still."

The previous year, while Safeco was under construction, they let some us take batting practice there a couple of times, and it kind of jolted us. The ballpark seemed huge, to the point that many of us players expressed concerns to the Mariners. I knew how poorly the ball carried outdoors in the Northwest, having played in Tacoma and Vancouver. I wasn't so much worried about myself, because I was a doubles hitter. But we were a team built, at least at the time, around home runs. I wondered, along with everyone else, how much the new stadium would sap our power. I thought it was too big. Griffey joked that I might get 90 doubles in that park and even a couple of triples because there was so much space in the outfield. But we all had doubts about how many home runs would be hit there, especially by right-handed hitters.

It turned out some of our concern was unnecessary. The dimensions that were portrayed to us during the BP sessions—which were as far as 422 feet to a part of left field—were only hypothetical and still under review. By the time the ballpark opened, they had cut that massive alley down from 422 feet to 409. Still, Safeco Field was no longer a hitter's paradise like the Kingdome had been. That took some adjustment. So did dealing with the wind, and the "marine layer" that kept the ball from flying. The glare in center field was a big problem for hitters for the first couple of years, too. But the fact that the new ballpark was like a country club—everything first class—made it a lot easier to accept.

Over the years, I think Safeco definitely got in some players' heads, especially before they moved in the fences prior to the 2013 season. It can be frustrating, especially for right-handers. It can affect some guys when you crush a ball and you're positive it's going to be a long home run, and it gets caught at the warning track. That happened to all of us. You have to have the mentality that your objective is to square balls up and not try to hit home runs. That's when things go bad. When you start trying to hit home runs, what happens is that not only don't you hit home runs, but your average goes down. It's a double whammy. The other thing is, when guys are struggling to hit home runs, they'll try to pull the ball. Another mistake. That doesn't work very well. A better approach is to work the middle of the field.

The weird thing is that I took to Safeco Field right away. In 41 games in 1999, after we moved in at midseason, I hit .394 at the new place (on the way to a final average of .337, fourth-best in the AL). And in the first full season we played at Safeco, 2000, I hit the most home runs of my career, 37. That's the only time I ever exceeded 30 homers. It was eight more than my highest total when the Kingdome was my home ballpark. That helped me lead the league in RBIs for the only time in my career with 145. That was the most in history for a player 37 years or older. I surpassed a guy named Babe Ruth (137 at age 37 in 1932).

I don't think it was the ballpark so much as the fact my swing just clicked that year, starting in spring training. I lifted more balls. My swing just felt nice and easy, very consistent. Most years, I hit a lot of line drives. That year, for some reason, I was squaring them the same way but they had the distance.

Today, they call it "launch angle." I had no idea what that was in 2000. But it was very consistent. I preferred to win the batting title over hitting a lot of home runs, so it's like I was shaking my head over so many balls in the air. At the same time, we didn't have Junior anymore. It helped the run production in the middle of the lineup, so I was okay with it. One thing about that year—it put on hold any thoughts I had about retirement. "Sometimes when you get older, you wonder how long you're going to be able to do it," I said. "When you perform and help the team, it makes you feel you can play for a few more years."

The Mariners quickly realized they needed to fit their personnel to the ballpark, and our new GM, Pat Gillick, was a master of that. The first issue he had to deal with immediately when he took over was what to do about Griffey and A-Rod. Both of them were entering the final year of their contract in 2000. Pat's path became clearer over the winter when Junior asked for a trade, which occurred on February 10, just before spring training.

The key player for us coming from Cincinnati turned out to be Mike Cameron, who took over for Griffey in center field. I won't say "replaced," because no one could ever replace Junior. But Cammy was an outstanding player who could really patrol the outfield and put up some good numbers at the plate, too. In one of his first games at Safeco, he robbed Derek Jeter of a home run and started to win over the Seattle fans. Eventually, he became a fan favorite, and it didn't take him long to become a clubhouse favorite, too.

It was amazing how quickly, and how well, Pat revamped the team, despite losing a superstar like Griffey. Every acquisition worked out perfectly, which just doesn't happen. He signed Kazuhiro Sasaki from Japan to be our new closer, and he saved more than 100 games his first three years. John Olerud was signed to play first base and was around .300 every year with solid production. Free agents Mark McLemore and Stan Javier were valuable players for us in multiple roles. Arthur

Rhodes helped solidify the bullpen. Aaron Sele was signed for our rotation and won 17 games.

In late May, Pat picked up Rickey Henderson, who was 41 and near the end of his career. But he could still play. Rickey still had a knack for getting on base and stole 31 bags for us in just 92 games. And he was Rickey Henderson! A legend. I always loved watching him play, and I couldn't believe we were on the same team. He was a cool, funny guy, always joking around and laughing, but serious about his preparation. I heard the story about how, when he got to the Mariners, Rickey saw Olerud and said, "You know, I played with a guy on the Mets that wore a batting helmet in the field, too." Of course, it was John. I'm not sure Rickey really said that, but it's still funny.

I was lucky enough to make the All-Star team again, and it was fun to have my son, Alex, on the field with me for introductions. Playing at Turner Field in Atlanta, I lined out to center field on the second pitch I saw as a pinch-hitter off Bob Wickman in my only at-bat. I'd decided I was going to be aggressive and swing at anything close. But the interesting part was that I took part in the Home Run Derby for the only time in my career. I had declined an invitation in 1996 in Philadelphia, but this time, in my fifth All-Star Game, I decided to give it a shot. It's a lot harder than it looks. I hit two home runs and was eliminated in the first round. As I said afterwards, "Boy, I was tired by my fifth swing!" I felt better when Chipper Jones and Vladimir Guerrero also finished with two homers, and Pudge Rodríguez had only one. Sammy Sosa ended up winning the title, beating Junior in the final round. The Home Run Derby was made for Junior—he won three times and once hit the warehouse behind right field at Camden Yards, the only person ever to do that. I was in awe of both guys watching them drive so many out of the park.

263

Another memorable moment in 2000 occurred in late July when I got a bases-loaded single in the bottom of the 13th inning to end the longest game in Safeco Field history (in both innings and time: five hours and 4 minutes). Then I quickly showered, hustled out of the clubhouse, and headed across town to ride in a float as the grand marshal of Seattle's Seafair Parade. I was a little late, but everyone understood.

Later, near the end of the season, I had an emotional moment when I played in my 1,536th game, breaking Griffey's record for most games as a Mariner. When the game became official in the fifth inning, the crowd gave me a long and warm standing ovation when I arrived in the on-deck circle as they showed a highlight video of my career. "We call Alvin Davis 'Mr. Mariner,'" Dan Wilson said. "I don't know what you would call Edgar. Maybe 'Sir Mariner' and 'Señor Mariner.'" The best part was that Holli sang the National Anthem before the game— and did a great job.

My favorite moment of 2000, though, was an opposite-field grand slam at Safeco to win a game over the Yankees on August 29. At the time, I called it "one of the biggest hits of my career," because it pulled us out of a terrible slump—13 losses in our previous 15 games that had nearly allowed a playoff berth to get away. But we went 20–11 after that to earn the wild-card berth in the American League (just a half game behind the A's in the division, after we'd led the division most of the year). That stretch included an eight-game win streak in mid-September after Lou called a meeting of about 10 veterans to tell us to relax and have fun. It helped put things in perspective after a couple of tough losses. "At times, especially losing times, it's like you don't have a life outside the park or the game," I told reporters. "We had to pull back some, lighten up, look at the big picture."

Going into the playoffs, I said I liked our chances better than our last postseason trip in 1997. We were more patient and had a better bullpen, along with better chemistry. In fact, I called it the best Mariners' team I had ever played on. We swept the White Sox in the opening round of the playoffs, in which I put up a .364 average and hit a tie-breaking homer in the 10th inning of the first game. But we dropped the ALCS to the Yankees in six games, giving up a 4–0 lead in the clincher to lose 9–7. That was frustrating—another shot at the World Series slipping away—but the way our team was gelling, it felt like we were on the verge of something even greater.

The next year, after Alex signed with Texas during the off-season, Gillick kept on tweaking and refining our roster. Jeff Nelson and Norm Charlton returned to shore up the bullpen even more. But the two huge additions were second baseman Bret Boone and a mysterious player from Japan named Ichiro Suzuki. That season was just astounding from the start. We became the first team in MLB history to win 20 games in April—and then won 20 more in May. We put together a 15-game winning streak midseason and wound up winning the division by 14 games, despite the fact Oakland won 102. We clinched a playoff berth on September 3—with 24 games still to play.

Did anyone see 116 wins coming? I'd be lying if I said yes. Most people figured we'd battle with the A's and Rangers for the division. Before the season, Pat Gillick compared us to the Super Bowl champion Baltimore Ravens—built around our defense and pitching. I remember in spring training, Lou said, "We're not going to hit a lot of home runs. We're not going to win with offense. We just have to play the game right and do the little things." In spring training, I remember there were bunting stations. The focus was on execution. That sat in our minds. We understood that we didn't have a lot of room to make mistakes, and we took that mindset and focus into the season. All year long, our execution was nearly flawless.

To have lost Randy during the 1998 season, Junior after the 1999 season, and Alex after the 2000 season—and then rack up 116 wins the very next year, well, that's hard to fathom. Our CEO, Howard Lincoln, said at one point, "The more I see, the more I am convinced that there is no connection between superstars and winning." I just know that Gillick found the perfect blend of talent.

The word I can come up with is "balance." We had power and speed, left-handed bats, right-handed bats, left-handed pitchers, right-handed pitchers. Everything was balanced—personality-wise, skill set. McLemore and Javier gave us great flexibility, two switch-hitters who played different positions and were actually good at it. They could sit for a few days and come back and do their job well, steal a base and play good defense. It was just a great fit all around the diamond, and Lou made it all work in harmony. I believe that winning leads to good chemistry, not the other way around, and this team was a perfect example.

I've got to say a few words here about Ichiro, right? He had been in our camp as a guest a few years earlier while playing for the Orix Blue Wave, but got food poisoning and didn't get to do much. No one knew quite what to think of him at first when he showed up in 2001. We knew he had won a bunch of batting titles in Japan and was a huge star, but we weren't sure if that would translate to the major leagues. I'll admit, I was skeptical at the beginning.

Early in spring training, he was hitting everything the other way, on the ground. I remember Lou got a little frustrated. One day Lou challenged him to pull the ball. He said to Ichiro, "Can you just give me an appetizer?" Ichiro crushed a home run over the right-field wall.

When he got back to the dugout, Ichiro said to Lou, "Are you happy now?"

One thing I learned quickly about Ichiro: he had a reason for everything, including the way he prepared for the season. He didn't talk much, so the communication wasn't there. If it was someone else, you could just pull him aside right away and say, "Hey, why do you do that?" Maybe then you'd be able to say, "Okay, that makes sense." But he was quiet, all business. It took a while to unravel the mystery that was Ichiro. And when I did, I gradually realized that he and I have the same kind of narrow focus. Both of us had the ability to tune out the noise and focus on the task in front of us. Between Moyer, Olerud, Ichiro, and myself, I saw that type of mentality on that team. It was like, I'm going to be here for eight hours, so focus on what needs to be done, develop a routine to make it happen, and stick to that routine.

When Ichiro came back to the Mariners in 2018 while I was hitting coach, we had more communication than I ever had when I was his teammate. His English is a lot better now—really good. But at the very beginning, back in 2001, I was questioning whether this experiment would work, just like Lou. Our attitude was, "Okay, let's see what you can do."

It didn't take Ichiro long to show us. On Opening Day, he started the winning rally against Oakland with a drag-bunt single, and it just took off from there. Along with Boonie, who had a career year, Ichiro was the difference in turning a good Mariners team in 2000 to a great one in 2001. When you have someone at the top of the order who could do what Ichiro did—hit .350, steal 56 bases, disrupt both the pitcher and the defense—it completely changes the whole picture. You know that guy is going to score a ton of runs. He's going to force the pitcher into more mistakes because of his speed. But even when they made a perfect pitch, Ichiro could beat out a slow roller, or sometimes even a routine grounder. He's a distraction on the bases, too, so they could never relax. He put so much pressure on the other team. In fact, Ichiro is what we needed on the 1997 team. We had all those guys that could hit the ball out of the ballpark. A leadoff hitter like Ichiro would have been huge.

We haven't even talked about Ichiro's defense. In one of our first series against Oakland, he threw a laser from right field to gun down Terrence Long, who was trying to advance from first to third on a single. But as our announcer, Dave Niehaus, put it, Ichiro's throw was like something out of *Star Wars*, right on a rope to third baseman David Bell for the out. That was something you never forget. You see a bunch of guys make good throws, and you say, "Okay, eh, good throw." But when someone makes a throw like that, and you see the difference in the way it comes out of his hand and how it travels and gets to the base, that sticks in your head. I know one thing: not many people ran on Ichiro after that.

Our whole team that year just had a great vibe. Cameron was a perfect fit, a fun personality and one of the entertainers on our team. He was a tremendous outfielder and had a ton of clutch hits. If someone was going to replace Junior, he was ideal. Boonie, after I challenged him in spring training to not just settle for okay numbers, had a one-of-a-kind season in 2001. He put up a .331 average, 37 homers, and 141 RBIs—plus being one of the best second basemen I've seen. It made him feel like he could be a big part of the team, which was natural with his personality. The thing about Bret, he was also the ultimate team player, and he gave everything he had on the field. He wanted to be out there, wanted to be in the tough situations.

John Olerud was a very quiet guy, not flashy at all, but you could see he had a lot of confidence. What I remember is that every at-bat for John was a quality at-bat. He'd see a lot of pitches and never chase. It seemed like he never swung through the ball; he always made contact. He'd foul balls back, but you didn't see many empty swings. Oly was a natural great hitter who knew his strike zone, constantly made contact, and used the whole field. His style just fit really well with our lineup, and it was great for me to have him hitting behind me. John was someone I learned a lot from just by watching. And I can't leave out Dan Wilson, who was the mind behind the success of our pitching staff. At the beginning of the year, we weren't too sure about our pitching, but we ended up with four starters with 15 or more wins. Dan was a huge part of that.

DAN WILSON
Former Mariners Catcher

We had a team full of veterans. I think what designates '01 is we all had specific roles. As veterans, we understood what our role was. We just went out each night and did it. Everything was covered, so it was just harmonious in a way. Our bullpen had the exact same thing. It was Rhodes for the lefties, Nellie for the righties, and Sasaki to close. Everything just fell into place. Our roles were so distinguished. McLemore was a utility guy and he played a lot, he spelled guys, and he appreciated his role. Even guys like Stan Javier, who was sort of the utility outfielder and would play sparingly, understood that and was comfortable with that. And did really well at it. Everyone had a role. It just kind of moved along.

In fact, we won the "Triple Crown" in 2001, leading the American League with a 3.54 team ERA, a .288 team batting average, and a .986 team fielding percentage. Only four teams in history had done that. We scored the most runs in the league (927) and allowed the fewest

(627), for a plus-300 run differential. That's how you finish 70 games over .500.

And if we hadn't lost our last game of the season to the Rangers, 4–3, we would have been the winningest team in baseball history. That would have also been the case if we had held a 12–0 lead over Cleveland in early August. Instead, we suffered one of the greatest collapses in major-league history and lost 15–14 in 11 innings. It was one of those games where you kept saying, "It's okay, we're going to be okay," and then, "Uh, oh, this shouldn't be happening."

As Norm put it, "It was like cutting your fingernail and bleeding to death. We couldn't stop it." But then we won our next three games. It seemed like nothing could stop our roll.

It was just amazing—one of those years where we didn't have any major injuries, we executed all year, and everyone played up to their capabilities. My year got off to a good start when I got a one-year contract extension in spring training that took me through 2002, with a team option for 2003. Then I had eight hits in my first 10 at-bats of the season. I went on to hit .306 with 23 homers and 116 runs batted in, despite a stint on the disabled list for a strained left quad in July, right after the All-Star break. It wasn't hard driving in runs that year with Ichiro and the rest of the guys always on base.

After a while, we started to believe we were going to win every game. Our motto became, "Two outs... so what?" We never felt we were out of it. We just rode that wave and had a great time at the ballpark. The peak moment was the All-Star Game, which just happened to be played that year at Safeco Field. The weather was perfect, the crowd was wildly enthusiastic, and the Mariners put eight players on the team. Myself, Ichiro, Olerud, and Boone all were voted in as starters, and Cameron, Kaz Sasaki, Jeff Nelson, and Freddy Garcia were named to the team by the AL manager, Joe Torre of the Yankees. To make things even better, Joe named Lou to his coaching staff. It was just a magical night. In the first-pitch ceremony, they had five Hall of Famers from five different countries. I got to catch Tony Pérez, a Cuban who had starred in winter ball in Puerto Rico and was a favorite of my grandfather's.

I remember how exciting it was when Ichiro led off against Randy Johnson—and beat out a grounder to first for an infield hit. It was Cal Ripken's 19th and final All-Star Game. He wound up hitting a home run to lead our AL team to a win and was named the Most Valuable Player. Cal was voted as the starter at third base, but in the first inning, Alex moved over to third and let Cal play shortstop, his original position. It was just a beautiful night, all the way around. Even Alex, who had been roundly booed earlier in the year when he came back to Seattle for the first time with the Rangers, got cheers as an American Leaguer on this night.

In every way, 2001 was shaping up as a magical season. We sold out the ballpark almost every night on the way to drawing 3.5 million fans. It felt like Seattle had turned into a true baseball city.

But everything changed, obviously, on September 11. We were in Anaheim, having racked up our 104th win the night before, when word began to spread of the attacks in New York. I got a call in my hotel room early in the morning from Ron Spellecy, our traveling secretary, telling me to turn on the TV, because the U.S. was under attack. Just like everyone else, I couldn't believe what I was watching. I immediately called Holli, and we talked about how terrible it was. I checked on my family that still lived in New York—the city of my birth. An uncle who usually worked near the World Trade Center happened to be off that day, traveling to Pennsylvania. Everyone else, including my father and sister, were safe, thank goodness.

You didn't know if you were watching a movie, or if it was real. It took a while to believe it was true. As a team, we were stranded in Anaheim for three days before we were finally cleared to fly home to Seattle. They had called off the games and halted baseball—rightly so— for a week. All we did was watch television to see what was happening. Everything felt so out of place and strange. It didn't feel like we were in the middle of the season. That mindset of following your routine, and of your focus constantly being on the game, just kind of disappeared. The games were no longer foremost on our minds—at least that was the case for me.

I know it's trivial compared to what it meant for the country, but the tenor of our season changed. The jubilant feeling that had marked our crazy success faded out. Everyone's mind was on what was going to happen next after the attack. It felt almost like the meaning of winning so many games wasn't as great, or as enjoyable. It was clouded by everything that was going on. I imagine that unconsciously affected our team and the momentum we had built up. Even when we came back and started playing again, the state of the country, and risk of more attacks, was the main concern.

I reached a milestone of great personal significance when I hit the 441st double of my career to surpass the total of Roberto Clemente, who meant so much to me and to Puerto Rico. But my reaction was subdued, because of the circumstances. As I told reporters just before the season resumed, "The season is kind of secondary right now. And it should be. Everyone is thinking about the people who died in New York and everywhere else. I know a lot of people in New York. I feel for those people going through such a bad time."

For the rest of the year, there was a lot of tension every time we went to a hotel. You'll remember that about that time, there was an anthrax scare, a fear that letters laced with anthrax were being sent out around the country. Well, when we got to New York for the ALCS in October, I checked into my hotel room and found a letter under my door. It looked to me like the handwriting was similar to what they had showed on TV on the anthrax letters. It had my name on it, which was odd, because I always use an alias when I check into a hotel on the road. How would anyone know I was there?

I called the security agent who works for MLB, a former FBI agent, and he told me not to pick it up, he would come and get it. He came to my room and picked up the envelope. I assume it wasn't anthrax, because I never heard back. But I wanted to be extra cautious. I never, ever had a letter under my door before. And the fact that it had my real name—the whole thing was kind of scary. Maybe someone was just playing a joke on me, but I didn't want to take any chances.

We clinched the division title in our second game back after 9/11 with a 5–0 win over the Angels at Safeco Field. No one felt it was appropriate to have the normal wild celebration in the clubhouse with everyone pouring champagne on each other. Instead, we had a heartfelt ceremony on the field where we hugged, kneeled on the mound, and observed a moment of silence. Then we walked around the field with an American flag held by Mark McLemore—a spontaneous moment that kind of symbolized what was important. It was very moving. When we got to the clubhouse, we had our champagne—a brief toast and then a sip out of plastic glasses. I said afterward, "I think we felt satisfaction for a special year, for doing things as a team that don't often happen, this kind of record and all. But thinking of that, we had to think of the people who died and their families."

Frankly, that break after 9/11 stifled our momentum a little bit. And heading into the postseason, the momentum switched to the

Yankees. It seemed like everyone was pulling for them because of all their city had gone through.

We got by the Indians in five games in the first round, although we needed to win our final two games to stay alive. I hit a home run to help us win Game 4 in Cleveland, a two-run shot in the ninth off Paul Shuey that I called my best swing of the season. It might have been the longest ball I ever hit, an estimated 458 feet. I had an RBI single late in the clinching game, a 3–1 win behind Moyer. Ichiro hit .600 in the division series with 12 hits, tying my record from 1995 against the Yankees (and surpassing my record .571 average that year). We played those games without our shortstop, Carlos Guillen, who was sidelined with, of all things, tuberculosis. The Yankees defeated the A's, also in five games. So for the second year in a row, we played the Yankees for the American League pennant.

The difference this time is that the Yankees, despite winning the past three World Series titles, felt almost like an underdog. They were the sentimental favorite. Whether or not that transferred to the players and provided extra motivation, leading to some of their comebacks in the games, I don't know. It might have, subconsciously. I just know that the energy was different in that series.

We lost the first two games at home, and Lou caused a commotion by guaranteeing that we would return to Safeco Field. That meant we had to win at least two at Yankee Stadium. That was classic Lou. He had total belief in our team. I remember before the first game at Yankee Stadium, he gave us a fiery talk. We still felt we could take the Yankees. The way we had played all year, we didn't have any doubt. We just had to play our game, do what we had done to win 116 games.

It just didn't happen, though. We won the first game in New York, but then let an eighth-inning lead get away on a Bernie Williams homer. We lost on a walk-off home run by Alfonso Soriano. The Yankees clinched the next night in a 12–3 rout. They out-executed us for the entire series. Case in point: we didn't score in the first three innings in any game in the series, so we always seemed to be playing from behind. We were 0-for-17 with runners in scoring position in our losses. I remember how they pitched to Ichiro, throwing at his legs and trying to make him jump. He had just four hits in 18 at-bats for a .222 average. Our team average was .211. I hit .150 (3-for-20) after putting up a .313 mark against Cleveland. Those Yankees teams just knew how to win (although they would lose the World Series that year in seven games to Arizona).

"You know, they play human all summer, and then in the postseason, they turn it up a notch," Lou said.

We weren't the same team we had been all year, when we won 21 more games than the Yankees in the regular season. Jay summed up our feeling: "This organization has come a long way since Lou came here, and we keep getting close, but we can't get that one out, or that one pitch, or whatever. It's very frustrating."

Bret added, "I think after the great season we had, we felt we could do a bit more in the postseason. Now, all you feel is, I don't know, empty."

DAN WILSON
Former Mariners Catcher

I think there was a combination of a lot of things. I think 9/11 was certainly one of those things. A lot of us were veteran players, a lot of us had families. I think it was a strange time. It made us circumspective in a lot of ways. It was different. That definitely had a role. Going to New York right afterwards certainly had its role. Winning the first game back, everything was kind of odd from that point on. But that's not an excuse. It just felt different. It's a shame. It's the one thing I wish, that we had been able to take it a little deeper.

It was a tough blow. All that success, all that fun all year that we thought was finally pointing us toward the World Series, and we came up short. It's like you forget about everything that happened. The 116 wins don't mean as much. Looking back, that should have been the year. That was our most balanced team. For most of the season, we had the momentum, and we had the expectation we were going to win. When you have expectations and it doesn't happen, that's when it hurts the most.

The good news is that we felt we had built the team to eventually knock that door down. But 2001 turned out to be the closest we would come.

Chapter 11

Walking Away

I'M VERY PROUD OF the fact that I played my entire career with the Seattle Mariners. My contract came up numerous times, and I could have become a free agent. But I always told my agent, Willie Sanchez, that I wanted to stay in Seattle, and to find a way to get it done. To be honest, I couldn't see myself playing or living anywhere else—at least not by my choice. If the Mariners had traded me, as was rumored to be in the works on many occasions, that would have been one thing. But to leave by my own decision, well, I always pushed that idea away.

But on one occasion, I came as close as I would ever come to at least entertaining the thought. It was at the end of the 2002 season, which was a really disappointing one for me and the team. Coming off our 116-win season, we were all pushing hard to not only get back to the playoffs, but take that next step. Instead, after getting off to a 17–4 start, and leading the division most of the year (by as much as 6½ games in May), we faded down the stretch and finished in third place. Despite winning 93 games, the second-most in franchise history, we ended up 10 games behind the A's and six games out of the wild-card.

We didn't make a trade at the deadline when our offense was struggling, which was frustrating to everyone, including me. "I see every other team getting their team ready for the last couple of months," I told reporters. "They're getting some help to make it to the playoffs. Sometimes it is a little frustrating when our team can be improved, and we don't make a move." We ended up fading in September with a six-game losing streak that included a four-game sweep by the last-place Rangers in Texas.

On a personal basis, it was an extremely frustrating year. It was also tinged with sadness, because Jay Buhner had announced his retirement at age 37 after the 2001 season. Jay meant so much to the Mariners, and so much to me, but his body just wouldn't let him continue. He had missed most of 2001 with a torn tendon in his arch, and much of 1998 because of Tommy John surgery. Jay joked that he needed two more operations—on his knee and shoulder—just to retire. Jay left a tremendous void on our team, both on the field and in the locker room. As I said when he announced his decision, "Jay is our leader. He has come through in so many key situations. When you get to know him, he really cares about people. He's willing to help anyone at any time. He's a great friend of mine."

Jay was a Mariner for 14 years, all of them overlapping my time with the ballclub. He came from the Yankees in 1988, and together we went through the ups and downs of trying to break into the starting lineup. And together, we also went through the ups and downs of the Mariners, including a lot of ups starting in the 1995 season. Many of the key players left, like Randy, Junior, and A-Rod. We didn't go anywhere.

But at age 39, I was thinking more and more about when I, too, would have to walk away. I knew I wasn't quite ready yet, though. When someone asked Jay why Seattle had adapted so well to the two of us, he said, "Gar will tell you the same thing: Who knows why we're still around? We were just the lucky two that lasted through it. I think a lot has to do with the way we play. We go out and play the game right. No matter what you think about me or think about him, you have to respect the fact we go out and play every day, play hard and leave our guts on the field."

JAY BUHNER
Former Mariners Outfielder

Edgar was one of the best teammates ever. Over the years, I'd watch him and the way he went about his business. His work ethic was off the charts. Edgar was a workaholic, always the first to come and last to leave. You never heard much from him. He spoke with his bat. Every time you looked around, he was in the batting cage or weight room. I learned more from watching how hard he trained when I thought I was pushing myself. I'd watch him and know I had to push it to the next level. But the greatest part of Gar as a teammate wasn't just what he did on the field, which was great, but the way he carried himself, his professionalism, what he did in the community. That was a special time—but he was a special player.

Not taking anything away from anyone. Look back at Junior and Unit and A-Rod—those guys all basically would do mega-damage and put up stupid numbers. It was like Nintendo baseball. But when Gar went into the on-deck circle, people took notice. "Oh, crap." Ask any pitcher. If it was a situation where you had to pitch to him, and you couldn't pitch around Gar, I guarantee they were saying, "Oh, crap." You knew Gar was going to make contact and put the ball in play, and nine times out of 10, he would square the ball up.

Edgar had a quiet presence in the clubhouse. He was really good at sitting down and talking to guys. He would say something like, "Hey, dude,

I've been watching you. You're not quite getting your foot down in time. Forget everything else and do that." He made things so simple. He was so good at watching guys and figuring out what could help them. Edgar didn't say much, but when he said something, you knew it was important and took it to heart. He soaked up everything like a sponge. Gar and Junior were both like that. You didn't think they were paying attention at times, but they were seeing everything.

Gar had some definite red-ass to him, too, like the boom box in spring training. It got everyone's attention. Or the beanball war we had with the Angels. [Angels manager Mike] Scioscia always drilled him. Then he snapped and tried to go after Scioscia. David Eckstein tried to hold him back. Edgar always called him Einstein. He said, "Get the hell off me, Einstein."

At the end of the day, there's not enough things I can say to eloquently talk about what a great pure hitter he was. The ultimate compliment is, you talk to any pitcher, especially the Hall of Famers, and they'll tell you flat-out they didn't want to face him. The pitcher would have to grind, grind. Edgar might not always come through and get a hit, but for the next guy up, with the pressure points, it made it easier because of Edgar's battle. Pitchers might subconsciously relax and let down after getting past Edgar. Those are the things that don't show up on paper, but a lot of us reaped the rewards of Edgar Martínez.

He knew his swing so well, he could make a correction in the middle of an at-bat. It was one thing to do it in the middle of a game; but an at-bat? No one did that but Edgar. His strength was middle or the other way, but he had power foul pole to foul pole. He was able to foul off bastard pitches until he got the one he wanted. And let's not forget his eye condition. People had no idea what he went through because of a very serious lazy-eye-tracking situation. If not for Dr. Nikaitani, it could have ended his career much earlier. He'd always make these weird noises at the plate, and then he'd start taking his left hand and hit his eye to get it to stop doing the crossing. Then he'd go back up and square the ball up. To do all that without a lot of technology to get better, it's amazing. Bleeping amazing. The game's hard enough, and he's playing with a serious eye condition and no wheels. And wearing people out.

Other than missing Jay and his antics, spring training was good in 2002—especially the day Muhammad Ali showed up at our training facility in Peoria and spent time in our clubhouse. We all stood and gaped at him in awe—including me. I told Lou I might be late for the game.

The season started off fine, too. In the 10th game of the year, I scored my 1,063rd run to surpass Griffey for the franchise record. "My on-base percentage helped, not my speed," I had joked earlier in the week when I tied the record.

With a sixth-inning double in that game, I was just starting to get my swing in a groove. And then, in my final at-bat of an 8–4 win over the Angels that gave us a four-game sweep of the series, I hit a ground ball to third base. As always, I busted out of the batter's box. On the way down the line, I felt a pop in my left hamstring—the same pop, in the same leg, I felt in 1993 in Vancouver. That injury, remember, had pretty much wiped out the season—a terrible, painful, frustrating year. My left leg was never quite the same after that, with my hamstring flaring up periodically over the years. But with treatment and training, I was able to keep it in check—until now.

I knew I was going to be out a while. I just hoped it wasn't as serious as the one in 1993. I was encouraged that in the morning I could walk with just a slight limp. Last time, I had needed crutches right away. But no such luck. It was actually worse. It turned out I had ruptured the hamstring tendon behind my right knee, and I underwent surgery a few days later. Dr. John Conway, the Texas Rangers orthopedic specialist, did the operation. It was a relatively new procedure that he had also performed on football players with the Dallas Cowboys and Kansas City Chiefs. In the old days, they used to just wait for the injury to heal. But instead Dr. Conway removed the semitendinosus, the smallest and farthest outside of the three tendons that make up the hamstring.

The recovery was supposed to be four to six weeks. Rubén Sierra, my old teammate in Puerto Rico, had been signed in the off-season by the Mariners and did a great job stepping into the DH role while I was out. Also while I was out, Mike Cameron bashed four home runs in a game against the White Sox on May 2 in Chicago, just the 13th player in history to do that.

Meanwhile, I worked hard on rehab to try to get back as quickly as I could, and everything was going smoothly. I was ahead of schedule, in fact. But just a few days before I was going to be activated from the DL, I was taking batting practice. On one of my final swings, I felt a sharp pain and had to be helped out of the cage. Dr. Pedegana said I had just broken loose some scar tissue, nothing serious, but my comeback was pushed back at least another week.

I knew from experience that just because everything was feeling good in practice, it didn't mean it would keep going smoothly. Sure enough, I got myself back on a path to come back again, only to have another setback when they had me run the bases for the first time. It just didn't feel right, so the Mariners put me on the 60-day disabled list. That meant that it would be June 11, at the earliest, before I could play.

As frustrating as that was, I felt better about my recovery than I did in 1993. That year, the hamstring tendon never stopped bothering me. This time, my initial thought was that I didn't know if I could even come back from this injury. But once the tendon was removed, I actually felt good—I just needed to get stronger, which I gradually did. But because of my age, the original timetable of four to six weeks was unrealistic. As usual, I probably pushed it too much.

I finally came back on June 14, after missing 55 games. And we were on a National League road trip at the time, so I was limited to five pinch-hitting appearances for the first week. Lou was ready to put me in the starting lineup when we returned home to Seattle. But in my final pinch-hit appearance, playing in Cincinnati, I tweaked my hamstring again and was sidelined for another week.

I flew to Dallas to see Dr. Conway, who had performed the surgery. He told our trainer, Rick Griffin, he had never seen so much buildup of scar tissue in a patient. I kept breaking through that scar tissue, which caused short-term pain. I hoped it wouldn't be a problem all season. "The doctor told me he's performed the surgery on 11 athletes and I'm the only one that had the muscle move like it did last week," I told a reporter. "It must be a Puerto Rican kind of muscle."

Luckily, the adhesions finally stopped pulling loose. I returned to the lineup on June 27, my first start since I hurt myself on April 11— and hit my first homer of the year. It only took me until Game 78. The crowd at Safeco gave me a standing ovation on my first at-bat, which was very emotional. I almost lost my composure before I pulled myself together. "I tried to stay composed," I said afterward. "I was faking it."

I was able to make it until the end of the year, but it was a struggle. I had to be very careful on the basepaths, because I didn't want to pull it again. In one game, we faced a pitcher with a high leg kick and Lou said everyone but me had the green light to steal.

"Edgar didn't even have the amber light," he said.

Someone said they cringed every time I churned down the line, and I said, "So do I." I was only half-joking. I wound up hitting .277 with 15 homers and 59 RBIs in 97 games—my first time under .300 since 1994. My slugging percentage (.485) was under .500 for the first time since 1994, too. I did manage to put up a .403 on-base percentage to run my streak of .400-or-better to eight seasons.

There was a rumor in late July that I was retiring. It even made ESPN. I don't know where that came from but I wasn't ready to stop playing. The farther removed I got from the injury, the better I felt at the plate. I felt like my leg wasn't going to be a big issue for me. I definitely wanted to come back in 2003.

The ballclub had a choice, though—an option on my 2003 contract for $10 million. If they didn't pick that up, I would become a free agent. Realistically I didn't expect them to pick it up, considering that I was going to be 40 years old and was coming off a major injury. But I was hoping we could work out something that was fair for both sides to bring me back in 2003. If not, I would have a tough decision. On the one hand, I really wanted to get to the World Series, and I felt I could still be productive. I was also 27 hits away from 2000, but that wasn't a huge factor for me. I knew that my son, Alex, was eight and at a critical age where he needed more interaction with me. I wasn't sure I wanted to go somewhere else to play.

"I want to do all I can to secure my family's future," I said. "As long as I can produce on a ballfield I will do that for my wife and kids. You can make a lot of money in this game but if you're not careful it could be gone in 10 years or 20.... But you can't buy time, and when you play it costs you time with your family, important time."

The reporters started asking me if I could see myself playing with another team if the Mariners and I couldn't get a deal done. Moyer, Wilson, and Olerud were also heading for free agency, so it was going to be a complicated winter for the Mariners to come up with enough money for all of us. "If I don't play here, I have to really think whether I want to play somewhere else," I said. "I really don't know at this point."

On the last day of the season in Anaheim, Lou let me carry out the lineup card, just in case it was my last game. "I don't know if they're trying to tell me something," I told the umpire.

At the end of the season, I had a meeting with general manager Pat Gillick and other executives to let them know I wanted to be back. They didn't give me a decision on my option, but I know they had other things to worry about. Lou was in the process of deciding whether or not he was going to come back as manager for the final year of his contract. I was really hoping they could work things out, because I loved playing for Lou. I felt he was the driving force behind us becoming a winning team and making the playoffs. I was the only guy on the team who remembered what it was like before Lou got there, and how we were never contenders. From the moment he arrived, you could see: this team was going to win at some point with him in charge.

In the end, though, Lou decided to leave. He said he wanted to be closer to his family in the Tampa area, particularly his elderly father. On October 14, the Mariners released him from his contract, and a week later Lou signed a four-year deal to be manager of the Tampa Bay Devil Rays. The Mariners received outfielder Randy Winn as compensation. Lou joked, "In my 10 years in Seattle, the Mariners never got a left fielder for me. Now they got a left fielder for me."

Lou's departure was a jolt to all of us. And all of a sudden, on top of my not having a contract yet, there was new element of uncertainty to deal with: Who would be the Mariners' manager in 2003?

We kept talking to the Mariners but couldn't reach a deal. Finally, it came to November 6, the final day before I had to declare free agency. Still no agreement, despite negotiating into the evening. I went out to dinner with Holli and I remember telling her, "I'm not going to sign this contract." For the first time in my career, the negotiations got to a point where I thought their offer wasn't fair. It was more on principal. I said, "If I have to go, I have to go. And if I don't get a job with anybody, that's what it's going to be." I was prepared for that. I told Holli I was probably going to be a free agent, and we probably would have to go to another city. Or maybe I wouldn't even get a contract.

When I awoke the next morning, I thought I was about to become a free agent for the first time. But I got a call from Willie, my agent, saying they had reached an agreement. Basically, I was a free-agent overnight. The deal included incentives that could make it worth $10 million for 2003, which is the amount my option was for.

WILLIE SANCHEZ
Agent

I've got to admit, the Players Association didn't care too much for me. They always wanted me to up the ante with Edgar's contracts. But I thought, some ballplayers just fit a certain city. Others don't care who they play for, just show me the money. He wasn't that way.

The Yankees were very interested the last few years when Edgar could become a free agent, and we leveraged that. It was the only time Howard Lincoln and Lee [Pelekoudas, assistant general manager] got mad at me. We had a very good relationship. Negotiations were difficult, but we always came to an agreement.

That time, though, we said we're going to declare free agency. You know the Yankees want him and that's where we're going to go. Lee and I used to play golf together. We had a great relationship. But he got mad. He called me a few names and threw the phone.

I called Edgar and said, "I think tomorrow we're going to declare free agency."

It wasn't 30 minutes later, Lee called me and said, "Okay, you SOB, you've got your money."

I said, "Lee, you know he deserves it."

Edgar was going to end his career with Seattle, the way he wanted. And Seattle didn't want to let him go.

I thought the contract was fair, and I was relieved. I would be back for a 17th season in Seattle. Certainly, there were no hard feelings over the negotiations. Howard Lincoln, the Mariners' CEO, said at the press conference, "We just had to get it done. I didn't sleep well when we didn't get an agreement, and I'm sure Edgar didn't either."

Well, that was true. "I didn't feel comfortable," I said at the press conference.

Now I was excited for spring training to start what I thought might—emphasis on might—be my final year. I believed my leg had healed well enough that it wouldn't give me problems. I thought our team, coming off a 93-win season, was going to be a contender again. All four of our potential free agents—Jamie, Dan, Oly, and myself—had re-signed with the Mariners. Winn was a nice addition, and so was reliever Shigetoshi Hasegawa.

The one thing we didn't add was a front-of-the-rotation pitcher, although Pat tried hard to sign José Contreras. The year before, we had nearly signed Jason Schmidt, but he chose the Giants, even though our offer was higher. Similarly, we had been unable to make a major acquisition at the trade deadline the previous couple of years, which was frustrating in the clubhouse. It felt like it was hard for the team to get the player we needed for years. We would talk about it and say, "Why can't we get the right guy?" But I learned over the years that it's not that easy to swing the right deal. It can be tough. At that time, however, it was frustrating to us, the players, because we felt we were so close.

A week after I re-signed, we found out who our manager was going to be: Bob Melvin, who had previously been the bench coach of the Arizona Diamondbacks. He was with the Diamondbacks when they won the World Series over the Yankees in 2001. Bob was low-key, quite a contrast from Lou, but I liked him a lot. Even though he was very calm, he was also very well-prepared. Bob was young, just 41—only 15 months older than me! (And only 13 months older than Jamie). He had never managed other than the Arizona Fall League, but he related well to the players.

Bob's attitude was that we, as players, know our role, and as long as we did it the best we could, he was okay with it. I remember early in spring training, I was walking between the field and the cage, and he pulled me aside. He told me that whatever I needed to do to prepare, go ahead and do it. There was a drill going on, and he said that if I needed to go to the cage instead, he was fine with that. That was nice to hear. Essentially, he was saying from the beginning that he trusted me, and trusted that I knew what I needed to get ready for the season. I appreciated that.

BOB MELVIN
Former Mariners Manager
Shoot, I'm a .230 lifetime hitter. Edgar is one of the greatest right-handed hitters of all time. I'm going to come in and give advice? I was young

manager. There were certain guys I wanted to let do their thing in light of the success they'd had, and he was at the head of it. I leaned on him more than he leaned on me.

I don't know how much has been said about his eyes, but when I was there, it was so bad. He was constantly having to do eye stuff. To be successful despite that is still amazing to me. It was amazing enough to put together the resume he did with 20/20 vision; to do it with his eye condition, it even makes the legend more remarkable to me.

I was there at the end of his career, and it was bad as it ever was, especially the last year. At times you'd see pitchers spinning curves at him to get him to duck out. The Angels did that quite a bit. They'd throw a breaking ball at him that would break over the plate and go after him that way. He would sit up there until two strikes and hit it up the middle for a hit. I was uncomfortable. I brought it up with the training staff. They wouldn't let him go out if he was in harm's way.

Edgar wasn't the most vocal guy in the world, but his actions spoke volumes. If he felt like he needed to say something to somebody, he'd do it quietly, without a lot of fanfare. I appreciated a guy like that willing to help out. He was not just concerned with himself, but the team. It's rare to get a guy like that. I've been doing this a while now, and there's only a handful of guys that even compare to Edgar and what he meant to a team.

I remember we were trying to bring Ellis Burks in to play for us. Edgar's a guy when you're recruiting somebody, you can use him as a resource. I remember telling Ellis, look, I know you're not a younger guy, but spending a summer with Edgar is like spending a summer with Picasso if you're an art major. There's not many guys you can learn from like him. That resonated with Ellis. He didn't end up signing, but he did a double take. He thought long and hard. That's how much impact Edgar Martínez had.

Bret Boone thought that we might have worn down chasing the wins record in 2001, which led to our second-half fade in 2002. We were determined not to have a repeat in 2003—but it happened again. We moved into first place on April 14, and kept at least a share of the lead until August 27. I made the comment that the feeling on the team was similar to 2001, and for a while it was. We were winning with pitching one day, defense the next, and hitting the day after. Our confidence was growing. Our lead grew to as big as eight games on June 13, which is about the time we ran off 11 wins in 12 games.

But after going a season-high 27 games over .500 at 76–49, we had a stretch where we went 14–20 to fall out of first place. Once again, we won 93 games, but all that did was get us second place in the division, three games behind Oakland and two games behind Boston in the wild-card. It's too bad MLB didn't go to two wild-card teams until years later, or we would have made the playoffs in 2003 and had a one-game playoff with Boston in 2002.

But that's not the way it worked. I was disappointed, because one reason I came back to play another year was to get that shot at a title. Personally, my year was satisfying after all the injury problems in 2002, and how discouraged I felt after surgery. To come back and be productive again after what I went through, well, there had been times I wasn't sure that was going to happen.

I made the All-Star team (for the last time), voted in as the starting DH, and hit 24 homers with 98 RBIs. I'm never completely satisfied if I don't hit .300, though, and I wound up at .294. When August ended, my average was at .303. But I hit .250 in September after I fouled a ball off my left foot on August 23 in Boston and suffered a stress fracture in my left big toe. The injury caused me to change my stance and swing pretty much flat-footed. Then I re-aggravated it by fouling another ball off the same spot.

Despite that, it was still a good year overall for me. I had a scare in April, when in the sixth game of the year I strained my left hamstring running out an infield hit in Texas. That forced me to miss my first home opener since 1994. Luckily, I avoided the disabled list, but one consequence was that I had to really be extra careful on the basepaths so that I didn't aggravate the hamstring. There were times I simply was unable to score from first base on a double, and I felt really bad costing guys an RBI. But I wanted to stay in the lineup, and Melvin and the medical staff urged me to show caution on the basepaths. The doctors had explained to me that because of the surgery in 2002, I lost one of the muscles in my hamstring. The two remaining muscles were taking a bigger load. That meant I had to work even harder to strengthen them.

I stepped up my training even more, but I still tried to be smart on the basepaths. Even when I felt good and I was tempted to push it, I realized that I couldn't. That's when I got myself into trouble. I got removed for a pinch-runner in the late innings a lot of times that year, which I understood. It was frustrating, yes. But I wasn't frustrated with Melvin. I was frustrated with the situation. Later in the year, I legged out an infield grounder and aggravated my left calf. I kept learning the lesson the hard way that no matter how good I thought I felt, I had to hold back on the bases.

My days of playing in the field were also pretty much over. That meant that every interleague road series meant a long stint on the bench. And then when I came back, it would take a while to get my rhythm back. As I said during one series, "I've never liked interleague play and I never will. I don't know if it's good for baseball; I only know it's not good for Edgar Martínez."

JAY BUHNER
Former Mariners Outfielder

Another amazing thing about Edgar, he was doing all this with no wheels. He could run a little early in his career, but we were not known as fleet of foot, him and me. He was not getting a lot of infield hits, and his legs got worse and worse. You could play the banjo on his frickin' hammies. But he worked his butt off. He took pride in all aspects of his game. The last thing he wanted to do was not score on a double and take an RBI away. That's why he was always in the weight room, always stretching, trying to get himself ready and prepared to the utmost of his ability.

A great day for me occurred on May 2, 2003, when I recorded the 2,000[th] hit of my career in Chicago against the White Sox. It was a line-drive single to left field off relief pitcher Gary Glover in the sixth inning. We won 9–2 and the team had 16 hits, so that made me feel even better. Considering the way my career started, and all the spots along the way where it looked like I might not make it—and then all the injuries—2,000 hits was something I never thought would happen. I felt a lot of pride.

Mike Cameron had a nice quote about me that day: "He's like a tree stump in the middle of our lineup all the time. It's kind of like having an inspiration with you all the time. It doesn't matter how tough the pitcher is, Edgar is going to battle him and, as often as not, hit him."

Some pitchers, of course, were tougher than others. Like Pedro Martínez, for instance. He called me the "toughest guy" he faced in his career. I felt pretty much the same way about him. On MLB Network, Pedro talked about how I would make him "throw at least 13 fastballs above 95 [mph]. I would be hard-breathing after that. Edgar was a guy who had the ability to foul off pitches, and it pissed me off when I had to throw 13 pitches to get a guy out."

That was very flattering, of course. But in 33 appearances against Pedro, I had just three hits in 25 at-bats with no extra-base-hits, seven walks, and 11 strikeouts. I did try to battle against him, though. He threw all his pitches for strikes. He elevated, he had great command, he threw 96, 97, and also had a great changeup. I didn't try to pull Pedro. I just fought. It was a fight with him. All my at-bats, it seemed, went deep in the count. It wasn't like I was grounding out on the first pitch. I just remember a full at-bat of fighting. I never could guess what he was going to throw. Pedro was very difficult to predict, so he was one of those guys where I'd be ready from the first pitch to just battle. If I didn't get a hit, at least I'd make him work.

Another really, really tough at-bat early in my career was Nolan Ryan. By the time I faced Nolan, he was already in his forties, but he still threw hard, with a really good breaking ball. I went 1-for-19 with 10 strikeouts off Nolan, so that tells you the kind of success I had—very little. Pitchers who threw from the angle he did—over the top—I generally had trouble with. And then you throw in the kind of stuff he had, I had a hard time squaring the ball up. Since my swing was inside-out, I'd foul balls off and be behind in the count. I'd try to make adjustments, but it didn't work with him.

Roger Clemens, who won seven Cy Young Awards, was the pitcher I faced more than anyone else in my career—108 plate appearances. I had pretty mixed results—a .245 average with four homers, six doubles, and 11 RBIs, with 16 strikeouts and nine walks. At the beginning, when he would get me out, I remember saying, "I see the ball well." But he had that angle, too—over the top—and I would foul balls off and get behind in the count. Later, he got that split-fingered fastball, and I had trouble hitting him. He would go more up and down with the split. That was the pitch I had the most trouble with. That, and knuckleballs. Tim Wakefield and Charlie Hough—they owned me.

I was glad I didn't have to face Randy Johnson very often. First, he was my teammate, and then he went to the National League. I had just four at-bats in my career against him, and got two hits, with a strikeout. That doesn't count the 2001 All-Star Game in Seattle, when he struck me out. As Junior did, Randy went out of his way to tout me for the Hall of Fame, which was much appreciated. He said, "Edgar Martínez is, hands down, the best hitter that I've ever seen. I'm glad I didn't have to face him too much. Having seen him play from '89 to all the way when I left, I got to see him a lot against great pitchers. Like I said, hands down, he is the best pure hitter that I got to see on a nightly basis. And I hope that his time comes soon, that he gets a phone call stating that he's a Hall of Fame player, because he is."

With Randy, you had to be ready from the get-go, just like with those other guys. He had a really good slider. So I thought to myself, I'm not going to wait for that slider. I would tend to swing early in the count. That slider down and in had good action, and he could throw it both sides of the plate. Randy was a really tough at-bat. He would come inside, too.

In fact, all those guys I was just talking about had an element of intimidation that helped their success. One thing in baseball I could honestly say: I never had any fear going into the batter's box. I don't remember one time saying, "Oh, this guy is scary. This guy is going to hit me."

For some reason, it never crossed my mind, and that was helpful. On the other hand, I was hit 89 times, tied for 132nd most in MLB history. I think it's probably because I use the other side of the field.

That caused a lot of pitchers to come inside. But that never made me feel gun-shy or back down.

Speaking of which… at the All-Star Game that year at U.S. Cellular Field in Chicago, I was beaned in the helmet on a 90 mph fastball by NL starter Jason Schmidt. I guess it looked bad, because I went down on the ground. But it just glanced off my helmet and I was fine. The trainer came out and checked out my vision and memory. He asked me to name my wife and son. I guess I passed, because I stayed in the game. I batted twice more and struck out both times, against Kerry Wood and Woody Williams.

"Edgar assured us he was fine," AL manager Mike Scioscia said after the game. "But I told him afterward, I don't know if you're fine because you swung through two pitches, and I've never seen you swing through two pitches."

We did make one trade-deadline deal in '03, and I was happy with it. When Carlos Guillen was injured, we acquired Rey Sánchez to play shortstop. He was my Dream Team teammate in Puerto Rico and a solid, dependable player. He did well for us, too, hitting .294 in 46 games.

I was at the stage of my career where statistical milestones were beginning to arrive. In August, I hit my 486th double to tie Lou Brock and Billy Herman for 49th on the all-time list. But I was never aware of my numbers and records until someone told me. Those kinds of things weren't my focus. I was still intent on getting better every day and improving my batting average—the one statistic that I did focus on.

Two decisions loomed as our 2003 season ended in another disappointing fade. One was whether Pat Gillick would came back as our general manager. The other was whether I would come back and play in 2004.

I liked Pat a lot and really respected the way he built our team. We had one blowup at the end of the 2003 season, which got a lot of attention, but I certainly had no hard feelings at all toward Pat. We had just lost a 4–0 game to the Angels that pretty much ended our chances of making the playoffs. The game lasted just two hours and seven minutes, and we made a lot of mistakes. Pat was angry with the way we played. He thought we had mailed it in. It was the last game of the road trip, so we were getting ready to catch a plane back to Seattle. In the clubhouse afterward, Pat ordered our traveling secretary to move up the departure time for the team bus by 15 minutes. That left just five minutes to dress, pack, and catch the bus, and a lot of guys weren't ready. That didn't sit right with me, and I said, loudly, "What's the hurry?"

He replied, "What was the hurry to lose this game today?"

I yelled back, "This team has busted its ass all season—all season!"

Eventually, we calmed down. I was just really frustrated with the way the season ended. He was frustrated we didn't make the playoffs. We were both coming from the same place, actually. It wasn't fair to him for me to say the things I did. I wasn't attacking him; I was just trying to stand up for our guys. We went through a lot during the year, and we played hard. The team was committed, and those guys were all trying to win. It was just a reaction, and not fair to Pat.

I apologized to him afterward. It was out of character. Usually, I just hold those things inside. I don't know why I spoke out then. It could have been that it was getting closer to the end of my career. I wanted to get in the playoffs and go to the World Series and all that so bad. I kept seeing those chances slipping away. The frustration got the better of me. Usually, I just don't let things bother me, and I keep my mouth shut. This time, I kind of snapped. Pat told me he was glad I spoke up. He said he knew we had busted our tails this year. He just felt we had not been focused in that game. He said, "I understand how you feel, but you have to understand, I want to win, too."

I was disappointed when Pat decided to step down after the season. Lou leaving last year, and Pat this year—those were big losses for the organization. He was 66 years old and at the end of his contract. Pat said that after four tries at getting the Mariners to the World Series, it was time for someone else to take a shot. Someone asked him at his press conference if the incident with me in Anaheim had a bearing on his decision.

"No, not at all," he replied.

I told a reporter, "If it was a sign of anything, it was that Pat still has passion for the game, still is driven to win."

And I added, "One of my top things is I want to win, and Pat Gillick was a guy to help you win. It hurts to have him leave because I think he was a big part of our success."

Now I had my own decision to make. As always, I sat down and discussed it with Holli, and I included Alex, too. He was nine and his input was critical as well. Tessa was just 19 months old at the time, so a little too young to have an opinion. Even though the Mariners fell short, I had enjoyed the season and the fact we stayed in contention all year. I felt my health was still more or less good. Even though I was just three homers away from 300 and nine doubles short of 500, those weren't big factors. It was more about whether I felt I could still be productive and help the team. I wouldn't be happy just chasing numbers.

I fell short of .300 in 2003, but I still finished fourth in the American league in on-base percentage at .406, seventh in walks with 92, and had the second-best batting average with men in scoring position at .352. Overall, it was a good enough season to convince me to come back for another season.

One way you could go is to quit while you're still reasonably close to the top of your game. But it's really hard to walk away when you know you can still play. And also, when you've played baseball since you were a kid, and still enjoy it. After giving it a lot of thought, I decided, "I can still play. I can still hit. I can still do a good job. So why not go back and play another year?" We discussed it extensively as a family during vacations in Arizona and Florida, and everyone felt good about the decision.

On November 4, two months before my 41st birthday, I signed a one-year contract with the Mariners to come back for my 18th major-league season. The negotiations once again went down to the wire, but we reached an agreement before I had to declare free agency. At my press conference, I said I was truly undecided when the season ended. But I couldn't think of a good reason to step away.

"It's hard to sit at home knowing you can compete and play, and you sit home retired," I said. "I didn't want to feel any regrets. That was one of the key parts of the decision, to make sure I'm not going to have any regrets."

I was pretty sure that 2004 was going to be my last year, but I wasn't ready to commit to it. If I had a good season and the team won, I might change my mind.

Bill Bavasi was named the Mariners' new general manager, and Paul Molitor was chosen as the new hitting instructor. He replaced Lamar Johnson, who was let go after the season. Paul would be the ninth hitting coach of my career, and I was excited to be working with him. When I heard he was being interviewed, I told Melvin, "What are you waiting for?" Paul had 3,319 hits in his career and would be elected to the Hall of Fame just a few weeks later. Considering Molitor spent just under 50 percent of his career as a designated hitter, his election was thought by some to give hope to me when my turn on the ballot came around. Paul accurately forecast my long quest for the Hall when asked about my chances.

"Edgar's been hurt somewhat by injuries, like I was, but he's gotten more productive as he's gotten older. I don't think being a designated hitter will keep him out. The question is whether his accumulation of numbers over time will satisfy voters. He keeps climbing certain ladders as far as hits and other milestones. His performance is Hall of Fame material. Whether he's borderline or how it bears out, we'll have to see."

PAUL MOLITOR
Hall of Famer and Former Mariners Hitting Coach

One of the highlights of my year in Seattle was getting a chance to be around Edgar on a day-to-day basis. He was one of the few right-handed hitters that I played against that I would intentionally get out to watch him work batting practice, just to see how he went about it. I thought he had one of the better approaches of any right-handed hitter I had played against or seen during my time in the major leagues.

Just to watch him go about how he tried to prepare even though he was winding down. How he thinks about hitting. To me, we get way too consumed with mechanics as opposed to just having a plan against a certain pitcher, how you're swinging, how they're throwing, and going up there and giving yourself the best chance.

So I marveled at what he was able to do for a long time, and to spend that season with him and being around him was really one of the highlights for me. I remember talking to him about his younger days and how he ended up being the type of hitter he was. I talk to guys today even about Edgar and those people that really knew how to let the ball travel and take advantage of the whole field. And somewhat unexpectedly, you'd think you'd have him

Edgar: An Autobiography

set up for something on the inside of the plate, and he'd hit it over the left-field fence. He was a guy who really could slow down his at-bats. He was a really tough two-strike hitter. He had the ability to lay off tough pitches. He'd put the ball in play and give himself a chance. A little better health along the way and we all know he could have done greater things.

I don't think anyone ever felt like they had a real good idea on the best way to get Edgar out. It was a constant need to change speeds and locations and stay away from patterns, because he would capitalize on all those things. People didn't watch him in batting practice because he hit them 500 feet. It was the craft, the crispness. I watch guys today [as Minnesota Twins manager], sometimes subconsciously keep track, and we have guys that have trouble hitting .300 in batting practice. Edgar, you watch him, and most of the balls that come off his bat, it's with a purpose, from his first swing of the day to the time he wraps up his day of work. I just think he understood how he could give himself the best chance each and every at-bat he went up there. And it played.

Prior to the 2004 season, we made a couple of nice free-agent signings—outfielder Raúl Ibañez and reliever Eddie Guardado (who became our closer when Kaz Sasaki went back to Japan). We tried hard to sign Miguel Tejada and almost brought back Omar Vizquel. We had agreed to a trade with the Indians, Vizquel for Carlos Guillen, but Omar failed his physical so that deal was called off. Instead, we signed Rich Aurilia to play shortstop.

We thought we had another contending club. But the 2004 season just didn't go as hoped or expected, for either the Mariners or for me. I had worked harder than ever to get ready for the season. I knew that at age 41, I had to. I hit well in spring training—.382 with a team-high 21 RBIs. Someone figured out that in my career I hit .360 in the

Cactus League in over 900 at-bats—roughly the equivalent of two full major-league seasons—with 73 doubles, 45 homers, and 214 RBIs. That was a by-product of keeping myself in shape over the winter, and a lot of years of playing winter ball, so I came to camp ready to hit. And, let's face it, it's easier to hit in Arizona. The ball travels well, and you're facing a lot of minor leaguers.

Once the 2004 season started, though, I could feel my age, more than I ever expected. How does that show up? You lose bat speed. You lose strength in your legs, and for me that was a big deal. My legs are where I got my power, as well as my bat speed. It just didn't feel the same. Not necessarily weak, but weak enough I could feel the difference. My vision was faltering as well. I couldn't pick up the spin of the ball like I used to. I could still hit the fastball pretty well, but the breaking ball was giving me trouble—especially as it got darker at night. So, of course, teams were throwing me almost nothing but breaking balls.

I was hitting .300 on April 28th, but then I fell below and kept dropping. It just wasn't feeling the same. Oh, there were a few good days mixed in. The best one, probably, was May 7, when I hit the 500th double of my career as well as the 299th homer to drive in four runs in a 6–2 win over the Yankees at Safeco Field. It all happened in front of the biggest crowd in Safeco Field history—46,491. They tried to give me a curtain-call after the inning I hit the 500th double, but I had gone inside the clubhouse to find a new bat to replace one I had broken earlier. I didn't even know about the ovation. I apologized after the game—I felt terrible. I nearly hit my 300th home run in that same game, but my drive to left field in the seventh inning was caught at the warning track.

Dan Wilson called it "vintage Edgar"—but those games were coming more infrequently. One was a few days later, in Minnesota, when I hit my 300th career homer off Brad Radke with two aboard. It wasn't as enjoyable as the 500th double, however, because we lost the game, our fourth straight. I knew—because everyone kept telling me—that I had become just the sixth player since 1900 with 300 or more homers, 500 doubles, 1,000 walks, a .300 batting average, and .400 on-base percentage. The others were Stan Musial, Rogers Hornsby, Babe Ruth, Lou Gehrig, and Ted Williams. Those names really hit me. What kept me in the minors so long was that people thought I didn't have enough power to play third base. To have numbers on a par with legendary hitters like that was immensely gratifying.

Still, I hit just .227 in May, and .229 in June. My lower back was really bothering me, to the point I had X-rays in late May. As the season progressed and I continued to struggle, I slowly realized, "Okay, this is not going to improve. This is going to keep getting worse."

Meanwhile, the team was struggling as well. We lost our first five games of the season, and by the end of April we were mired in last place at 8–15. We never got out of the cellar and finished 63–99, 29 games out of first place. Just four seasons after winning 116 games, we put up the worst Mariners season since 1983. That played on my mind, too. In June, we traded our ace, Freddy Garcia, to the White Sox for three young players. It reminded me of the kind of deals we used to make early in my career, when the team wasn't going anywhere. It wasn't a good feeling, especially since going into the season we honestly thought we had the talent to make a run for the playoffs.

Early on in the year, I decided that this was definitely going to be my last season. If we were playing better, maybe it would have been different. But that conclusion began to crystalize in my head.

And I was okay with it. It would have been tougher if I had said after 2003, "I'm not going to play." Then I'd always wonder. Instead, I got that confirmation that, "Yeah, this is it." It was a sad thing, sure; but it was a good thing for me, too. There were no regrets at all.

On August 9, I announced at a press conference that I was retiring at the end of the year. I decided it was better to end all the speculation about my future. This way, I would be able to soak in the final seven weeks of my career. Even though I felt comfortable with the decision, it was still emotional. I choked up several times as I was explaining my decision.

"It is hard, very hard," I said. "I feel in my mind and my heart I want to keep playing. But my body is saying something differently, so I feel this is a good decision."

At the time of the announcement, the Mariners were 41–70, and my average was at .258. I would wind up hitting .263 in 141 games, with 12 homers and 63 RBIs. It was the worst full season of my career. I struck out 107 times—the only time I ever went over 100.

"I've proved to myself that I won't be able to play anymore," I said.

Yet I felt great about my career. I felt great about the fact that I did it all in Seattle, while watching a lot of other players—great players—come and go. At the time of the announcement, I had played with 355 of the 508 players in team history—70 percent. I could just never see myself playing in another uniform. I was proud to be a lifelong Mariner.

One of the few people who stayed in Seattle that whole time was Dave Niehaus, our great announcer. He called it one of the saddest days of his career when I retired. I'll always be linked to Dave because of his classic call of my double in 1995:

"Right now, the Mariners are looking for the tie. They would take a fly ball, they would love a base hit into the gap and they could win it with Junior's speed. The stretch... and the 0-1 pitch on the way to Edgar Martínez. Swung on and LINED DOWN THE LEFT-FIELD LINE FOR A BASE HIT! HERE COMES JOEY, HERE IS JUNIOR TO THIRD BASE, THEY'RE GOING TO WAVE HIM

IN! THE THROW TO THE PLATE WILL BE... LATE! THE MARINERS ARE GOING TO PLAY FOR THE AMERICAN LEAGUE CHAMPIONSHIP! I DON'T BELIEVE IT! IT JUST CONTINUES! MY OH MY!"

I was so sad when Dave died in 2010. I remember near the end of the 1994 season he came to the back of the plane and we talked about the team and what we needed to do to take the next step. You could tell how much it meant to him, and the passion he had for the Mariners. And Dave had such a great skill to call the game and convey the excitement to the fans. Every time I hear his call of the double, I still get chills.

I was totally at peace with the decision to retire. Holli was pregnant, with our third child due in February. It was a good time to be home with the family. The team was clearly going to be in transition, and I wasn't prepared to go through another rebuilding phase. Mostly, I realized that I couldn't compete the way I used to, or the way I needed to. Before, I could always make a mechanical adjustment whenever things weren't going well. But with my leg issues and now my back as well as my eyes, no mechanical adjustment was going to help.

"Retirement was an ongoing conversation over the last three years," Holli told the *Seattle Times*. "Edgar would come home at times very frustrated by some physical limitation, and we'd talk about it again. But he loves the game, and that love always convinced him to keep on trying. Yet this year has been tough on everyone, and I think Edgar decided it was time. And I think there's 100 percent peace with that decision."

I remember watching Jay go through this exact situation two years earlier. That's when I really started thinking about what it would be like for me.

"Baseball is magic," I said at the press conference. "You feel sad when a player retires. But you feel good for them, too. They don't have to chase any more sliders."

Of course, I had nearly two months to go. And a few more sliders to chase. But there were some good moments, too. For the next 24 games after I made the retirement announcement, I hit .349. Maybe getting it out in the open cleared my mind.

In my first game after the press conference, Melvin moved me up to third in the order, to ensure I'd bat in the first inning. He wanted me to get an ovation, which I appreciated. They ran a tribute video on the scoreboard. Then I stepped up and somehow managed to hit a home run. Melvin called it "storybook" and said he had goosebumps the size of oranges. I kind of felt the same way. I joked that I had changed my mind about retiring. We won the game 4–3, with rookie Bucky Jacobsen getting a two-run home run as well.

The Mariners had called up Bucky, a big first baseman who was tearing up Triple-A in Tacoma, in July. This was after they'd released John Olerud, another sign that an era was ending in Seattle. Bucky was hitting .312 with 26 homers in just 81 games for the Rainiers. Naturally, they wanted to take a good look at him to see if he was going to be in their plans next year. Bucky was having knee problems, so the most logical place to play him was DH.

Melvin felt bad whenever he held me out of the lineup, but I totally understood. I wasn't going to be part of the future. Bucky, who was 28, might be. I wanted to help him out as much as I could. Bucky was a good kid, and you could tell he had a lot of power. He used the whole field and had a good approach. I tried to help him out by giving information about certain pitchers, or advice on routines. Bucky put up good numbers—a .275/.335/.500 line with nine homers in just 42 games—but unfortunately he needed knee surgery after the year and never made it back to the majors.

BOB MELVIN
Former Mariners Manager

That was very uncomfortable. When you're around long enough, you deal with guys who are legends that are at the end of their career. At some point in time, you have to go give someone else an opportunity. Where we were that season in the standings had a lot to do with that. If we were in a different position like the year before, Bucky wouldn't have had the same opportunity.

Those are very difficult. It's one thing when you have a guy as good as Edgar was. It's another thing to have a guy who is such a big personality and such a big part of Seattle, and toward the end of his career. Like I said, it's very uncomfortable. But that's an organizational decision, not just the manager.

Edgar didn't make it hard. I don't know that he was comfortable with it, but he never made any waves. There was not anyone on that team that in big situations I felt better about than Edgar. But at that point, we knew he was retiring. We had to look at Bucky.

BUCKY JACOBSEN
Former Mariner

That year was the first time I got a big-league spring training invite. I remember coming into the locker room in Arizona. I was getting ready to play for the team I grew up cheering for in Oregon. I remember looking to my left and seeing Edgar Martínez. Oh, my gosh. One of my idols. I walked away and wandered around to find my locker. I figured it was on the other side of the room. I walked through the entire room, and sure enough, it was right next to his. I introduced myself and said, "My name is Bucky. I want to let you know I'm a huge fan. I've been watching you play my whole life. It's crazy my locker is next to you." He was super cool, just like Edgar always is. He was putting pine tar on his bat. I was just in awe of him.

As we went through spring training, I remember watching him hit, paying attention to him in the cages, and trying to pick up stuff he was doing. I didn't talk to him too much. I knew I was a non-roster invitee. I wasn't making the team. I hung around guys my own level. Spring training was fun, but I was not a peer as much as a dude who got to practice with his idols.

When I got called up right after the Triple-A All-Star break, at this point my locker was not next to him. The veterans all had their spots, and there were extra lockers for the new guys called up. I remember the first game I played first base and he was DHing. I was in his hitting group. I'm taking BP with Ichiro and Edgar. What in the world is going on? Again, he's just Edgar, the coolest guy. I don't know why I thought he'd be anything different, but it was a surprise to me how cool he was, how he treated me as a teammate, rather than a guy who had his baseball card as a kid.

I remember I hit my first homer in my second game. He was on first base. I hit a pitch six inches off the inside corner, over the left-center-field fence into the bullpen, off CC Sabathia. As I'm rounding second, I'm thinking, I've got to remember that swing. It might be the best swing I've ever taken. Usually, I hook that ball foul. I was on cloud nine. Before the inning was over, I was standing on the railing watching the game. A buddy of mine took a picture from the front row—it was Edgar after he came up to me and put his elbow on my shoulder and said, "Bucky, how did you hit that pitch to left-center?" Wait, is this literally the best inside-out hitter of all time, in my opinion—maybe him and Jeter—really asking me how I got to an inside ball? I was in a weird daze. This was the Twilight Zone.

My memory is not that great, but anything I did with Edgar, I'll never forget. I remember watching him in BP. The last round, he'd have the guy throw in, in, in. He wanted to get inside it and hit it like the double that saved baseball in Seattle, and have it slice back fair. Most guys barrel-whip it and hook it foul. I asked him about that, and for the rest of my life, my hitting life, I tried to do that. My first big-league bat order was for Louisville Slugger M356. The M stands for Martínez. It was a big barrel and thin handle, which I liked. But there was a part mentally that I got to use the same style as Edgar Martínez. I went so far as to copy the bats he was using.

As the season went on, my knee was jacked up. I had been DHing in Triple-A, and by that time Edgar was straight-up DHing, so only one of us could play. Earlier, there had been a bunch of times I'd show up and look at the lineup, and quite a few times my name was in the lineup and Edgar's wasn't. He would take ground balls at first, and I told him one day, "Hey, Papi, to see my name and not yours, I don't necessarily feel I deserve that."

He said, "Don't worry about it. I've had a long career. You do you. Don't worry about me. I've got everything taken care of."

The next day was a day off, and I was walking through the mall. I saw a TV in the Rainforest Café, and it said, "Edgar Martínez retires." I'm like, "What?" I went in and asked them to turn up the sound. They said he was retiring at the end of the season, not now.

The next day at the yard, Melvin pulls me into his office and says, "We want to get you into the lineup, but we've got to get Edgar in the lineup, too, especially when we're home. Can you play first?" I said, put me in anywhere. He told me to tell him if the knee gets too bad.

In my head I was saying, "I'm never going to say my knee's not good." For the rest of the year, I'd DH on the road and play first when we were at home. That didn't last very long, though. They shut me down for surgery in September.

That same buddy that had taken a picture of me standing at the plate hitting my first home run also got a picture of me crossing home plate, my foot just about to touch, with Edgar standing with both hands up for a high 10. The next picture is him with his elbow on my shoulder. The last day of his career, I brought those in and asked him to sign them.

It says, "Many more to come. Your friend, Edgar." It's a prized possession. It hangs on the wall at my house. He was a super cool guy. I was actually taking at-bats from him. He knew his time was coming, but he treated me better than I could have ever expected. We were from different generations, not boys, but he treated me like a peer. I don't consider myself one, but for him to treat me like one, it speaks volumes to how good a guy he is, in addition to being a Hall of Famer and one of the best to ever swing a bat.

Even though the Mariners were mainly trying to avoid 100 losses in 2004, there was another drama going on to distract us all. Ichiro was making a strong run at one of the biggest records in baseball—most hits in a season. George Sisler had set the record with 257 in 1920, but 84 years later, Ichiro was on pace to break it. As someone who never reached 200 hits in a season, I had a great appreciation for the accomplishment. Especially with the way pitching was changing. Teams were going more and more to relief specialists. Everyone you saw from the bullpen was throwing harder and harder. From the sixth inning on, you were seeing different pitchers every inning, and sometimes batter to batter. It was amazing to me Ichiro was able to accomplish that feat under those circumstances. To succeed at that level, you have to know yourself really well. You have to know your swing. You have to be consistent and disciplined. And all that is what Ichiro is.

I had mixed feelings during the final stretch of the season. I tried to enjoy everything, soak it all in, but when you're not producing the way you think you should be, it's hard. Especially when the team is losing so much. At times, I didn't want it to end. Other days I'd think, okay, I'm ready for this to be over. It was back-and-forth with my thoughts. I was struggling a little bit with what was happening.

But there were some good things that happened, too. Every ballpark we went to for the final time, they made an announcement to honor me or presented me with a gift. That was heartwarming. When President George W. Bush came to Seattle for a fundraiser, he told our team president, Chuck Armstrong, he wanted to meet with me. So I went to Boeing Field and had a nice visit with the president, which was an honor. I had met his dad at the All-Star Game in San Diego in 1992. President Bush congratulated me on my retirement. We exchanged signed baseballs and took a picture together.

When Jay Buhner was inducted into the Mariners' Hall of Fame in August, I caught his ceremonial first pitch. Playing with Jay was one of the highlights of my career. The way he played hard every night, and played through injuries, he showed all of us the way to play the game.

It was only fitting that I had one final injury of my own to play through. In mid-September, I fouled a ball off my right big toe and fractured it. The surprise was that it wasn't on my left foot, since every other significant injury I had in my career was on my left side. There was some fear they would have to shut me down, which meant I would have to retire early. But after missing five games, I was able to go until the end.

On our last flight into Seattle, after playing in Oakland in the final road game of the year, the flight crew hung a big sign inside the cabin that said, "Thanks for the memories." En route, the team had a champagne toast for me, with Melvin and Boonie saying a few nice words. I got on the PA system in the plane to say a few words of appreciation myself. And because of my interest in aviation, the pilots invited me into the cockpit for the landing. They helped me bring the plane down, which was cool. The plane taxied through an arch of water created by an airport fire truck. Vulcan Air, the charter company, had painted "Edgar Martínez, No. 11" on the side of the plane.

"Does this mean I get to keep it?" I joked.

The whole thing was very touching. The players gave me a very nice send-off gift—a trip to Europe, and a case of French wine. That was just the start of an amazing weekend.

The Mariners had scheduled Edgar Martínez Day for Saturday, October 2, the next-to-last game of the season. Meanwhile, Ichiro kept gunning for Sisler's record. For a while, it looked like the two events might converge. When we began the final homestand of the year on Friday, October 1, Ichiro was at 256 hits—one shy, with three to play. If he went hitless in that game, it was possible it could happen on Saturday. But Ichiro, fittingly, rose to the occasion on Friday night. He tied the record with a single his first time up, a ball that hopped over the head of Texas third baseman Hank Blalock. His next time up in the third inning, Ichiro hit the ball hard to the left of the second baseman and into right field. No. 258!

We all streamed onto the field to congratulate him, and Ichiro went over to the stands to honor the members of George Sisler's family in attendance. His daughter, three grandsons, and one great-grandson were on hand. It was a thrilling moment. Later in the inning, I singled Ichiro home with what turned out to be the final RBI of my career. In the eighth inning, I got another single, off Travis Hughes. It was the 2,247th, and final, hit of my career. We won to ensure we would not lose 100 games—which meant something to us.

I'll admit, I kind of liked that all the furor over Ichiro's record diverted the attention away from me. My concern was that I not get too emotional on Saturday, so I'd be able to get through my speech. I wanted to make sure I showed appreciation to all the people who meant so much to me over the years. Family, teammates, friends. I didn't want my emotion to get in the way of doing that.

It turned out to be a wonderful day, full of touching surprises. And, yes, it was emotional. The only disappointment came in the fifth inning, when I came to the plate with the bases loaded. It would have been nice to come up with a big hit one last time. But instead I grounded back to the pitcher, Kenny Rogers. We lost, 10–4. So much for a storybook ending.

Unfortunately, in baseball there's always a pitcher out there who's trying to shatter your dreams.

Actually, it *was* a storybook ending in almost every way. When we took the field in the ninth inning, Melvin put me at third base—the position where I began my career. I hadn't played third since July 2, 1997, in San Diego. The fans started chanting, "Ed-Gar! Ed-Gar!" like they had so many times. A few days earlier, someone had asked me if those chants ever distracted me. I answered honestly: "I'm so focused on the at-bat, they don't even register." I said I had been driving in the car recently and a song came on the radio. A person with me said, "Oh, that's the song they play when you go up to hit—'Salome,' by Chayanne." My response was, "They play a song when I go up and hit?" I didn't even realize that.

Standing at third base after all those years was very strange. The hitter looked so far away. First base looked so far away. I know that if the ball had been hit to me, I would not have been able to make the throw. But I found out later Dan Wilson, our catcher, had asked the batter, Mark Teixeira, not to swing. He assured Mark that our pitcher, Aaron Taylor, would throw a ball.

After one pitch, Bob sent Willie Bloomquist out to replace me at third, and the sellout crowd saluted me with a prolonged ovation. But the fun was only starting. After the game, the Mariners held a 90-minute ceremony to honor me. The first shocker came when Commissioner Bud Selig announced that the award for the top designated hitter each year would now be called The Edgar Martínez Award. That was the first I had heard of it. It was an incredible feeling that brought me to tears. I couldn't believe it. It was almost like I was there, taking it all in, but it wasn't registering. It took a while to sink in.

I received many other accolades, so many my head was spinning. Governor Gary Locke designated October 2nd through the 9th as Edgar Martínez Week in the state of Washington. Seattle mayor Greg Nickels presented a sign for Edgar Martínez Drive, which would be the new name of Atlantic Avenue outside the ballpark. When they had told me they were renaming a street in my honor, it was another shocking— and humbling—moment.

Mariners CEO Howard Lincoln presented me with a beautiful portrait by local artist Michele Rushworth that showed my batting stroke. Team president Chuck Armstrong announced a $100,000 donation by the Mariners for the Edgar Martínez Endowment for Muscular Dystrophy Research at Children's Hospital.

It was all overwhelming. Finally, all my teammates gathered around me. Also on hand were teammates from earlier in my career, dating back to my first season, 1987. Bret Boone introduced me: "Ladies and gentlemen, I present to you the greatest Mariner of all time."

I tried to thank all the people I could, from Mariners executives to the medical staff, as well as past and present teammates. Two people I singled out were Marty Martínez, the scout who had signed me way back in 1982 and taken care of me early in my career, and Orlando Cepeda, one of my idols growing up. I also thanked my family, my kids, and, of course, Holli. "I love you," I said to her. "Without you, I am nothing."

Finally, I took a lap around the field, waving to and high-fiving fans. Through it all, I felt a sense of peace. I knew I could walk away and not look back and wish I could still play.

But I had one more game. If I wasn't sure I was done before, I was now. We lost 3–0 to the Rangers, our 99th defeat, and I went 0-for-4. In fact, I grounded into double plays in the last two at-bats of my career, the final one in the eighth inning off reliever Doug Brocail. I hit the ball hard, but right back to the pitcher. "The good thing is that I won't do that anymore," I said after the game. "I won't kill any more rallies or chase any more pitches out of the zone."

In my second at-bat, I drove a ball to the warning track, but it was caught by the left fielder. Once again, no storybook ending. I hit it well, but my weight shift was too soon. I was hoping a breeze would carry it out, but no such luck. Still, I was pleased with my concentration level in the game. I tried to enjoy the fact it was my last game yet also treat it like just another game, so I could focus on my at-bats. Oddly, I wasn't that emotional during the game. I think that's because I had played it all out in my head so many times that it was almost like I had lived it already. And I guess I got it all out of my system on Saturday.

I would make one final appearance on the field as a still-active player. Bob Melvin sent me out to the mound in the top of the ninth inning to change pitchers. I called for Randy Williams to replace Matt Thornton as the crowd roared and roared.

"It's kind of funny," I told Bob Finnigan of the *Seattle Times* after the game, "that my last time on the field I would be making a change.

314

After playing baseball since I was 10 years old and having it a part of my life, now I am making a big change."

Unfortunately, it was the last game for Melvin, too. He was fired the next day. One thing I'll never forget: after the game, Bob had me sit in the chair in his office. I think he wanted to tell me, this is where you belong one day.

Eventually, I would indeed get back in a major-league uniform. But at that moment, it was nowhere in my mind. I had many other things in store. I knew I wasn't going to be back for a while.

Chapter 12

Life After Baseball

WHEN THE 2005 SEASON started, I was sitting at home watching it on television with an infant baby in my lap. So, yes, my life had changed a bit.

The Mariners asked me if I wanted a position in the organization, but I wasn't ready for that yet. I knew that Jacqueline was due in February, and I was looking forward to spending more time with Holli and what would now be three kids—two of them very young. I was also looking forward to pursuing business interests, as well as some hobbies I never had time for.

Still, it felt very strange when spring training rolled around, and I stayed home. All through the minor leagues, then the majors, my life had revolved around the same routine: training during the off-season so I'd be prepared when February rolled around. If you do that for 20-plus years, leaving for spring training is part of your life. When it's gone, it's like someone took something away from you. It left a big empty space. So I felt a little lost, a little bit confused, and missing something. The fact that you're spending more time with your kids and your wife makes it better. But you're still missing something you've done, and have loved to do, for 30 years.

A few weeks after my last game, I went to St. Louis to accept the Roberto Clemente Award during the World Series. As I said, that was very meaningful because it was for community service, which I took very seriously. Holli and I were involved in many charities, including Parent Project Muscular Dystrophy, Children's Hospital, Overlake Hospital, Make-A-Wish Foundation, Wishing Star Foundation, United Way, Esperanza, Page Ahead Children's Literacy Program, Big Brothers Big Sisters, Boys & Girls Clubs, and Mariners Care. We were proud to serve as honorary co-chairs of Overlake Hospital's Capital Campaign in 2003, and also as honorary chair of Children's Hospital's Wishing Well Night at Safeco Field, where we raised more than $120,000 in 2002. And now that I was retired, I had even more time for community involvement.

In November of 2004, I found out I had received nine write-in votes in the Washington state governor's election, which was amusing. And in December, I got to raise the 12th Man flag before a Monday night Seahawks game against the Dallas Cowboys at CenturyLink Field. That was a lot of fun. But mostly, I was trying to figure out how to live life without baseball. It was a weird feeling. I was so routine-oriented. I had a purpose for every hour of the day. All of a sudden, I didn't have to do all those things. The eye exercises, the affirmations, the cage work. "Okay, what do I do now?" I remember traveling with Holli, and she would laugh, because I struggle with simple things. It was definitely an adjustment to have so much time on my hands, and not have a purpose for all that time.

I gave myself a couple of months to just think about things and relax. We traveled, played golf, all the things I couldn't do during the summer when I was playing. I had always loved the ocean and boating, so we did some of that, too. I had two boats, a 37-foot powerboat that I kept in Seattle named *Seaswing*, and a faster one I kept in Puerto Rico named *Martillo*. That translates to "hammer," for the way it hit the water.

Another thing I did over the years was take flying lessons. I'd been fascinated by aviation since I was a kid. I used to play games with flight simulators all the time. So I went to Boeing Field and took lessons. But they kept getting interrupted by various trips and vacations, and I'd fall behind. I did do a solo flight, which was a lot of fun—but not very smooth. I kind of threw the plane down. I remember thinking, "If I'm going to do this, I really need to put a lot of time into it." Flying is not something you want to do halfway. I wasn't sure I wanted to put 100 percent effort into it, which I realized was risky. So eventually, I gave it up.

One thing I didn't do much was watch the Mariners. They had hired Mike Hargrove as the new manager, and signed Adrian Beltre and Richie Sexson as free agents. But I never liked to watch games, even when I played. I wanted to occupy my mind with something else. I'd watch documentaries, the History Channel, the Learning Channel. I didn't watch ESPN, though. In fact, I didn't watch any baseball. I wanted to keep my mind learning things. I would read about business, finance, investments—that became my passion. I'm not big on anything that had to do with fiction—books, movies. I like to laugh, so sometimes I'll watch a comedy movie. But mostly I wanted to watch and read things that involved learning something. I guess it's because in baseball, you just play a game. You're mentally active, but it all revolves around strategies of the game. Learning something outside that life—that was important to me.

Like every former player, I tried golf. It was great, but I realized you get bored quickly. I felt I needed to be busy doing things that would

319

give me the same drive and adrenalin that I had competing. I used to think, constantly, "What do I have to do tonight to get three hits, or four hits?" Now I was thinking, "Okay, what do I *want* to do?" I had trouble adjusting to that. When you compete for so long, you get used to saying, "What do I have to do?" and not so much, "What do I want to do?"

It wasn't so much that I *missed* that focus—I *needed* it. I didn't even last a year trying to relax and decompress after I retired. My mind had to be working on something. I tried to replace that feeling with other things. I did those flying lessons. I got very deep into investing and was very hands-on with my advisors. That helped a lot. So did going back to school to take an 18-month executive business administration program at the University of Washington. That's the same subject I was studying when I left college to sign with the Mariners. While I was a little rusty with doing schoolwork—it had been more than 20 years since I left American University in Puerto Rico—I found that program to be very enjoyable and fulfilling. It's funny—when I was in school as a youngster, I didn't want to go. But when I got older, I actually wanted to go to school. You enjoy it more—and get more out of it—when you want to, instead of have to.

I also became very involved with my business interests. I had invested in an embroidery company called Caribbean Embroideries in Puerto Rico in 1992 with a partner. Eventually, I bought more equipment and opened a branch in Seattle. I began spending more time with this company after I retired, going into the office like a real businessman. At this point, the company was struggling a bit, because people were starting to order from China, which cut into our market share. So I went into partnership with another company, Image Source. We changed our name to Branded Solutions and began to expand our product line. Business improved, but in 2010 I decided to sell my share to my partners, to give myself a little more flexibility. I still serve on the board of directors, though.

I got involved in the mezcal business with a line of artisanal mezcals called El Zacatecano. Mezcal is a distilled alcoholic beverage made from agave that is similar to tequila, but smokier and made from a different type of agave. El Zacatecano is one of the oldest and most popular mezcal brands in Mexico. With my partner, Gene Juarez—well-known for his salons and spas—we decided to bring El Zacatecano to the states. Gene and I traveled to Mexico to visit the plant where it's made.

I also invested with Gene and others in Plaza Bank, which we founded in 2006 to serve the Hispanic community in the Puget Sound area. We eventually sold that to a bigger bank in California in 2018, but helping run these companies, along with a few other smaller ones I invested in, satisfied my competitive itch. So did my involvement in the stock market and learning all aspects of that form of investing. If you come to my house, you'll see that the television is tuned to the financial stations all day long while I'm here. I have great partners and advisors, all very knowledgeable, who have taught me a considerable amount about investment and running a business.

At the same time, Holli and I have tried to stay heavily involved in the community. One passion of ours was the Edgar and Holli Martínez Foundation, which we launched in 2008 to encourage diversity in teaching. Holli and I have both always had a strong belief in the impact of education. In talking to educators and scholars as well as people who have worked on educational foundations, we became convinced that our focus should be teachers of color. There weren't enough of them in the classroom, so our cause became to help promote and encourage more teachers of color. The evidence was clear that students of color do much better when they have a teacher that looks like them. Holli was the driving force behind the foundation as its executive director through 2012, and she did a fantastic job. She had recently gone back to school herself and graduated magna cum laude from the University of Washington's Bothell campus, with an interdisciplinary major called Society, Ethics, and Human Behavior. Then Holli continued her learning and received a Master of Public Administration degree from the University of Washington in Seattle in 2012.

The cause of equity in education was our motivation. Over the course of seven years, we were able to give scholarships, as well as coaching and ongoing professional development, to more than 100 teachers all over the state of Washington, who in turn gave back to their communities. Recipients are encouraged to teach in low-income school districts. We learned that the first two years are the most difficult for new teachers. Within those two years, a high percentage stop teaching. So we focused on giving them support and training early in their careers, to get them through this period.

In 2015, we transferred the foundation to the Technology Access Foundation (TAF) and College Success Foundation, which has maintained our framework as the Martínez Fellows program. The whole project continues to be very rewarding. It's inspiring to see these teachers, often the first in their family to attend college—sometimes with young kids of their own—and how they are impacting the younger generation. It's so inspiring to see the effect they have in the classroom, because of the training we give them. Our hope is that they learn to really care about the kids. Holli and I would go to the classroom and watch them teach, which never failed to be a moving experience.

Another cause particularly near and dear to our hearts, among all the charities we support, is muscular dystrophy. I got to see firsthand the challenges of this disease on both the afflicted person and the family. Elionel, the son of my brother, Elliot, was diagnosed with muscular dystrophy as a youngster in Puerto Rico. It was only natural for me to try to help out and raise money in pursuit of a cure. I have hosted a charity golf tournament that has raised more than a million dollars to help fight muscular dystrophy. When I retired in 2004, the Mariners established the Edgar Martínez Endowment of Muscular Dystrophy Research at Seattle Children's Hospital.

As I said, this is very personal for me. Elliot left a good job in Puerto Rico to move here because he realized the programs for MD— the treatment, the access for his son, the schools—are better in Seattle. He took a chance to relocate here without a job and has become very successful in home construction. I'm proud of him and also of Elionel.

As the kids grew older, I began to think of getting back into baseball. I realized that if I did so, I wanted to be on the field, not in the front office. After I sold the business, I began to contemplate how this might take shape. When Holli started working full-time, I started thinking seriously of putting the uniform back on. Once again, I was feeling like a needed a new challenge.

I talked to the Mariners, and they agreed to let me try it out on a part-time basis. That way, I could continue with my business interests and see how I liked the teaching side of baseball. In 2008, when John McLaren was manager, I attended spring training to work with the Mariners' young players. It felt a little strange to put the uniform back on—but at the same time, it felt right. I continued to go to spring training each year to help out, and I enjoyed it. Then, a few years later, I felt it was time to expand my role, and the Mariners made me a roving minor-league instructor. When the season started, I would go to our various minor-league affiliates in places like Pulaski, Virginia; Appleton, Wisconsin; Adelanto, California; and Jackson, Tennessee;

in addition to nearby Tacoma and Everett in our state. The travel was tough, driving in rental cars and trying to find the airport. I discovered that the fun part came once you got to the ballpark and got to work with the kids, which I enjoyed.

JOHN McLAREN
Mariners Coach, 1993–2002, and Manager, 2007–08

Edgar came over to talk to our minor leaguers about hitting and approach. Afterward, I asked if anyone had any questions. Bryan LaHair raised his hand and asked what was the toughest pitch for him to hit. Edgar smiled and said, "No question, it was the hard sinker." Then LaHair raised his hand again and asked what was his approach to guys who threw the hard sinker. Edgar said he never tried to do too much. He just tried to get a single up the middle. If he tried to do too much, he'd get himself out. The answers Edgar gave to the young people were fabulous.

I really enjoyed that, and it was a productive way to fill my time. Holli was working full-time, Alex had graduated high school, and the girls were busy with their school activities. I found I was spending a lot of time by myself, and this helped fill the void. One day in June 2015, I was meeting with Mariners general manager Jack Zduriencik. We were discussing our minor-league prospects as well as the current team, which was struggling. Jack brought up the subject of becoming the Mariners' hitting coach. I told him I'd like to do it someday.

"How about now?" he said.

I wasn't expecting that at all. I wasn't sure I was ready to jump all the way in like that. But at the same time, it sounded really appealing. The more I thought about it, the more I liked the idea. I told Jack I needed to talk it over with Holli and the family. Holli told me she thought it made sense, and if I wanted to do it, go ahead. So I told Jack the next day that I would accept.

It was a little bit awkward to start in the middle of the season, replacing Howard Johnson, but my focus was on turning the team around. The other part of it was, if I never tried it out, how would I know if I was going to like the job? If I had told Jack, "No, I'm not ready right now, let's try it next year," maybe he brings in someone else, and they do such a good job I never get a chance. So I figured the best course was to jump right in. And I loved being back in the cages, the grind of the everyday schedule. The only difference at age 52 was that instead of just worrying about myself, I had 12 or 13 guys to be concerned about all at the same time.

A lot of my focus as a hitting coach was to make sure the players kept a positive frame of mind. As I said, that's something I really admired about my longtime hitting coach in Seattle, Lee Elia. My belief was that major leaguers had the skill, or they wouldn't be here. It's their mind that is limiting them from achieving the full potential of their skills. A lot of that was negativity—I can't hit, I can't see the ball, whatever. Sometimes, it was the mindset that, "I don't need help." I tried to show them I had the information and knowledge that could help them get better. Some players were really receptive, others not so much. But I thought I could probably help players in that area. The ones who weren't interested in working on their mental game, I worked on their mechanics and tried to find something in their mechanics to get them in a better mindset, so they'd say, "Now I'm ready."

One player who bought in right away was Mark Trumbo. We worked on some mechanical things, but he was very receptive about the mental side of the game. We talked a lot about visualizing his swing. You could see him in the on-deck circle sometimes close his eyes. You could tell he was working on it. He hit .302 over his final 74 games that year, then led the major leagues in home runs the next year and made the All-Star team. Mark said he was just continuing some of the things I had taught him. That was gratifying.

LEE ELIA
Former Mariners Hitting Coach (via the *Seattle Times*)

If I were a player, I'd crawl over glass to get a chance to listen to Edgar talk hitting. No one knows the art of hitting any better. He always had that passion. There were certain things he did that rubbed off on other guys. Maybe one little question, that knack of saying one little thing, with the guys we had. He'd mention it to me, and I'd mention it to them, and the next thing you know, it would click.

Hitting coach is a tough job. All players are different. From my own career, I already knew that some had a very open mindset, while others were very closed. I expected that. What has changed since I played, however, is the vast amount of information available to players—and they use it. They are very into things like analytics, launch angle, exit velocity. Those words didn't even exist when I played, but they look for that information all over. They can find it on the internet. They can talk to a private coach who has helped someone else. They are always seeking that information in search of an edge.

Honestly, I didn't have a problem with that. I'm sure I would have been doing the same thing if that information had been available when I played. We as coaches don't have all the answers. In some ways, it's a generational difference. Older coaches tend to attach a little more to the old styles. I believe the coach has to adjust to the players, and that's what I tried to do. I was very open to exit velocity, the angles. I tried to learn as much as I could, because the information was all out there. Then I tried to blend my belief of how I can help with trying to be more efficient in teaching the biomechanics of modern baseball. How can we make your swing more efficient? You have to kind of help them feel like it's their idea, not yours. It always boils down to trying to make them feel good.

I enjoyed it, I really did. I felt we had a lot of success. After I took over in 2015, we scored nearly 1.2 runs more per game the rest of the year. In 2017, we finished seventh in the American League in runs scored and hit 200 homers for the sixth time in club history. There were also some struggles, particularly in 2018. I tended to be hard on myself. When a particular player wasn't doing well, I'd ask myself, "How can I help him so he doesn't have to go through this?" And I'd take it personally in the sense that, if I'm not doing my job, then I'm affecting his career. And I'm affecting the team. It was hard not to take it personally, though you realize you're not up there hitting. Sometimes you say to yourself, "I've given them the information, but they're not receptive, or they're not executing." Yet I was still hard on myself. I'd say, "I have to find another way to get to him. What I'm doing is not working, so what can I do to get through?"

I believed in the old saying: When a player does well, the player deserves the credit. When a player does poorly, the coach didn't do his job.

I had the opportunity to work with a couple of superstars, Robinson Cano and Nelson Cruz. My philosophy was to treat them like superstars. That doesn't mean to give them special treatment, but you treat them with respect. It's a matter of understanding they are where they are because they've done a lot of good things. Just respect them for that. And when they were down, it was often a matter of asking questions:

What do you do when you're doing well? And if I don't think he's telling me what I think is missing, I'll say to him: "This is what I see when you're going well." If that clicks with them, they try it. If it doesn't, we keep searching. Most of the so-called superstars, they have similar characteristics. They're open to learning. They have great work habits. They put in the time and work. They want to get better. When you put all those things together, they're easy to work with.

One player who was in a category all his own was Griffey. I never coached Junior, of course, but I played alongside him for a decade. Junior was like Michael Jordan—one of a kind. Junior knew what Junior needed to do—and everyone around knew that he knew. So you kind of left him alone. He was the most talented player I ever saw, in all areas. His skills playing the game, of course, but also the mental side. He had incredible instincts and positivity. Put all that together and it made Junior a one-of-a-kind player. If I had coached him, I probably would have just left him alone.

One huge topic of debate these days is the massive amount of shifting that teams do—moving infielders from one side of the field to the other to make it harder on hitters. My thinking on this has evolved over the last few years. Not too long ago, I said, "You can beat the shift. Any major-league player should be able to beat the shift." My thinking was, just hit the ball the other way, and the shift will stop. But eventually, I gave up that idea, particularly for the power hitters. I still think guys should be able to hit the other way. But my focus became, "Okay, if you want to pull, let's find a way for you to pull better. Not just hitting a ground ball to second base. Let's find a way to help you lift it in the air and find the gaps." In other words, I worked with them on pulling the ball more efficiently.

One thing I'll admit that does bother me about today's game is the two-strike approach. When I played, you cut down your swing with two strikes and just tried to make contact. If you put the ball in play, you increase your chances of getting a hit. Most players today have the same swing with two strikes as no strikes. They feel like they can't change their swing. There's not as much of a negative stigma attached to striking out as their used to be. If a hitter strikes out a lot, that means they are probably seeing more than four pitches. There's some value in that. What I struggle with, though, is not making any adjustment with two strikes. What I did when I reached two strikes was to cut down. Slow down your mechanics. My two-strike mentality was almost like I was getting the sign for a hit-and-run. On a hit-and-run, you're going to wait longer and just make contact. If your mechanics are good, the ball is going to take off.

Off the field, one thing that happened in 2016, when I started my first full season as hitting coach, was that the Mariners put me back in their commercials to advertise the team. When I was playing, I had appeared in a whole string of commercials, which were produced by the advertising firm Copacino+Fujikado. For some reason, people seemed to have really liked me in those spots over the years. The commercials were funny, but I always felt so awkward. It never came naturally to me. Over time, you feel more comfortable—but never totally.

The "light bat" ad—which was actually for Eagle Hardware and not the Mariners—is the one people remember the most. In that one, I use power tools to build a lamp with a handle that's a bat. My tagline, which kind of became a catchphrase in Seattle, is, "It's a light bat." And to answer the question I get a lot, no, I don't have the lamp. I wish I did, though.

There was a good one I did in 1998 where I was helping the rookies from other countries learn Northwest lingo. I taught them phrases like, "How 'bout them Cougs?" and, "I took my gooey duck to Puyallup." The other spot that people quote all the time is "the clapper," which involved a gadget that turned the lights on and off at Safeco Field with a clap. It worked great until the fans started clapping during a game, and the lights went off and on. My closing line in that one, which is also quoted a lot, was, "That's a problem."

When I came back as hitting coach, they had me do a funny one where Robinson Cano goes in front of a mirror, and I'm on the other side mimicking every move he made. We had to do a lot of takes on that one—to keep from laughing, and to stay in synch, which wasn't easy. And at the end, I got to say "It's a light bat" again—and this time for the Mariners.

KEVIN MARTINEZ
Mariners Senior Vice President, Marketing and Communications

When we first started doing these commercials with the Copacino+Fujikado Agency in 1996, we realized we had a lot of really great guys who were fun to be around. The challenge we put to ourselves was, how do we show this through our advertising to our fans? Jim [Copacino] and his team came up with these vignettes.

We had a feeling Edgar, Jay, Dan, and Junior would all shine, each in his own way. Edgar did have some magic about him on the screen. He's incredibly charming. He's got a warmth to him, and friendliness, a very gentle way of speaking. Edgar almost finishes his words with a hint of a smile. He makes you feel good. I even chat with Edgar and feel that way when he's not an actor in a commercial. He has this real genuine quality that draws people to him.

He was just a pro about it. I don't think if you said to Edgar, "Do you want to do a bunch of commercials?" he'd say, "Let's do that, it'll be great." He did it because we said it was important and the fans would enjoy it. He's not looking for a secondary career in acting. But he was a complete pro. He was a delight. Everyone on the production crew adored working with Edgar. He was just a gentleman. He'd nail every line like he was taking an outside pitch to right field.

I think the first commercial he did was when Edgar was in the batting cage with [coaches] Matt Sinatro and Lee Elia playing cards behind him. He's hitting, hitting, and they don't even look up. We realized right there, "Gosh, he's really good on camera, charming and warm."

The next year, he delivered one of the classic lines in Mariner commercials. We were highlighting what he did between at-bats as the DH. In the final scene, he's calling a pizza place—"I'll take 18 pizzas, two pepperoni..." And he says, "Yes, we have a coupon." It was an ad-lib on the set. It was great. He was super-flexible, willing to try things.

His most famous line, of course, was, "It's a light bat." And that wasn't even a Mariner commercial, even though a lot of people think it was; it was for Eagle Hardware. We thank the Eagle Hardware folks for that. When people are asked what is their favorite Mariners' commercial, many respond, "That's easy, light bat." No, that's Eagle. It's one of the all-timers.

We would write the spots with Edgar's personality in mind. When we got to 1999, the spot created the Safeco Field roof opener. We kind of fell in love with the idea of him being a gadget guy, fashioning a clapper for the stadium lights to use for late-night batting practice. Of course, the crowd starts rhythmically clapping during a game, and the lights go on and off. Edgar's line was another classic: "That's a problem."

We kind of created this persona for him. He's done three post-career commercials. In 2009, we reunited Edgar and Jay Buhner for the 100th player commercial in the series. In that spot, Jay and Edgar are walking down a hallway with all these pictures of famous Mariners' commercials. We revealed the person who wrote them all—a chimpanzee at a typewriter named Sprinkles.

WILLIE SANCHEZ
Agent

I think Edgar enjoyed the commercials, because he loved Seattle. It's all hypothetical, of course, but if you put him in New York, would he have shined the way did in Seattle? I don't think so. Here's a big-time player, a Hall of Famer, in a small market being a hero. I'd say all the time, "Do you want to go to a big-time market and be an everyday player, or be a big guy here?" I think that stayed with him. He just felt comfortable.

The managers I worked under as hitting coach, Lloyd McClendon and Scott Servais, were both great. When I came in mid-season in 2015, Lloyd told me, "Do what you know. You've got the hitting. Go do it." Scott was great, too—very open-minded, very open to information coming his way. He asked a lot of questions. I couldn't have asked for a better group to work with, from general manager Jerry Dipoto to Scott and all the coaches.

But after the 2018 season, I sat down with Jerry and Scott to talk about my future. I had begun to realize that I wanted to spend more time with Holli and the kids. When I came home from games at Safeco, everyone would be asleep. I'd get up in the morning to see Holli and the kids, but then they would go off for the day, and I'd have to leave for the ballpark before they got back. Then I'd come home late, and the whole process would repeat itself. That's not to even mention the long road trips when I wouldn't see them at all.

I asked for a new role that would allow me to stay involved with the ballclub but give me more flexible hours. The season had been frustrating, particularly the second half, when our offense really struggled, but that wasn't why I made the decision. I really enjoyed working with the players and the staff and welcomed the challenges. It was totally a family decision. I was at a stage of my life where I wanted to be around a little more.

The Mariners were great about it. We worked together to form a new role for me that I'm really excited about. It allows me a chance to work with hitters at every level of the organization. It's a broader role that allows me to do what I love—teach hitting—but with less travel and more opportunity to see my family.

The Mariners had retired my No. 11 in 2017, another amazing honor. But I'm not quite ready to take the uniform off yet. It's been nearly 50 years since my grandfather gave me my first baseball uniform back in Dorado. I couldn't have ever dreamed where the sport would lead me—to a highly rewarding professional career, to the magical 1995 season that saved baseball in Seattle, to the ultimate honor of making the Hall of Fame, to a wonderful wife and family I love so much, and to a beautiful city that has become my home. The fans have always been incredibly supportive, and my goal is still to bring a World Series title to Seattle for them. I'll do everything in my power to make it happen.

My career wasn't always smooth, and there were bumps, setbacks, and challenges every step of the way. But that just made the triumphs and accomplishments even sweeter. I can honestly say that I worked as hard as I possibly could to maximize my skills and did everything in my power to help the Mariners win. In fact, I'll continue to do so.

It's been quite an adventure since the day that I hid on the roof of my grandparents' home, setting into motion the chain of events that led me to Bellingham, and then Seattle, and then Cooperstown. And you know what? I wouldn't change it for anything.